Edited by Dr. Juerg Steffen

Relocation to Austria

An Introduction for High Net Worth Individuals and Entrepreneurs

2nd Edition • Revised and Expanded

IDEOS

ZURICH • LONDON • HONG KONG • NEW YORK

Published by Ideos Publications Ltd. in Zurich.

For general information on our other products and services please visit: *ideospublications.com*

All books published by Ideos Publications are also available as eBooks.

The CIP Catalog record for this book is available from the British Library.

ISBN (Hardback): 978-3-9524742-6-6

ISBN (eBook): 978-3-9524742-8-0

Data correct as at 1 January 2018

Contents

Preface

Dr. Juerg Steffen, Chief Operating Officer, Henley & Partners

Although this is sometimes forgotten, Austria has long been a country at the crossroads of north, south, east, and west. Since Roman times, travelers and merchants have been stopping over at Vindobonum, the old name for Vienna. During the Habsburg empire it unified many different ethnicities including Slavs, Hungarians, Poles, and Germans. Today, at the heart of the EU, it is one of the most visited countries in the world, combining old-world charm with modern comfort and safety.

But more than making a temporary visit to Austria, many people choose to relocate permanently to this country. With its pristine lake and mountain scenery, its culinary delights, a solid and reliable health system, and world-class teaching and research facilities, Austria of today is one of the most sought-after countries in which to settle. Its strategic central location makes it an economically appealing hub to many multinationals. For eight consecutive years, Mercer, an international consultancy, has consistently ranked Vienna the city with the highest quality of life, putting it ahead of New York and London. As a resident of Austria, I can only agree.

During my time as a banker and then as a consultant, I came to realize that many people who want to change their domicile have a difficult time navigating all the complexities that relocation entails. Issues related to healthcare, the schooling system, inheritance tax, registration formalities, and banking confidentiality, etc., are all topics that should be carefully considered before making such an important move.

This book is an attempt to help those considering relocation to Austria to make an informed and balanced decision. While the book touches on many useful topics, it is nonetheless advisable to consult with professional firms (lawyers, consultants, etc.) to delve deeper into the details of one's own individual situation.

I would like to thank all those who contributed to making this second, improved version of the book such a success. First and foremost, I heartily thank the authors, without whom this book would not have been possible. They are true experts in their respective fields and I am grateful for their theoretical but also practical approach to the challenging topics they cover in their chapters. I would also like to thank the publishers and my office, particularly Philip Reuchlin and Daniel Pfeifer, for their hard work in making this book a reality.

I hope you, dear reader, will find it informative and enlightening. I would like to welcome any questions or comments you may have.

Dr. Juerg Steffen
Vienna
1 February 2018

1 Introduction to Cross-border Relocation

Dr. Christian H. Kälin, Henley & Partners

Progressing globalization, and the integration of Europe in particular, has had a significant impact on the mobility of many citizens. Many aspects of life are no longer confined to one's home country, but extend worldwide, across borders. Modern careers often inherently require travel, and many companies prefer employees who are internationally mobile. Similarly, financially independent persons are increasingly considering changing their place of residence internationally; the integration of Europe makes this much easier.

With the course of European integration, political stability not only facilitates relocation within Europe, but also contributes to the development of infrastructure, such as improved transport and communication facilities, increased cross-border activities, and the acquisition of property abroad. Overseas property is often purchased as a second home, a holiday home, or even as an entirely new residence. The single currency and free movement of persons and capital within Europe have led to increased property purchases by non-residents, especially in southern Europe, where France, Spain, Italy, and Portugal have particularly benefited. Austria has always been a popular holiday destination in Europe, as well as being an attractive option for permanent residence, and the latter option is becoming ever more appealing.

1.1 Relocation and international tax planning

For successful international relocation, various aspects should be considered. First and foremost, the residence and immigration regulations of the desired country must be studied carefully before relocation. The EU has simplified the relocation of citizens within Europe. In addition, in many countries the acquisition of property is now possible without restriction for foreigners.

It should also be noted that the acquisition of real estate does not affect immigration and residence regulations. In the US, for example, one must obtain a visa should one wish to extend one's stay.

In contrast to the US, countries such as the Bahamas, Malta, and Monaco as well as Australia, Croatia, Panama, Portugal, and Cyprus make it easy for the financially independent to relocate if they can prove that they are not employed in the new country. Residence permits for unemployed persons are usually issued as soon as proof of financial means is available; Croatia requires at least EUR 25,000, while countries such as Monaco and Bermuda require EUR 500,000 or more. In addition, a police certificate must be provided. It is important in such cases to ascertain whether proof of adequate accommodation is required at the time of visa application, or whether property acquisition or the renting of accommodation can be organized after receipt of the visa. It is very easy for EU or European Economic Area (EEA) citizens seeking to relocate to Austria to do so, since they can rely on the concept of free movement of persons and therefore have a right to residence. These citizens can concentrate on other aspects of their move, such as tax planning, inheritance planning, and property acquisition.

In principle, one should not be considering a change of residence solely for tax purposes; nevertheless, the impact of relocation on taxation should not be overlooked. If one buys a property only as a vacation home and spends only a few weeks of the year there then nothing changes in terms of personal taxation. By contrast, if one spends several months at the holiday home, the subject of personal taxation becomes relevant. Specifically, individuals who spend more than three months in a country — even without gainful employment — should be concerned with the issue of tax residence. Individuals who spend more than six months in a country are generally considered to be tax resident and therefore must expect unrestricted taxation. If, however, an individual relocates to a country with a mild tax climate as his/her main residence, considerable tax savings are made possible. In uncomplicated tax planning scenarios, relocation to Monaco, the UK, Malta, or Austria, for example, can offer such savings.

Migration is, however, often not without consequences. Many high-taxing countries have enacted laws that make the transfer of residence to a milder tax climate unattractive for their citizens. This is done through an 'exit tax'. In Germany, for example, the Foreign Taxation Act applies. Under certain circumstances, unlimited German tax liability may continue despite the transfer of residence to another country. Essentially, full German taxation still applies although taxes paid in the new country of residence may be accounted for. This rule may remain valid for between five and 10 years after the transfer of residence and can be circumvented only with targeted structuring and, most importantly, ceasing regular or long visits to one's home country.

Although bilateral agreements are designed to avoid double taxation, the relevant national tax laws must be scrutinized before relocation to avoid any unpleasant surprises. Particularly relevant are the double taxation agreements, now multilateral tax treaties. It may happen, for example, that two states operating under different national laws both classify a taxpayer as a resident and therefore as fully taxable. In principle, for as long as a double tax agreement exists, tax is due where one is tax resident. In this scenario, tax liability applies to the total worldwide income and possibly, as the case may be, to the net wealth. The second state is referred to as the source country and has the right to tax only the assets located in, or income generated in, that country.

In addition, there are some exact rules — assignment or tie-breaker rules — relating to double or multilateral tax scenarios. For example, if one has a fixed place of residence in two countries, one must indicate the country that is one's main place of residence. If this cannot be easily determined, it is necessary to establish the habitual place of residence or, finally, a decision may be taken based on nationality. If the jurisdiction is still not established because of dual citizenship, the matter must be clarified between the two states through a mutual agreement procedure.

Tax treaties can often present an advantage for the taxpayer. An example would be if one wanted to leave the old state of residence swiftly because of tax reasons.

Here, Austria is an interesting example because it has a relatively good network of double taxation agreements that are not subject to special restrictions as in the case of some Swiss double taxation agreements. In the case of Switzerland, foreigners are taxed at a flat rate. For this reason, it is sometimes better to move to Switzerland and be taxed as normal than to use the flat tax rate. Nonetheless, where possible it is better to obtain a tax ruling before taking up tax residence in another country.

By contrast, one is less protected if one takes up residence in a state that does not have a tax treaty with one's former state of residence, for example, when emigrating from Germany to Monaco. As no tax treaty applies between these two states, taxpayers find it difficult to end tax residence in the old country of residence. Often, the only way to avoid being taxed by high-taxing countries from which one has relocated is by taking the radical step of cutting all connections to one's country of origin. This applies particularly to Germany, but also to many other high-taxing countries.

The Standard for Automatic Exchange of Financial Account Information, introduced by the Organisation for Economic Co-operation and Development (OECD), outlines automatic exchange of financial account information between countries through a set of rules detailed in the Common Reporting Standard (CRS). The CRS requires financial institutions to report account holder information to local tax authorities who, in turn, automatically exchange that information on an annual basis with the tax authorities where these account holders are tax resident. The first phase of the CRS was initiated in 2017 and is in the process of coming into force in almost every significant economy except the US.

With the introduction of the CRS, alternative residence or citizenship — and the fiscal and security benefits associated with them — is being taken more seriously by those wanting to operate globally, reduce their exposure to external threats, increase their international flexibility, and explore new opportunities.

The CRS has been widely welcomed as a positive, globally coordinated move towards greater financial transparency and accountability. Rightly or wrongly, however, some wealthy individuals and families who reside in developing countries fear that the necessary regulations and safeguards taken to protect privacy may not be sufficiently effective, thereby making personal and financial information available to criminal elements and threatening their safety and security. Concerned individuals may look into relocating and becoming tax resident in a country where the vital controls and regulations around cross-border sharing of information are in place. Austria is particularly safe in this regard and, for this reason, will be in the coming years of increasing interest to wealthy families as a secure place of residence.

1.2 Estate planning and inheritance tax

Inheritance law, inheritance tax, and the corresponding estate planning and inheritance tax planning are closely intertwined with the topic of tax planning. Inheritance and gift taxes depend on the last place of residence of the deceased or benefactor, but where the heirs or beneficiaries are located or which citizenship they hold can also be relevant. Germany, specifically, is the only country in which inheritance tax must be paid by the heir if he/she is tax resident in Germany. Tax relief in the case of inheritance is therefore possible only if both the deceased and the heir are not resident in Germany. In the US, it is relevant if anyone concerned has US citizenship. Applicable inheritance law as well as possible inheritance and gift taxes can have both positive and negative effects on a change of residence, depending on the country of residence. Some countries permit other asset dispositions because of death, for example, the right to a compulsory share, greater freedom of testament, or reversed, stricter forced heirship rules.

Thorough estate planning is particularly recommended in the context of international relocation. It is useful to consult experts in the present country of residence as well as in the destination country. In addition, the corresponding structuring of real estate, wherever located, should be factored in.

Migration is often the only way to legally reduce the tax burden in high-taxing countries; nevertheless, one shouldn't seek to relocate solely for tax reasons. If a second home already exists, the decision is somewhat simpler, since one is familiar with many of the usual areas of uncertainty, for example, quality of life or real estate options.

1.3 Acquisition and structuring of real estate

Many real estate purchases are entered into despite the buyers not having the necessary knowledge about tax and/or other implications. In the case of a relocation, not only should the climate and the living conditions in one's new home country be considered, but also that some practices are different from those in one's former home country. The proverb 'different countries, different customs' should not be disregarded — one should be particularly aware that different legal regulations apply in the case of transfer of residence, particularly in the fields of property and tax law. It is therefore critical when planning relocation to consider not only the local justice system, but also the laws and regulations of the destination country, for which one should obtain detailed information and adapt or plan accordingly. In any event, in most countries one must comply with certain basic rules to secure property acquisitions. In this respect Austria is exemplary, since land purchases can typically be handled safely and without any problems.

In the case of relocation and associated private property purchase, the main objective should be an improved quality of life. It is often the case, however, particularly in cases of cross-border relocation, that not all potential problems are considered, which is why it is important to seek professional counsel from lawyers, tax experts, architects, and reputable real estate companies. Ideally, each expert should not only be knowledgeable about the local conditions but also have experience in advising on relocation to the destination country. The resulting additional costs are compensated for in most instances by a fast and impeccable structuring and execution of the purchase.

In addition, the acquisition of real estate is always a capital investment; conservation of value and value growth, as well as tax and inheritance aspects, are therefore important factors to consider. Before acquiring a property, it is important to clarify these essential basic conditions to ensure protection from unexpected legal and tax consequences. While this applies to real estate in general, it is particularly relevant to foreign real estate.

When selecting a property, not only do the local legal and tax factors play a role; one should also investigate the development plans for the immediate surroundings. This is particularly important in a new country with which at first one is not as well acquainted as one's former homeland. For example, a beautiful property can quickly become unattractive if a highway is built nearby, or if a neighbor's construction project limits or even blocks an idyllic view. Major projects for which one should keep an eye out include the construction of future highways, airport extensions, high voltage lines, and landfills, because all these can affect one's quality of life and the value of one's property. Further considerations that would affect the price level at the time of purchase and in the future are site quality and infrastructure. One should ask oneself, for example, Where is the property located: is it on a quiet, peaceful street? What is the quality of the surrounding infrastructure? What is the distance to the nearest school, doctor, or hospital, and to basic amenities such as post office, bank, and shops? How accessible is the connection to national roads and highways? What is the journey time to the nearest airport? How well developed is the public transport system?

1.4 International insurance

Various aspects of insurance must be understood when planning international relocation, the most notable being health insurance. All too often, health insurance is not prudently factored in or included in advice to internationally mobile clients, which is possibly the reason there are relatively few companies worldwide that can truly and independently advise on this sensitive but important topic.

Finding good health insurance is not as simple as one might think, making it all the more important to identify a reliable insurer when relocating to ensure that, in the event of illness or an accident abroad, insurance cover is adequate and readily available. When considering providers and their offerings, try to identify which insurer places the fewest restrictions on one's choice of doctors and/or hospitals. Those who live, work, run a company, or retire abroad should be covered as widely as possible, ideally globally.

If a stay in a foreign European country is temporary, one can rely on the emergency care of basic state insurance for at least minimum coverage. In addition, travel insurance can be obtained for illness and accident cover with almost every local healthcare provider. In the case of a definitive residence insurance, however, it is advisable to be thoroughly informed about local insurance. As soon as the relocation process is officially completed, ensure that the planning and implementation of the changes to one's health insurance plan are also completed. Otherwise one risks not only being limited to consulting free doctors and hospitals, but in a worst case scenario, having temporarily no insurance cover at all.

For international relocation, other insurance policies should be considered too, however, since these are usually free of the restrictions found in health insurance they can, and often should, be completed or changed after the relocation. While the best deals are often concluded on the spot, it is important to assess whether the cover applies abroad as well. For example, a policy may cease to provide cover upon migration, or there may be a geographic restriction for a motor vehicle insurance. Confirmation that insurance cover will still exist ought to be obtained in writing so that, in the event of a possible damage claim, cover can be proved beyond doubt. One is usually well advised to select an internationally active insurance company, particularly for the insurance of special valuables such as art or jewelry. Insurance coverage is in many instances applicable worldwide and can be maintained even in the event of subsequent migration, such as in the case of an international health insurance policy.

1.5 Financial planning

Last but not least, pension and financial planning need to be re-parameterized during international relocation. As tax and legal framework conditions change during relocation, so should financial planning be adapted to the new situation.

For relocation purposes, financial planning starts with the reference currency, which often changes when one migrates across borders. If, for example, one moves from the US to Austria, the new reference currency is no longer the US dollar but the Euro. The re-evaluation of financial assets in the relevant currency is best planned and implemented with a qualified investment manager. This is less relevant in the case of relocation within the Eurozone, but here, too, a different currency weighting may make sense because time spent traveling may increase. Asset and pension planning can therefore be improved.

Often, capital that is tied up in pension funds regulated in state-regulated systems can be dissolved. The reallocation or liquidation of one's retirement provisions such as pension claims, life insurance, or pension funds is worth considering, since this can lead to tax breaks, particularly in the country of migration, and have a positive effect on liquidity planning. This may in some circumstances need to be adjusted for the new place of residence since expenditure may increase or decrease.

Furthermore, it may be sensible or necessary to 'buy into' the pension system of the new country of residence, and this may be advantageous from a tax perspective. In all events, these points should be very carefully checked.

It is very important to include estate planning and inheritance structures (for example, partnerships, foundations, trusts, and family holding companies) in financial planning for relocation. For example, a migrant setting up home in Malta, the UK, Ireland, St. Kitts and Nevis, or the Bahamas can structure assets in such a way that the appointment of a freely selectable successor is made possible. This is only rarely the case in countries such as Austria or others that follow a civil law tradition that includes forced heirship. Asset protection is also a significant factor in relocation and this is an especially important topic in the US. The American legal system facilitates civil lawsuits to such an extent that it makes sense to protect one's assets or part thereof, such as property ownership, from vulnerability by setting up appropriate structures. Correspondingly designed asset protection trusts, as well as specifically structured life insurance policies, are particularly suitable for this purpose. Even though this problem applies mainly in the US, it is becoming increasingly an issue in Europe and thereby putting European assets at risk.

International relocation should for all these reasons be planned carefully and accompanied by professional support to best position oneself to take advantage of all the positive aspects of relocation. As this introduction shows, many details must be considered, clarified, and checked. One should review not only tax advantages or disadvantages, but also factors such as legislation, financial and estate planning, and asset protection. Finally, it is important that one is aware that in the acquisition of real estate there is potential for growth in value. Relocation is not only an opportunity to enjoy an international lifestyle and all potential tax advantages, it also presents the possibility of optimizing personal wealth and providing for oneself and one's family in an international dimension. Austria offers optimal conditions in this regard.

About the author

DR. CHRISTIAN H. KÄLIN, TEP, IMCM, Chairman of Henley & Partners, is considered one of the world's foremost experts in investment migration and citizenship-by-investment, a field he pioneered. Holding master's and PhD degrees in law from the University of Zurich, he is a sought-after speaker and advises governments and international organizations. He is the author, co-author, or editor of many publications, including standard works such as the *Global Residence and Citizenship Handbook*, the *Henley & Partners – Kochenov Quality of Nationality Index*, and the *Switzerland Business & Investment Handbook*.

2 Transfer of Tax Residence to Austria: Tax Consequences

Dr. Yvonne Schuchter-Mang, LeitnerLeitner

The decision of whether to move to Austria depends on various parameters. Tax burden and the country's tax regime also play an important role in the decision-making process, particularly for wealthy private persons.

This chapter aims to provide a brief overview of the Austrian tax system. In addition, the prerequisites for a (successful) relocation and the tax consequences resulting from the transfer of residence to Austria are outlined for different asset categories. In this context, special focus is placed on wealthy individuals deriving their income solely from asset management and not from active work income.

2.1 Overview of the most important taxes

Income tax

The income of individuals is subject to income tax. Income tax is a direct and federal tax that is economically borne by the taxpayer. There are no local income taxes. The Fiscal Equalization Law details the rules on the division of income tax between the Federal Government, the provinces, and the municipalities (Community Federal Tax).

In general, the income tax is levied by assessment, based on income tax returns filed by taxpayers.[1] Income tax is usually withheld at source, however, particularly income from capital investment, from the disposition of real estate, and from employment.

1 For more details on income tax collection see 'Declaration obligation and collection of income tax'

Taxable income is the total income from all categories of income set off against losses arising from these categories after deduction of special expenses, extraordinary expenses, and certain exempt amounts.

Corporate income tax

Corporate income tax is the tax levied on the income of corporations. The definition of corporations especially covers legal entities governed by private law (for example, limited liability companies (GmbH), joint stock companies (AG), private foundations, or associations with independent legal existence). Speaking in general, corporations are regarded as independent taxable entities that bear the burden of taxation itself. Corporate profits are thus subject to corporate income tax. Dividend payments to individual shareholders or portfolio corporate shareholders are subject to a capital withholding tax (capital yield tax) at the time of distribution.

The current corporate income tax rate is 25%. Corporate income tax is levied by way of assessment based on corporate tax returns. Any profit derived by a corporation, regardless of whether distributed or retained, is subject to the flat rate of 25%.

Value-added tax

Value-added tax (VAT) is a consumption tax that applies to the supply of goods and services by businesses. VAT is an indirect tax, since it is collected by businesses from the end consumer who bears the ultimate economic burden of the tax. Businesses that carry out taxable transactions must pay invoiced VAT to the tax authorities by way of assessment.

Because of the VAT Directive of the EU, VAT within the EU is largely harmonized.

The current standard VAT rate is 20%. However, reduced rates of 13% or 10% are applicable for certain types of transactions (for example, residential leases, groceries, etc.).

Inheritance and gift tax

Since 1 August 2008, inheritance and gift (donation) tax is no longer levied in Austria. Consequently, transfers *mortis causa* and donations *inter vivos* after 31 July 2008 are no longer subject to inheritance and gift tax.

To enable the tax authorities to control certain transfers of assets, on 1 August 2008 a new notification obligation was introduced for *inter vivos* gifts. An exemption from the gift notification obligation applies, for example, to:

- Donations or gifts between related persons,[2] if the cumulated value of all donations within one year provided by one person to another does not exceed EUR 50,000
- Donations or gifts between other persons, if the cumulated value of all donations within five years provided by one person to another does not exceed EUR 15,000
- Donations or gifts of (domestic and foreign) real estate
- Occasional donations or gifts with a fair market value of EUR 1,000 as a maximum

Donations *inter vivos* are subject to gift notification if, upon receipt, the recipient or the donor has an Austrian residence, habitual place of abode or seat or place of effective management. It must be highlighted that a second residence is sufficient for the gift notification obligation (please note that this holds true even if the taxpayer applies the Secondary Residence Decree).[3] The recipient, the donor, as well as lawyers and notaries involved in preparing the relevant contracts or in charge of the gift notification are jointly liable for the gift notification.

Donations and gifts must be reported to the fiscal authorities within three months of the day the gift or donation is transferred to the beneficiary.

Any violation of the gift notification requirement constitutes a breach of financial regulations which is punishable by a fine of up to 10% of the fair market value of the donation. A donation notification exempting the taxpayer from punishment (voluntary disclosure) may only be submitted within 15 months from the date of donation.

Real estate tax

Real estate tax (*Grundsteuer*) is imposed on Austrian situs real estate covering agricultural and forestry assets, real estate as well as business premises. According to the Austrian financial constitutional law, real estate tax is a municipal tax. Thus, tax revenues are levied by and are at the exclusive disposal of municipalities.

---

2 Related persons are, for example, spouses (also after divorce), registered partners, children, grandchildren, parents, siblings, aunt/uncle, niece/nephew, cousins, daughters-/sons- or sisters-/brothers-in-law, adoptive parents or adopted children, foster parents or foster children, etc.

3 See 'Secondary Residence Decree'

The base for real estate tax assessment is the so called *Grundsteuermessbetrag*, a value assessed by the competent tax authority. A specific multiplier of up to 500% is applied to this amount at a municipal level. Special reduced rates are available for agricultural and forestry properties, single family homes, and residential rental properties.

Real estate tax is generally levied on an annual basis. The tax is due quarterly in four partial amounts (or as an annual payment if the tax does not exceed EUR 75).

Real estate transfer tax

The transfer of Austrian situs real estate (land and buildings) is subject to real estate transfer tax. Taxable events include the sale, exchange, and contribution to capital upon formation of a company. Real estate transfer tax is also triggered if Austrian situs real estate is transferred to a private foundation or a comparable foreign foundation or trust irrespective of a written contract. Transfers of beneficial ownership are also taxable. Furthermore, the transfer of at least 95% of the shares in a partnership or a corporation owing Austrian situs real estate is also subject to real estate transfer tax.

The taxable base is usually the value of the consideration given for the transfer, but at least the land value (*Grundstückswert*), which is generally derived from the fair market value. The land value applies to gratuitous transfers, reorganizations, and if at least 95% of the shares in a partnership or a company owning Austrian situs real estate are transferred, united, or taken over by one shareholder. The unit value (*Einheitswert*) applies only to the transfer of agricultural and forestry land.

The applicable tax rate depends on the type of transaction. If the consideration amounts to more than 70% of the land value, the applicable tax rate is 3.5% (based on the consideration). If the value of the consideration is between 30% and 70% of the land value, a rate of 3.5% applies to the consideration while the remaining part of the land value is subject to the progressive tax rates for transactions without consideration. If the consideration amounts to 30% of the land value or less, the entire land value is subject to the progressive tax rates. The progressive tax rates amount to 0.5% for land values ranging from EUR 0 to EUR 250,000, 2% from EUR 250,000 to EUR 400,000, and 3.5% from EUR 400,000. In the case of reorganizations, a general rate of 0.5% applies.

If Austrian situs real estate is transferred to a private foundation or to a comparable trust without consideration or at a consideration between 30% and 70% of the land value, the real estate transfer tax is increased by 2.5% of the difference between the land value and any consideration.

Additional registration fees (*Grundbuchseintragungsgebühr*), and other fees and charges, in total about 2%, should be taken into consideration when calculating the costs incurred at the acquisition of Austrian situs real estate.

A tax return must be filed by the 15th day of the second month following the month in which the taxable event took place. The tax must be paid one month after its assessment. The taxpayer is generally the purchaser, but the seller is jointly and severally liable for the payment of the tax. The control of the tax is facilitated by requiring courts, notaries, and keepers of real estate registers to notify the tax office of any taxable acquisitions.

Fees and other transfer taxes

Insurance premium tax

A special insurance tax (*Versicherungssteuer*) is levied on the payment of insurance premiums. The rate of this tax amounts to 4% for life insurance and insurance against disability if the term of the insurance is more than 15 years (or one year if the policyholder and the insured person have reached 50 years of age); otherwise, the rate amounts to 11%. In certain cases, moreover, a subsequent taxation is triggered for life insurances of 7%. For health insurance the insurance tax rate is 1%. For all other forms of insurance the rate is 11%, with a few exceptions.

The insurance tax is withheld at source if the insurance company is resident in Austria. The same is true for an insurance company resident in the EU or in the European Economic Area (EEA) if the insurance company has appointed a tax representative in Austria. Otherwise, the policyholder must pay the tax.

Standard consumption duty

The standard consumption duty (*Normverbrauchsabgabe*) is levied on the final supply of new passenger vehicles and motorcycles by an Austrian entrepreneur. Supplies to dealers, leasing companies, taxis, car rentals, and driving schools are exempt. The standard consumption duty is also triggered if new or used cars are imported to Austria. Electric cars are exempt from the standard consumption duty.

The taxable base is the consideration paid within the meaning of the VAT law or, in some cases, the fair market value. VAT at the rate of 20% is currently calculated from the price including the standard consumption duty. The tax rates vary between 0% and 32%, depending on the average CO_2 emissions.

Stamp duties

Stamp duties are levied on selected legal transactions that are concluded in written forms (for example, protocols, official documents, easements, lease and rental agreements, guarantees, and assignment agreements). Apart from a few exceptions, the obligation to pay fees is triggered only if a written certificate exists. The rates vary between 0.8% and 2% of the underlying transaction value. In some cases, the stamp duties are levied at flat rates.

2.2 Unlimited income tax liability: domicile or habitual place of abode in Austria

Overview

Table 2.1 An overview of income tax liability

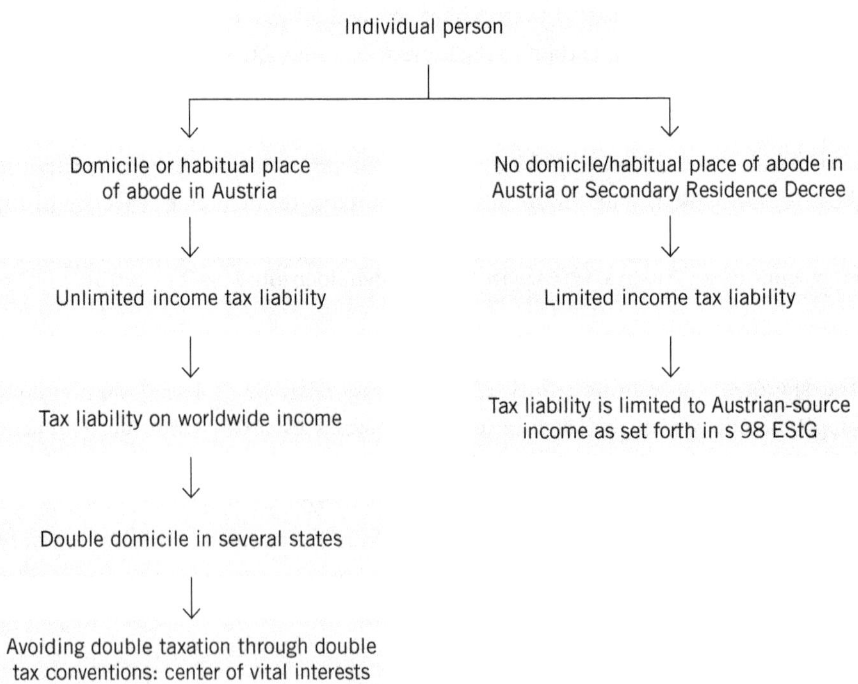

Individuals who have their domicile or habitual place of abode in Austria are subject to unlimited income tax liability, i.e. their worldwide income is subject to income tax liability in Austria.

If there is no domicile or habitual place of abode in Austria, the individual is subject only to limited tax liability in Austria, i.e. only special Austrian situs income sources trigger income tax in Austria if they are explicitly listed in s 98(1) of the EStG. The same holds true for an individual who has a domicile in Austria, but whose center of vital interests is abroad when applying the Secondary Residence Decree.[4]

Unlimited income tax liability begins with the establishment of a domicile or habitual place of abode in Austria and continues until the individual gives up the domicile, leaves Austria permanently, or dies.

According to the general tax provisions, the transfer of residence to or from Austria must be reported to the competent tax office within one month.

When an individual transfers his/her tax residence to Austria, at the time of the transfer of residence a tax-neutral step-up to the fair market value is granted for capital assets generating income from capital investment or derivatives, and for substantial shareholdings in corporations, i.e. the tax relevant acquisition costs of such assets is the fair market value at the time of the transfer of residence.[5]

On the contrary, circumstances leading to a restriction of the Austrian taxing right, i.e. the transfer of residence to another country with respect to capital assets generating income from capital investment or derivative financial instruments as well as substantial shareholdings in corporations, trigger exit taxation in Austria. A sale of such assets is thus simulated when the Austrian taxing right is restricted, for example, if the tax residence is transferred abroad.[6]

Domicile

A domicile is any place where an apartment or house is possessed under circumstances that indicate that the apartment or house will be maintained and used not merely on a temporary basis.[7] It is therefore crucial that:[8]

- The individual has the power to dispose of the domestic house or apartment
- It can be clearly identified that the taxpayer would like to keep it and uses it as such

4 *Zweitwohnsitzverordnung*

5 For more details see 'Capital gains from the sale of assets generating income from capital investment (realized increases in value)'

6 For more details see 'Capital gains from the sale of assets generating income from capital investment (realized increases in value)'

7 S 2(1) BAO

8 Loukota, (2004) *SWI* 53

A domicile is relevant to tax matters only if the taxpayer can use the apartment at any time for his/her own purposes. The apartment must therefore be available to the taxpayer all the time. The decisive factor is the actual (and not the legal) authority of disposal over the apartment.

Consequently, a domicile may be any room that is dedicated to residential purposes (for example, a summer residence or even a hotel room that is rented on a long-term basis). The apartment is considered possessed by the individual if the individual actually uses or has the right to use the apartment for his/her residential purposes. An Austrian domicile is constituted if the individual, from the beginning of his/her stay in Austria, intends to maintain the Austrian apartment for more than six months. Under a specific decree of the BMF, an Austrian secondary domicile is not considered a domicile triggering unlimited income tax liability in Austria on worldwide income if the requirements of the Secondary Residence Decree are met.[9] Unless the requirements for the application of the Secondary Residence Decree are met,[10] a holiday apartment might also constitute a domicile for tax purposes as, according to jurisprudence, the duration of the stay is not of significant importance for the assessment.[11] According to the jurisprudence, however, a minimum usage level of the apartment is required for establishing a domicile in Austria.[12]

Furthermore, a domicile does not exist if an individual regularly rents apartments, holiday houses, or hotel rooms but does not regularly use the same apartment, holiday house or hotel room.[13,14] The disposal of an apartment is deemed to be permanent if it can be used for at least six months.[15]

Real estate in Austria that is rented out to third parties does not constitute the domicile of the owner in Austria. The same is true for unfurnished apartments because they can not be used for residential purposes.[16]

According to fiscal practice, spouses in intact marriages derive their tax domiciles from each other. This applies to minor children too. Children who have reached their majority and run their own households establish an independent domicile

9 See 'Secondary Residence Decree'
10 See also 'Secondary Residence Decree'
11 VwGH 22 March 1991, 90/13/0073
12 UFS 27 June 2008, RV/0172-S/06 as well as UFS 12 December 2006, RV/3046-W/02: at least two or three months
13 See Loukota, (2004) *SWI* 53
14 Renting a hotel room on a long-term basis may lead to a domicile in Austria (see Ritz, BAO, s 26 No 2 with further details)
15 See, for example, Stoll, BAO, 335; Ritz, BAO, s 26 No 9
16 See EStR 2000 No 21 et seq.

even if they still have an allocated room in the house of their parents. The room in their parents' house may, however, qualify as an additional domicile. According to fiscal practice, students who are financially dependent on their parents and are renting their apartments at their places of study may maintain their domicile if accommodation in their parents' houses is nonetheless permanently available.[17]

If an individual residing abroad inherits a domestic apartment, in order to establish a fiscal domicile in Austria he/she needs to take action that indicates that the apartment is actually used for his/her own purposes.

The registration with the registration office (usually the competent municipality) is not decisive for establishing a domicile in Austria. In cases of doubt, however, the registration may be taken as circumstantial evidence.[18]

Secondary Residence Decree

Special rules apply if a taxpayer has had his/her center of vital interests outside Austria for more than five years (*Secondary Residence Decree*).[19] In this case, maintaining an Austrian secondary domicile triggers unlimited income tax liability in Austria on his/her worldwide income for only the calendar years in which he/she (i) has used the apartment (only, or as well as other apartments) for more than 70 days and (ii) keeps a record of the dates on which he/she has used the Austrian secondary domicile.[20,21]

His/her center of vital interests is in the country in which he/she has — in the light of overall conditions and circumstances — the closest personal and economic relationships. Facts such as the arrangement of family life, societal, personal, cultural or religious interests and activities, circle of friends or acquaintances, professional activities, income sources, and property ties are all relevant for the determination of the center of vital interests.

In general, an individual is deemed to have the strongest personal connections to the country in which he/she lives together with his/her family.[22]

When the tax residence is transferred abroad and the conditions of the Secondary Residence Decree are met, the consequences of the Secondary Residence Decree apply from the beginning of the following calendar year.[23] If, however, the taxpayer

17 See EStR 2000 No 22
18 See, for example, VwGH 3 July 2003, 99/15/0104
19 Federal Law Gazette II 2003/528
20 See Loukota, (2004) *SWI* 53 et seq.
21 BMF 21 April 2010, EAS 3149
22 See also 'Tax residences in the light of double taxation conventions'
23 S 2 Secondary Residence Decree

relocates his/her center of vital interests back to Austria within five years of his/her departure, the preconditions for applying the Secondary Residence Decree cease to exist. As a result, income tax must be paid on the worldwide income retroactively for prior years of assessment.

The Secondary Residence Decree applies only if the taxpayer keeps records of the days actually spent in the domestic apartment. If no proper records are kept (intentionally or unintentionally), the taxpayer becomes subject to unlimited income tax liability in Austria. This means that the effects of the limited income tax liability cannot occur against a person's will. Random calendar entries do not meet the documentation requirements necessary for the application of Secondary Residence Decree.

For the calculation of the relevant days to apply the Secondary Residence Decree, all days on which the apartment is used (whether it is used on a daily or hourly basis) must be taken into account (overnight stays are not decisive for the calculation). If more than one apartment is available to the taxpayer, all days on which the apartments in Austria are used must be added up. Hotel stays must not be included in the calculation. Spouses and (registered) partners need to keep separate records.

If the spouse or (registered) partner is not permanently separated from the taxpayer and uses the domestic residence for more than 70 days per year, thereby being subject to unlimited income tax liability in Austria, the Secondary Residence Decree is not applicable to the taxpayer. As a result, both spouses or (registered) partners are subject to unlimited income tax liability.[24] In other words, the Secondary Residence Decree cannot be applied unilaterally by only one spouse or (registered) partner.

Habitual place of abode

The habitual place of abode is the place where an individual is present under circumstances which indicate that the individual will stay at that place not just temporarily.[25] Thus, an individual may have several places of residence, but can have only one habitual place of abode. Whether a stay is temporary or not is assessed on a case-by-case basis. Physical presence in Austria in excess of six months results in unlimited income tax liability in Austria on worldwide income in any case.

---

24 S 3 Secondary Residence Decree
25 S 26(2) BAO

Generally, a continuous presence of six months is required. However, periods of temporary presence in Austria will be added up if the individual has an obvious intention to return to, and continues the stay in, Austria at the time the individual leaves Austria. If the period of actual presence in Austria exceeds six months, the individual's habitual abode is deemed to have commenced at the beginning of the six-month period. The six-month period does not have to be within the same calendar year.

The habitual abode ends at the time the individual leaves Austria not just temporarily. It is therefore assumed that the habitual abode ends once the individual has left Austria for a period of more than six months.[26]

Tax incentives for moving in

The Federal Ministry of Finance may grant relief to individuals who become a tax resident of Austria to carry out research or development activities or who are sportsmen or artists by profession to compensate for the additional tax burden attributable to the move. The possible relief, however, does not apply for Austrian income sources subject to limited income tax liability according to s 98 of the EStG.[27]

This relief may be granted as a deduction of certain expenses for wage tax purposes or a lump-sum tax rate of at least 15%.

The tax incentive is available only upon request. The decision on a possible tax incentive is at the discretion of the Federal Ministry of Finance. Such requests are handled very restrictively.

Gift notification obligation and Second Residence Decree

As outlined in 'Inheritance and gift tax', these are no longer levied in Austria since 1 August 2008. However, a gift notification obligation has been introduced regarding gifts *inter vivos*.

Thus, gifts must be reported to the competent tax office if either the donor or recipient of the gift has a domicile or habitual place of abode in Austria at the time of the donation. The gift notification obligation also applies if the Secondary Residence Decree applies for the donor or recipient of the gift since this decree applies only for income tax purposes.[28]

26 BMF 10 July 2000, EAS 1681
27 S 103 EStG
28 See for example, *Jakom*/Marschner, EStG 2017, s 1 No 41

2.3 Tax residences in the light of double taxation conventions

Individuals may have several domiciles in different states. In some countries the establishment of a domicile may lead to unlimited tax liability (as in Austria), and therefore to the taxation of the individual's worldwide income.

It is therefore not rare in practice for the same person to be subject to unlimited tax liability in two or more states. This may lead to the circumstance that in two states worldwide income is taxed. More frequently, persons are subject to unlimited tax liability based on their domicile, place of abode or citizenship, or any other personal connection in just one state, receiving income from another state. In that other state they are subject to limited tax liability.

To avoid double taxation, many states have concluded bilateral international tax conventions to eliminate it. These agreements are known as double taxation conventions determining the extent to which each state may levy tax and defining methods to avoid double taxation. Thereby, the double tax convention defines a residence and a source state.

The resident state has extensive taxation rights, whereas the taxation rights of the source state is usually limited to certain domestic income sources (for example, dividends, interest, and royalties). The allocation rules often set forth that the source state's tax may not exceed a certain rate. The avoidance of the remaining double taxation is dealt with in the method article (the exemption method versus the credit method).

In the case of an individual being a resident in both contracting states (due to a domicile, place of abode or citizenship), tie-breaker rules will determine the residence state of this individual. The first criterion that applies to determine the residence state is the permanent home. If an individual owns a permanent home in both contracting states, that person will be a resident of the state with which, in the light of overall conditions and circumstances, his/her personal and economic relationships are closer, i.e. the state where his/her center of vital interests is located.[29]

The center of vital interests is established in the state in which an individual has the closest personal and economic relationships.[30] For the determination of the personal relationships, facts such as arrangement of a person's family life as well as social, personal, cultural or religious interests and activities, including any membership of associations or clubs, will be taken into consideration. Crucial determinants for the economic relationships are the individual's professional activity

29 Art 4(2) lit a OECD-MA
30 EStR 2000 No 7593

as well as sources of income in a country.[31] According to Austrian jurisprudence and fiscal practice, in cases of doubt, personal relationships (especially the arrangement of a person's family life) are decisive for determining the center of vital interests.[32] The center of vital interests for families with school-age children is generally in the state where children attend school. The size of an apartment or house may also be an indication for the center of vital interests. Furthermore, the center of vital interests requires a certain degree of sustainability; permanent presence, however, is not necessary. Relocation of the center of vital interests is usually not assumed in the case of short-term stays in Austria (if the individual retains a permanent home in another state).[33]

If it is not possible to clearly determine the center of vital interests, or in cases in which the taxpayer has no permanent home in any state, the person's habitual abode will be determinative according to convention law.[34] Therefore, the state of residence shall be the state in which an individual spends more time[35] and usually lives.[36] For persons who are solely concerned with the administration and management of their assets (with grown-up children), the duration of physical presence in the relevant countries may be decisive for the determination of the state of residence according to tax convention law if the center of vital interests cannot be clearly identified by other circumstantial evidence.

In a case in which the habitual place of abode exists in both (or neither) of the contracting states, the individual may be deemed a resident of the state of citizenship.[37] Thus, nationality or citizenship under domestic law is decisive in this case.

The extensive taxation rights are allocated to the state of residence by the double tax convention, as determined according to the above-mentioned tie-breaker rules (for example, capital gains, income from capital investment, etc.), while the other state may have only source taxation rights.

Apart from double taxation conventions, double taxation might be eliminated on request by unilateral measures based on general national taxation rules (for example, if a treaty does not offer sufficient protection against double taxation, or if no tax treaty convention is in place, or does not apply).[38]

31 VwGH 25 June 2008, 2008/15/0166

32 VwGH 22 March 1991, 90/13/0073; Lang, *Introduction to the Law of Double Taxation Conventions* 79

33 For documentation of the center of vital interests see the checklist provided in the appendix

34 Art 4(2) lit b OECD-MA; also see Lang, *Introduction to the Law of Double Taxation Conventions* 79

35 OECD-MK, art 4 No 17

36 See Lehner, in Vogel and Lehner, *DBA*, art 4 No 204; Kaeser and Wassermeyer, in Wassermeyer, Kaeser, Lang and Schuch, *Doppelbesteuerung*, art 4 MA No 76 et seq.

37 Art 4(2) lit c OECD-MA

38 S 48 BAO; Lang, *Introduction to the Law of Double Taxation Conventions* 26

One example of such a unilateral measure might be the application of the Secondary Residence Decree, which is of great importance should an individual move to Austria but still have a domicile, a habitual place of abode, or citizenship in a state with which Austria has not (yet) concluded a double tax convention (for example, the Principality of Monaco).

2.4 Unlimited personal income tax liability on worldwide income in Austria

Unlimited income tax liability means that the worldwide income of an Austrian taxpayer is subject to income tax. Taxable income is the total amount of all seven categories of income after the deduction of special expenses, which include loss carry-forwards, extraordinary burdens, tax-exempt amounts, and losses incurred in these categories.[39]

The seven income categories for individuals

Austrian income tax law contains an exhaustive list of categories of taxable income; income not falling under any of these categories is not taxable. For individuals, the categories are:

Table 2.2 Taxable income for individuals

<table>
<tr><td>Income from agriculture and forestry</td><td rowspan="3">BUSINESS INCOME</td><td rowspan="4">MAIN CATEGORIES</td></tr>
<tr><td>Income from professional and other independent services</td></tr>
<tr><td>Income from trade and business</td></tr>
<tr><td>Employment income</td><td rowspan="4">NON-BUSINESS INCOME</td></tr>
<tr><td>Capital investment income</td><td rowspan="3">ANCILLARY CATEGORIES</td></tr>
<tr><td>Income from rents, lease payments, and royalties</td></tr>
<tr><td>Other specified income</td></tr>
</table>

39 S 2(2) EStG

Austrian tax law includes special provisions to calculate the profit for the business income categories (either through corporate or tax law accounting regulations or accounting on a cash basis). Income from non-business income categories is defined as the surplus of revenue over expenditure.

Business related income generally differs from non-business related income according to the difference between the value of the enterprise's assets at the end of a financial year, and the value of those assets at the end of the preceding financial year, plus withdrawals, less contributions to the capital of a business during the year. Moreover, business income must be computed based on a profit and loss account. Generally, the increase or decrease in value of private assets is not taxable.

Capital gains realized for private assets are subject to income tax if they are realized within the speculative period of one year or stem from the alienation of shares forming substantial shareholdings (of at least 1% in capital). Moreover, capital gains (and losses) realized from the disposition of portfolio shareholdings and investment fund units purchased after 31 December 2010, as well as from other capital market products, i.e. bonds, debt securities, index-linked notes, and derivative financial instruments acquired after 31 March 2012 (new holdings), are subject to income tax irrespective of the holding period.[40] Furthermore, capital gains derived from the alienation of privately held real estate are taxable irrespective of the holding period at a flat income tax rate of 30%. Lower rates may apply for real estate purchased before 1 April 2002 or if the real estate was not subject to capital gains tax in Austria before 1 April 2012. This tax is withheld and paid to the relevant authority by the notaries and lawyers conducting transfers of real estate on or after that date.[41]

The ancillary categories of income are subsidiary to the main categories of income, therefore interest on bonds and bank deposits is treated as income from capital investment to the extent only that the respective investment is not attributable to business assets.

When calculating total income, negative income may be offset against positive income from other income sources (loss compensation). This, however, does not apply to so-called loss-sharing models. Furthermore, loss compensation is restricted for losses from capital investment,[42] as well as for services and short-term sales transactions that do not result from capital assets.

40 See also 'Capital gains from the sale of assets generating income from capital investment (realized increases in value)' and 'Grandfathering Rules for the taxation of capital gains from capital investments' for more details

41 See 'Capital gains from the alienation of real estate' for more details

42 See 'Losses from income from capital investment'

As a rule, loss carried forward across accounting periods is available only for business income.[43]

Declaration obligation and collection of income tax

In general, the tax year is the calendar year.[44] If an individual changes his/her residence for tax purposes into or out of Austria during the calendar year, this results in two different assessments: one for the period of residence for tax purposes in Austria and the other for the period of non-residence for tax purposes in Austria.

Income tax is usually levied by way of assessment based on income tax returns. Generally, tax returns are due by 30 April of the year following the tax year or on 30 June of the year following the tax year if the tax return is submitted electronically. If, however, the taxpayer is represented by a professional Austrian tax advisor, the deadline is extended to 31 March of the second year following the end of the respective year of assessment.

If a taxpayer expects tax arrears for a year of assessment, it is recommended to make prepayments until 30 September of the year following the year of assessment, as tax authorities start imposing interest on arrears as of 1 October of the following year.[45]

During the year, the taxpayer must make prepayments based on the taxable income of the preceding income tax assessment. The prepayments are in each case due on 15 February, 15 May, 15 August, and 15 November.

Generally, individuals who are resident for tax purposes (unlimited tax liability) in Austria must file an income tax return if:[46]

- The tax office requests the taxpayer to file a tax return
- The income entirely or partly consists of business income and the profit had to be or was computed by way of accounting
- The income (not including income from employment) exceeds EUR 11,000
- Income from capital investment is not subject to withholding tax, unless taxation at the general rate pursuant would not result in a tax liability
- Real estate income tax is self-computed but not paid or is paid but is not final

Taxpayers whose income consists solely of income from an Austrian employment subject to wage withholding tax generally do not need to file an annual income tax return. However, an employee must file a tax return if, for example:[47]

43 S 18(6) EStG
44 S 2 EStG
45 Currently the interest on arrears amounts to 1.38% pa
46 S 42 EStG
47 S 41 EStG

- The employee receives income from:
  - Other sources of income exceeding a total of EUR 730
  - Two or more employers, and such income has been taxed separately
  - Capital investment which is not subject to withholding tax
  - The sale of privately held real estate and real estate income tax was not paid, or the payment of real estate income tax was not final
- A decree on tax-free amounts was considered in the computation of wage tax
- Certain tax credits (sole earner credit, sole educator credit, etc.) have been claimed, but the prerequisites for such allowances to apply were not met
- The employee and the employer collaborated with the intent to pursue an illegal advantage resulting in a reduction of wage tax, and the employee may be held directly liable for wage tax

Income tax on income from employment is basically withheld at source (wage tax). Hence, employees are generally not required to file income tax returns. An employee may file an income tax return on a voluntary basis, and request assessment of tax by the tax office within five years from the end of the assessment basis. The tax assessment based on a voluntary income tax return may result in a credit or a refund of income tax, for example if the employee's income has changed during the calendar year or the employee did not receive remuneration during the entire calendar year.

Income from capital investment is in many cases subject to a final withholding tax. As a result, no assessment for such income is necessary.[48]

The taxation of privately owned assets

Capital investment income

With effect from 1 April 2012, a new regime for the taxation of capital investment income came into force. The new tax regime sets forth three types of capital investment income: (i) income from investment of capital, (ii) capital gains from the sale of assets generating income from capital investment (realized increases in value) regardless of the holding period,[49] and (iii) income from derivative financial instruments.[50]

48 See 'Income from derivative financial instruments' for more details

49 See the favorable grandfathering rules in 'Grandfathering Rules for the taxation of capital gains from capital investments'

50 S 27 EStG

Table 2.3 Three types of capital investment income

Capital investment income

- Income from investment of capital
- Capital gains from the sale of assets generating income from capital investment (realized increases in value)
- Income from derivative financial instruments

Special tax rate of 25% or 27.5%

Exceptions: for example, bonds and real investment funds not offered to the public, interest on private loans, uncertificated derivative financial instruments

Capital investment income is generally subject to a special tax rate of 25% or 27.5%. If the capital assets are held with a domestic bank, the income generated is generally subject to a final withholding tax[51] of 25% or 27.5%. Since this withholding tax is final, the income does not have to be included in the income tax return. However, the taxpayer may file a tax return and apply for taxation and the applicable regular income tax rate (if the applicable tax rate is below 25% or 27.5%).[52]

Income from investment of capital

Income from the investment of capital includes, inter alia:

- Dividend income: dividends and other earnings from shares in a domestic or foreign stock company or a company with limited liability, similar earnings from shares in commercial cooperatives, and similar earnings from participation rights, and other financing instruments as well as participation rights
- Interest income: interest on bonds, bank deposits, time deposits, savings books, and other income from capital receivables of any kind, for example, under loans, bonds (including zero bonds), mortgages, and savings with a credit institution (except accrued interest). Pro rata interest accrued until the disposal of a debt capital instrument that is passed on to the buyer at the time of the sale increases, on the one hand the disposal proceeds of the seller, and on the other hand the acquisition costs of the buyer, but is not treated as interest income for income tax purposes

51 *Kapitalertragssteuer*

52 See 'Tax consequences' and 'Withholding tax and final taxation' for more details

- Distributions from Austrian private foundations, or foreign foundations, or trusts that are comparable to an Austrian private foundation: income from capital investment does not, however, include the distribution out of the substance, i.e. the assets that have been transferred to the private foundation. Accordingly, distributions are tax neutral if they exceed the balance sheet profit at the beginning of the business year, increased by profit reserves and hidden reserves of the assets transferred to the private foundation. Tax neutral treatment requires that the private foundation particularly accounts for the transfers to, and the distributions of, such transfers by the private foundation in a special account
- Special consideration or benefits paid alongside, or instead of, income from capital investment, for example, in kind benefits or other amounts due to indexation[53]
- Amounts of withholding tax borne by the withholding agent or a third party
- Difference payments under security lending and repo transactions
- Certain difference amounts between insurance proceeds and insurance premiums paid

Capital gains from the sale of assets generating income from capital investment (realized increases in value)

Capital gains from the sale, redemption or other settlement of assets generating income from capital investment (shares, bonds, etc.) are income from capital investment in the form of realized increases in value irrespective of the holding period. Mere valuation gains of privately held assets are not subject to income tax.

A sale within the present context is also constituted by circumstances that restrict the Austrian taxing right over these assets resulting in exit taxation.[54] An exemption from immediate taxation (where applicable in instalments) is available if:

- The taxpayer moves abroad to another EU/EEA member state
- The asset generating income from capital investment or the derivative financial instrument is transferred gratuitously (for example, by inheritance or gift) to another individual who is resident in another EU/EEA member state

In these cases, the taxpayer may request, in the tax return of the relevant year, that the tax is deferred until the assets are sold.

53 *Wertsicherung*

54 S 27(6)(1) EStG

An actual sale is also constituted and Austrian income tax is levied retroactively if the taxpayer moves to (or transfers the asset or derivative to) a state which is neither an EU nor EEA member state. The statute of limitation expires 10 years from the end of the year in which the retroactive event occurs.[55]

If the Austrian taxing right is restricted in relation to another EU/EEA member state because of other reasons, the taxpayer may request payment of the tax due in instalments over seven years (the first instalment is due at the end of the month in which the tax assessment is issued, further instalments are due on 30 September of the years following).

Income tax triggered by the taxpayer moving abroad is not subject to final withholding tax (although the taxpayer must include the income details in the tax return) unless the taxpayer gives an exact exit date to the withholding agent.

If the taxpayer moves to Austria, capital assets or derivative financial instruments are assessed at their fair market value, i.e. the tax relevant acquisition costs are equal to the fair market value when moving to Austria. If, when moving to Austria, the capital assets are transferred to or held with an Austrian depository bank it is crucial that the bank is informed in advance about the actual day of transferring the tax residence to Austria. If not, the tax withheld at source when realizing taxable capital gains is not correct and therefore not final, initiating the obligation to include such sales in the income tax return of the taxpayer.[56] If the taxpayer, before moving to Austria, moved abroad from Austria and requested that the exit tax be deferred, the initial acquisition costs (but not more than the fair market value) of the asset or derivative remain relevant for tax purposes (no 'step-up'). In this case, the later sale of the assets or derivatives is not a retroactive event. If proven by the taxpayer, increases in value that occurred in the EU/EEA area may be deducted from the capital gain.

A sale in this context is also triggered by a withdrawal from deposit of asset generating income from investment, unless the assets are transferred:[57]

- To another deposit of the same taxpayer held with the same depository bank
- To a deposit of the same taxpayer held with an Austrian depository bank, provided that the taxpayer instructs the transferring (domestic or foreign) depository bank to inform the receiving depository bank of the acquisition costs of the assets

55 S 209(5) BAO
56 S 97(1)(b) EStG
57 S 27(6)(2) EStG

- From an Austrian depository bank held with a non-Austrian depository bank of the same taxpayer, provided that the taxpayer instructs the transferring Austrian depository bank to inform the tax office of his/her name and tax identification number, the transferred assets, the acquisition costs of the assets, and the new depository foreign bank, within one month
- From a non-Austrian depository bank to a deposit with another non-Austrian depository bank of the same taxpayer, or gratuitously to a deposit of another taxpayer, provided that the taxpayer informs the tax office of the transferred assets, the acquisition costs of the assets transferred and the recipient of the assets, as well as the new depository foreign bank, within one month
- Gratuitously from an Austrian depository to a deposit of another taxpayer if (i) proof of the gratuitous transfer is provided to the depository, or (ii) the taxpayer instructs the transferring depository to inform the tax office of his/her name and tax identification number, the transferred assets, the acquisition costs of the assets, and the new depository bank, within one month

Capital gains resulting from the sale of other assets (except for derivative financial instruments) are subject to income tax only if they are realized within the speculation period of one year (for example, capital gains derived from the sale of physically actual precious metals).[58]

Income from derivative financial instruments

Income from derivative financial instruments (for example, forwards, options, futures, swaps, index-linked notes, etc.) is also regarded as income from capital investment irrespective of the holding period.

Income from derivative instruments comprises particularly the following items:[59]

- Difference payments
- Option premiums
- Income from another form of settlement under forward transactions and other derivative financial instruments

Other derivative financial instruments within this context are derivative financial instruments, irrespective of whether the underlying consists of financial assets,

58 See Kirchmayr and Polivanova-Rosenauer, (2010) *ÖBA* 781; Strunz, (2010) *SWK* 1388
59 S 27(4) EStG

commodities, or other assets, so that all types of linked notes (index, alpha, leverage, sport, etc.) are covered.

It must to be noted that exercising an option leading, for example, to an actual delivery of the underlying is not a taxable event. In this case, capital gains/losses are realized only when the underlying is sold. If the underlying is not a capital asset (for example, precious metals) a taxable speculative transaction might be triggered by its sale if it is sold within the speculative period of one year.[60]

Tax consequences

Generally, all three types of capital investment income are subject to a special income tax rate of 25% or 27.5%. The special tax rate also applies to income from foreign income sources. In this case, the special income tax is subject to income tax assessment and therefore must be included in the income tax return of the taxpayer.

If the special income tax applies, it is levied by way of withholding on income if it is paid out by the debtor of the dividends or the interest has its seat or place of effective management in Austria, an Austrian depository, or an Austrian paying agent. An Austrian depository or paying agent may be a credit institution, an Austrian branch of a non-Austrian credit institution, or an Austrian branch of certain investment service providers.

A special income tax rate of 25% applies for interest income on cash deposits and other non-securitized receivables with credit institutions except difference payments under security lending and repo transactions. In all other cases, the special income tax rate amounts to 27.5%.

The special income tax rate of 25% or 27.5% is not applicable to income from the investment of capital and realized capital gains in the following cases:

- Income from 'private loans' (unsecuritized loans and receivables not based on a banking transaction)
- Income from bonds, linked notes, and real estate investment funds if they were not legally and factually offered to the public (i.e. to an indefinite number of persons) at the time they were issued
- Income from unsecuritized derivative financial instruments (exception: the Austrian paying agent levies the final withholding tax voluntarily)

60 S 31 EStG

- Profit shares from silent partnerships
- Discount amounts of bills of exchanges and other orders
- Compensations and lending fees from repurchase agreements (securities loan) if the borrower is not a credit institution
- Differences arising out of endowment insurance as well as realized value increases achieved by the sales of entitlements of insurance contracts

If the special income tax rate of 25% or 27.5% does not apply, the normal progressive income tax rate with a maximum rate of 50% (55%)[61] is applicable. Such income must be included in the income tax return and is subject to normal income tax assessment.

If the taxpayer's personal progressive tax rate is lower than the 25% or 27.5% special income tax rate, the taxpayer may opt also to request taxation at the progressive rate for income that would otherwise be subject to the special rate.

For capital investment income that is subject to the special income tax rate of 25% or 27.5%, the special income tax rate is calculated based on the gross amount. Expenses in connection with the capital investment income (for example, custody or bank fees, asset management fees, etc.) are thus not tax deductible. The same is true for all acquisition-related costs (for example, transaction costs or subscription fees for funds).

Withholding tax and final taxation

Withholding tax at the rate of 27.5% is generally final, i.e. the income does not have to be included in the income tax return. Withholding tax does not apply to investment income that is not subject to the special tax rate of 25% or 27.5%.

No withholding tax is levied, however, on income from capital investment generated from assets held with foreign banks (except for dividends paid out by domestic corporations). This income must be included in the taxpayer's income tax return, will be taxed at the special income tax rate of 25% or 27.5%, and is subject to income tax assessment.

Losses from income from capital investment

With effect from 1 April 2012, special loss set-off provisions apply to losses from capital investment. Generally, a loss set-off is available over all three categories of income from capital investment. Thus, for example, a loss from the alienation of

61 The rate of 55% applies to income parts over EUR 1 million in the calendar years 2016 to 2020

a portfolio shareholding may be offset with interest payments from a bond. The loss set-off is, however, available only to realized capital gains and losses resulting from capital assets and derivative financial instruments if they are not subject to grandfathering rules.[62] Moreover, the loss set-off in particular is subject to the following limitations:[63]

- Losses from the sale of assets generating income from capital investment or derivative financial instruments may not be set off against interest income resulting from cash deposits, and non-securitized other claims with credit institutions
- Income from capital investment that is subject to the special income tax rate of 25% or 27.5% may not be set off against income from capital investment that is not subject to such special tax rates (for example, interest from private loans or interest or capital gains from private placements of securities)
- Losses from capital investments may not be set off with other categories of income (for example, rental income or income from the alienation of real estate)
- Losses from capital investments may not be set off with interest income from bonds, debentures, and linked notes that are subject to grandfathering rules
- Losses from the sale of assets generating income from capital investment or derivative financial instruments may not be set off against distributions of foundations
- Participation in losses under a (typical) silent partnership may not be set off against other income but must be set off against future profits under the same silent partnership

A loss carry-forward for capital losses is not available.[64]

If the capital investments generating income from capital investments are held with an Austrian depository, the Austrian depository must effect the loss set-off automatically, throughout all deposits held by an investor with that depository, by levying the final withholding tax (*Kapitalertragsteuer*). However, income from deposits is excluded from the set-off of losses if the deposit:

- Is held as a business asset
- Is held in trust
- Has more than one owner

62 See 'Grandfathering Rules for the taxation of capital gains from capital investments'

63 S 27(8) EStG

64 The academic literature has raised constitutional concerns because of the absence of the possibility of a loss carry-forward with regards to capital investment income

In these cases, the loss set-off is available only by filing an income tax return (option for loss set-off) and therefore by ordinary income tax assessment.

Grandfathering rules for the taxation of capital gains from capital investments

Portfolio shareholdings and investment (and real estate) fund units acquired up to 31 December 2010 are subject to special grandfathering rules. This means that these assets are not subject to capital gains tax if sold after the lapse of the one-year speculation period.

Specific transitional rules apply to qualified shareholdings, i.e. shareholdings that have amounted to at least 1% at any time during the last five years. Capital gains from the sale of shareholdings that met the requirements of a qualified shareholding on 31 March 2012 are subject to the capital gains tax irrespective of their holding period, even if they were acquired before 1 January 2011. However, if a qualified shareholding acquired before 1 January 2011 amounted to less than 1% on 31 March 2012, the new regime is not applicable to capital gains from the sale of such shareholding if the sale occurred after the five-year holding period (or a longer period that may apply to certain shareholdings due to the Austrian Restructuring Tax Act). There is no withholding obligation on capital gains from the sale of a qualified shareholding held with an Austrian depository after 31 March 2012 that was acquired before 1 January 2011.

Other asset generating income from capital investment and derivatives (including foreign exchange), acquired before 1 April 2011, is also subject to special grandfathering rules. Therefore, if such assets are sold after expiry of the speculative period of one year, they are not subject to capital gains tax. If such assets were, however, acquired after 30 September 2011 but before 1 April 2012, as income from speculative transactions they are subject to capital gains tax irrespective of their holding period. From 1 April 2012, the special income tax rate of 27.5% (until 31 December 2015: 25%) applies. Capital gains or losses from such assets are not, however, available for the general loss set-off as set forth in 'Losses from income from capital investment'.

Excursus: taxation of investment funds

Regarding the taxation of domestic or foreign investment funds, a distinction between two levels of taxation must be made:

- Taxation at the level of the investment fund: An investment fund may derive ordinary income (interest, dividends) and/or realized capital gains (including income from derivative financial instruments/extraordinary income)

- If ordinary income and/or capital gains realized (including profits from derivatives/extraordinary income) are distributed to the investor, the income derived by the fund is subject to income tax at the level of the investor based on the principle of transparency (i.e. the investment fund itself is not a taxable person). If the fund units are held as private assets, both ordinary income and realized distributed capital gains from capital investments are subject to the special tax rate of 27.5%. If the fund unit is held with an Austrian depository, final withholding tax will be withheld by the Austrian depository. This, however, does not apply to domestic dividends, for which the final withholding tax is withheld directly at source by the distributing company
- If the income is retained at the level of the investment fund but not distributed, investors are taxed based on deemed distributions. If the investment fund is a reporting fund, i.e. if the investment fund has appointed a fiscal representative in Austria who notifies the reporting office[65] in time about the taxable income of the investment funds, the full amount of ordinary income net general and special expenses is to be distributed. Only 60% of the capital gains realized are deemed, however, to be distributed until they are actually distributed or the fund unit is sold. Mere valuation gains are not liable to tax. The acquisition costs of the fund units are increased by taxable deemed distributions, and decreased by tax neutral actual distributions, to prevent double taxation. Deemed distributions resulting from income from capital investments at the level of the fund are subject to the special tax rate of 27.5%. If the investment fund unit is held with an Austrian depository, the tax is withheld at source, and it is final
- In contrast to direct investments, an extensive loss-compensation between all types of income as well as a loss carry-forward into future periods is provided for investment funds. In addition to this, costs that accrue in the fund (for example, transaction costs, custody fees, etc.) are tax deductible
- If reporting requirements are not met, however, deemed distributions will be determined by lump-sum assessment. Deemed distributions are thus assumed to amount to the higher of (i) 90% of the difference between the first and the last redemption price of a calendar year and (ii) 10% of the last redemption price of a calendar year. Such income is deemed to be distributed on 31 December of each year of the holding period if the fund units are held

65 *Oesterreichische Kontrollbank*

by the investor on 31 December. Actual distributions are not deductible from the lump-sum assessment of deemed distributions. Instead of the lump-sum assessment, the investor may bring qualified evidence for the actual deemed distribution. The acquisition costs of the fund units are increased by taxable deemed distributions to prevent double taxation. Deemed distributions are subject to 27.5% special tax rate. If the investment fund unit is held with an Austrian depository, the tax is withheld at source, and it is final

- Taxation at the level of the investment fund unit: The investment fund unit is subject to capital gains tax if it is sold. For investment fund holdings acquired after 31 December 2010 (new holdings), the capital gains realized are subject to the special tax rate of 27.5% irrespective of the holding period. The taxable amount is the difference between the sales price and the (adjusted) acquisition costs. If the investment fund unit is held with an Austrian depository, the tax is withheld at source, and it is final. However, if the investment fund unit was acquired before 1 January 2011, the capital gains realized are not subject to income tax due to grandfathering rules[66]

Rental income, lease payments, and royalties

Rental income, lease payments, and royalties are subject to the progressive income tax rate (maximum 50% or 55%). In general, taxable income is calculated according to the net-income method as the surplus of receipts over expenses incurred in acquiring and maintaining income. Taxable income is the aggregate net result of all categories of income minus losses, special expenses, exceptional expenditure, and certain other allowances and gains.

Only expenses related to the rental and leasing activity such as operating costs, repairs, interest expenses for a debt-financed acquisition, including 1.5% depreciation for buildings, may be deducted as expenses.

As a rule, for privately held real estate the annual depreciation rate is 1.5 % of the acquisition costs of the building. Generally, the part of the land for which no depreciation is granted is estimated at 40% of the acquisition costs if no other evidence is presented. If the acquisition takes place during the first half of the year, the full annual depreciation rate may be deducted; otherwise only 50% of the annual depreciation rate is deductible.

66 See 'Grandfathering Rules for the taxation of capital gains from capital investments'

Capital gains from the alienation of real estate

Capital gains derived from the alienation of real estate (including land, buildings, as well as leasehold rights) are taxable irrespective of the holding period at a flat income tax rate of 30%. The taxable capital gain is generally the differential amount between the sales proceeds and the historical acquisition costs. Lower rates may apply to real estate that was purchased before 1 April 2012 or has not been subject to income tax in Austria before 1 April 2012. In this case, taxable income may be calculated based on a lump-sum method.

This tax is usually withheld at source and paid to the relevant authority by the notaries and lawyers conducting transfers of real estate, on or after that date.

Capital gains derived from the sale of the principal residence or buildings built by the taxpayer are exempt from capital gains tax (under certain conditions).

Capital losses incurred on the sale of real estate may not be set off against other categories of income and may not be carried forward. If, however, the taxpayer opts for taxation at progressive income tax rates instead of the flat rate of 30%, losses derived from real estate may be set off against other income categories.

APPENDIX

Checklist for the transfer of residence of an individual to Austria

1. Documentation of the transfer of the center of vital interests to Austria, for example:
    a. Information from family and friends about the new domicile in Austria by circular letter/email, including the new contact details (address, phone number, etc.)
    b. New letterhead and business cards with the Austrian address; change of the email signature including the new contact details
    c. Written information about the new contact details in Austria to business partners (especially banks, retirement funds, or social or private insurance companies, etc.)
    d. Written invitations (for example, parties, events, etc.) should include the new Austrian contact details

   e. Establishment of new memberships to Austrian institutions, clubs, organizations (for example, charitable, cultural, religious, sports, etc.). Terminate or suspend memberships to institutions, clubs, and organizations, in the previous residence state (if possible)
   f. Season tickets for cultural or sports events in Austria
   g. Documentation of the (effective date of) the relocation:
      - Registration of domicile with the competent registration office[67]
      - Deregistration of domicile in the previous residence state with the competent registration office
      - Completion protocol regarding the new domicile in Austria (after building or refurnishing the new home in Austria) including documentation when the keys of the real estate have been transferred to the new owner and photographic records
      - The invoice of the relocation company should be kept on file
      - Documentation of the relocation of 'personal items' to Austria (for example, private photo albums, letters, works of art, etc.)
      - Photographic records
   h. After the relocation date, the measure of physical presence in Austria should be clearly greater compared to the measure of physical presence in other states; calendar documentation is recommended
2. To do's regarding passenger cars:
   a. Registration of passenger cars with an Austrian car insurer, and application for an Austrian license plate
   b. When a passenger car is imported from abroad and used in Austria, the standard consumption duty[68] must be paid. Therefore, a tax declaration must be filed with the competent tax office. The payment of the standard consumption tax is a precondition for motor vehicle registration in Austria
3. Open a bank account with an Austrian bank (current account, cash, and credit cards)
4. Establishment of healthcare infrastructure in Austria (contact medical doctors in Austria, particularly general practitioners, specialists, etc.)
5. Establishment of a telephone landline in Austria
6. Contract with an Austrian mobile phone provider (if possible also for emails)

---

67 *Magistrat, Gemeinde*
68 *Normverbrauchsabgabe*

7. Reorganization of ordinary mail: redirection order to new domicile in Austria, change of address with regard to:
   - Subscriptions to newspapers and magazines
   - Credit card statements
   - Utility and repair bills
   - Bank and other account statements
   - Communication from tax offices and social insurance institutions
8. Notification of the transfer of residence to Austria, of the competent Austrian tax authority, and the tax authority in the exit state:
   - Notification period: within one month of the relocation
   - Information regarding income sources and the amount of income expected for the following two years
   - Evaluation regarding exit taxes and tax neutral step-up to the fair market value for certain types of assets
9. Recruitment of house staff in Austria

Note: The above list is intended as a guide only. To evaluate whether a transfer of the center of the vital interests has occurred, the facts and circumstances must be considered on a case-by-case basis. The individual items in the checklist are listed in random order of importance and the list should not be considered final. Depending on facts and circumstances, different weights in terms of importance may be assigned to the individual criteria. It is also possible to add to the criteria. For these reasons the list cannot replace individual tax advice.

References

Monographs

Lang, *Introduction to the Law of Double Tax Conventions* (2nd edn, Vienna, 2013).

Commentaries

Kanduth-Kristen, Laudacher, Lenneis, Marschner, and Vock, *Jakom Einkommensteuergesetz* (10th edn, 2017).

OECD, *Model Tax Convention on Income and on Capital* (condensed version, 2014).

Ritz, *Bundesabgabenordnung* (5th edn, Vienna, 2014).

Stoll, *Bundesabgabenordnung* (Vienna, 1994).

Vogel and Lehner, *Doppelbesteuerungsabkommen* (6th edn, Munich, 2015).

Wassermeyer, Kaeser, Lang, and Schuch, *Doppelbesteuerung* (3rd edn, Munich/Vienna, 2015).

Tax Journals

Kirchmayr and Polivanova-Rosenauer, 'Steuern aktuell: Budgetbegleitgesetz 2011–2014: Besteuerung von Kapitalvermögen' (2010) *ÖBA* 781.

Loukota, 'Bes chränkte Steuerpflicht bei inländischem Wohnsitz' (2004) *SWI* 53.

Strunz, 'Vermögenszuwachssteuer: Von der Perspektive einer Neugestaltung der Besteuerung von Kapitalvermögen. Reformbestrebungen bei der Veräußerungsgewinnbesteuerung' (2010) *SWK* 1388.

Abbreviations

art	Article
BAO	Federal Fiscal Code
BlgNR	supplement number
BMF	Federal Ministry of Finance
DBA	double taxation agreement
EAS	Express-Antwort-Service
EEA	European Economic Area
EStG	Individual Income Tax Law
EStR	Income Tax Guidelines
EUR	Euro
etc.	et cetera
GP	legislation period
i.e.	that is/namely/in other words
InvFG	Investment Fund Act
IWB	*Internationale Wirtschafts-Briefe* (tax journal)
MA	model agreement
ÖBA	*Österreichisches Bankarchiv* (tax journal)
OECD	Organisation for Economic Co-operation and Development
OECD-MA	OECD-model agreement
OECD-MK	OECD-commentary on the model agreement

pa	per annum
s	section
SWI	*Steuer & Wirtschaft International* (tax journal)
SWK	*Steuer- und WirtschaftsKartei* (tax journal)
UFS	Independent Tax Senate
VAT	Value-added tax
VfGH	Supreme Constitutional Court
VwGH	Supreme Administrative Court

About the author

DR. YVONNE SCHUCHTER-MANG is a tax advisor and has been advising high net worth individuals, private foundations, and trusts since 2005. She has been a partner at LeitnerLeitner since 2015. Before joining LeitnerLeitner, Dr. Schuchter-Mang worked in the Banking and Finance team of a Big Four company in Vienna. Prior to this, until 2011 she was a university assistant at Salzburg University's Institute for Tax Law, headed at that time by Prof. Sabine Kirchmayr. She has been an Austria correspondent for the International Bureau of Fiscal Documentation since 2005 as well as a *Fuchsbriefe* correspondent since 2010. Dr. Schuchter-Mang's main areas of expertise are the taxation of private foundations and trusts, the taxation of income from capital, international tax law, and the regularization of financial assets and foreign trusts, foundations and corporations, and other foreign asset structures. She regularly publishes on related topics in specialist journals and books and lectures at, among others, the Academy of Austrian Tax Advisors.

3 Tax Frameworks for Doing Business in Austria

Michael Pucher & Maximilian Lausenhammer LL.M., LeitnerLeitner

The decision regarding the most advantageous holding location and locations for doing business is based on various conditions and must be considered while taking into account the overall picture. Austria does provide a variety of advantages from a purely tax perspective which are, inter alia, participation exemption for dividend income, over 90 double tax treaties, cross-border pooling of (profits and) losses, and various state subsidies (for example, research premium). Overall, Austria can be considered an attractive location from a tax perspective, particularly because of its group taxation regime and the multitude of tax treaties, which should reduce the overall withholding tax burden. Furthermore, legal certainty may be obtained for specific tax issues by issuance of an advanced ruling by the tax authorities.

3.1 Tax framework for doing business in Austria

Legal forms

The choice of legal form is usually based on a variety of different considerations. Typically, these are the limitation of liability, minimum capital requirements, creditworthiness, employee representation in the organs, the right to draw profit, audit and financial statement publication requirements, and taxation.

Business activities in Austria are carried out by either sole entrepreneurs or companies. A sole entrepreneur is an individual carrying out business activities. The term 'company' refers to a legal entity. Austrian law provides for, inter alia, the following types of companies; these are commonly used for establishing a business in Austria:

- General partnership — *Offene Gesellschaft* (OG)
- Limited partnership — *Kommanditgesellschaft* (KG)
- Limited liability company — *Gesellschaft mit beschränkter Haftung* (GmbH)
- Joint stock company — *Aktiengesellschaft* (AG)

Some information about the legal and tax framework for sole entrepreneurs (SEnt) and companies is provided in the table below.

Table 3.1 Outline of the legal and tax framework

FORMS	LIABILITY OF SHAREHOLDERS	MINIMUM CAPITAL (EUR)	MINIMUM OF FOUNDERS AND SHAREHOLDERS	REGISTRATION ON COMMERCIAL REGISTER (EUR)	TAX TREATMENT	TAX RATES (%)
SEnt	No shares, personal liability of the sole entrepreneur		1	Obligatory, if turnover > 700,000 per year	Tax liability of sole entrepreneur	0–55[1]
OG	Unlimited		2	Obligatory	Transparent, tax liability of partners	0–55[2] or 25[3]
KG	Unlimited (general partner) Limited (limited partner)		2	Obligatory	Transparent, tax liability of partners	0–55[2] or 25[3]
GmbH	Limited	35,000	1	Obligatory	Non-transparent, dividend taxation at the level of the shareholders	25[4]
AG	Limited	70,000	1	Obligatory	Non-transparent, dividend taxation at the level of the shareholders	25[4]

1 Personal income tax rate (0%–50%). The rate of 55% applies to income parts over EUR 1 million in the calendar years 2016 to 2020
2 The rate of 0%–50%/55% applies insofar as the partners are individuals
3 The rate of 25% applies insofar as the partners are corporations
4 Corporate income tax rate

The shareholders can provide the companies (GmbH, AG) with capital through contributions or loans (for the deductibility of the interest, see also 'Interest deductibility on debt financing'). Furthermore, Austrian tax law does not have a 'check-the-box regime' as the US does.

The following sections in this chapter refer solely to the GmbH and the AG as companies, if not explicitly stated otherwise.

Joint stock company (AG)

The stock company is designed for larger business enterprises. The AG is a separate legal entity with its capital divided into shares. Both individuals and legal entities may be shareholders of an AG. The liability of the shareholders is limited to the amount of their contribution to the share capital. For the establishment of an AG, a minimum share capital of EUR 70,000 is required. Shares may be issued either as par-value shares[5] or as fractional shares.[6] An initial audit[7] by an independent certified public accountant is required if the AG is founded with contributions in kind.

Generally, the establishment of an AG is more expensive than the establishment of a GmbH. The following procedure is required for the establishment of an AG:

- The drawing-up of the articles of incorporation
- Subscription of shares
- Appointment of the supervisory board and auditors
- Appointment of the management board by the supervisory board
- Application for registration in the commercial register at the competent local court

The AG may be founded by individuals and legal entities. It is required that the articles of incorporation are authenticated by judicial or notarial record and must determine the nominal amount of the subscribed shares of the founders, the amount of the issued shares, and the classes of shares.

Limited liability company (GmbH)

In general, Austrian subsidiaries of non-resident companies are predominantly established in the legal form of a GmbH, since the provisions for the articles of incorporation are more flexible. The transfer of the shares of the GmbH is generally considered to be quite expensive and complicated since it can be transferred by notarial deed only, and the GmbH is therefore designed for a smaller shareholder structure.

---

5 *Nennaktien*

6 *Stückaktien*

7 *Gründungsprüfung*

The minimum share capital amounts to EUR 35,000 whereas one half of the amount must immediately be paid in cash. The shares of a GmbH cannot be listed on a stock exchange. The GmbH may be established under a privilege for newly established GmbHs and must provide a minimum share capital of only EUR 10,000, of which at least one half must be paid in cash.[8] The privilege is revoked under certain conditions or after a certain time. The shareholders' liability is generally limited to the total unpaid share capital. The shares per shareholder are limited to one; however, the shares may have different par values. If more than 50% of the initial stated capital is contributed in kind, an initial audit is required.

The establishment of a GmbH by two or more persons requires the drawing up of the articles of incorporation before a notary public; if the GmbH is established by a single individual or legal entity, a statement of formation[9] before a notary public is sufficient. A GmbH is established after it is entered in the commercial register at the competent local court.

Taxation of companies

Tax liability

The taxation depends on whether the company is set up in the legal form of a partnership or corporation. Partnerships are generally transparent entities for tax purposes. This means that the income of the partnership is not attributed to the partnership (OG or KG), but to the partners directly. Thus, the partners, if individuals, are subject to unlimited personal income tax liability on income derived by the partnership. If one of the partners of a partnership is a corporation (GmbH or AG), the income share of that partner is subject to corporate income tax liability.

On the contrary, corporate entities, for instance the AG and the GmbH, are regarded as non-transparent under Austrian tax law. Therefore, the income derived by the corporation is taxable at the level of the corporation. Any profit derived by a corporation is subject to corporate income tax at a flat rate of 25%, regardless of whether the profit is distributed to shareholders or retained. Domestic earnings from dividends (distributed gains) are taxed for income tax purposes with withholding tax amounting to 27.5%, respectively 25% when the shareholder is a corporation.

A corporation having its statutory seat or place of effective management in Austria is subject to unlimited corporate income tax liability, which provides for a taxation of income on a worldwide basis (subject to applicable tax treaties).

8 *Gründungsprivileg*
9 *Erklärung über die Errichtung*

In the case of a corporation which does not have its statutory seat or place of effective management in Austria, it can be subject to limited income tax liability if it carries on a business in Austria through an Austrian permanent establishment or an Austrian partnership (see 'International business-related issues').

Statutory seat and place of effective management

According to s 27(1) of the Austrian Federal Fiscal Code (FFC) the statutory seat of corporate entities, partnerships, and asset funds[10] is located at the place which is determined by law, contract, statute, deed of foundation, or similar documents. If such a provision is not stipulated or is missing, the seat is determined by the provisions of the place of effective management (see below). Corporate entities are still subject to unlimited corporate income tax liability in Austria if their seats are located in Austria, even though their place of effective management is elsewhere. In this case, the right of taxation for the contracting states is allocated according to the rules of the respective double tax treaties.

The place of effective management according to s 27(2) of the FFC is the center of the overall management[11] and is determined by its effective conduct. Notwithstanding the provisions of the statutory seat, the place of effective management cannot be stipulated, and all relevant facts and circumstances must be examined to determine the place of effective management.[12]

In practice, if the place of effective management cannot be explicitly allocated, the center of the overall management is determined based on the following three-step scheme:

Step 1: Determination of significant decisions regarding the day-to-day business
Step 2: Determination of the factual director of the entity
Step 3: Determination of the place where the factual director takes decisions regarding the day-to-day business

In the case of double residence (i.e. the statutory seat is situated in a different contracting state from the place of effective management), the OECD Model Tax Convention prioritizes in its tie-breaker scheme the place of effective management over the statutory seat.

10 *Vermögensmassen*
11 *Mittelpunkt der geschäftlichen Oberleitung*
12 *Gesamtbild der tatsächlichen Verhältnisse*

Principles of determination of the tax base

The income of a GmbH or an AG is, in any event, to be regarded as 'business income' regardless of the nature of the income. Hence, income from the lease of real estate or income from capital assets is qualified as business income. The tax base is to be determined on the basis of the net equity comparison method[13] according to s 5 of the Austrian Income Tax Act (ITA), i.e. profit is defined as the difference between the net equity at the end and the beginning of the business year.

For sole entrepreneurs and partnerships deriving business income, the net equity comparison method must be applied if they are obliged to keep books (i.e. corporations are required by law; sole entrepreneurs and partnerships if they realize a turnover of more than EUR 700,000 for two subsequent years or of more than EUR 1,000,000 in one year). Under this method, 'profit' is defined as the difference between the net equity at the end and the beginning of the business year.

Basically, the valuation and determination of the net equity is based on the Austrian generally accepted accounting principles (GAAP) codified in the Austrian Commercial Code (UGB) which needs to be adjusted in the reconciliation of book and taxable income[14] for tax purposes.

In respect of the determination of the tax base, supply of equity by the shareholders is tax neutral according to s 8(2) of the Austrian Corporate Income Tax Act (CITA). However, a contribution in kind triggers a realization of the hidden reserves at the level of the shareholder if the prerequisites of the Austrian Reorganization Tax Act[15] are not met (see 'Reorganization'). On the other hand, the mere transfer of use[16] of assets and rights by the shareholder to the company is tax neutral. By contrast, a transfer of use in a cross-border situation (i.e. a domestic shareholder grants a transfer of use to a foreign company) is taxable.

The tax base is generally determined for the current financial year and includes the last 12 months; therefore, the fiscal year usually complies with the calendar year. In some special cases the period is shorter than 12 months (for example, intra-year establishment of the company) or can be extended to a period of more than 12 months in the case of winding-up procedures. The standard balance sheet date is 31 December of the respective year, but it can be changed with the consent of the tax authorities (an economic reason is necessary).

---

13 *Betriebsvermögensvergleich*
14 *Mehr-Weniger-Rechnung*
15 *Umgründungssteuergesetz*
16 *Nutzungsüberlassung*

Expenses

In general, all business-related expenses are tax deductible; however, the following selected expenses (inter alia) are not tax-deductible:

- Expenses for social representation (including entertainment expenditure and business meals). These expenses can be tax deductible up to 50% if it can be proven that the expenses were predominantly for business reasons
- Income taxes and expenses relating to the taxpayer's personal life. This includes expenses for the construction of 'luxury property' by the company for its shareholder if this property is built based on the needs of the shareholder and its rentability on the general real estate market is limited or precluded. Special diligence must be placed on this issue, since it can result in hidden profit distributions and is frequently checked by the tax authorities in tax audits
- The grant or receipt of contributions in cash or in kind, which is a punishable offence (for example, bribery); fines and penalties imposed by courts, administrative authorities, or institutions of the EU; fines imposed under fiscal criminal law; and payments made during a diversion program to avoid criminal prosecution
- Employees' salaries and remunerations exceeding EUR 500,000 per person per year (see section 4)
- Interest payments for the debt financing of the acquisition of shares if these shares were held directly or indirectly by an affiliated concern, company, or a shareholder who exercises a directly or indirectly controlling influence (for an exception, see 'Interest deductibility on debt financing')
- Interest and royalty payments if the receiving company is (i) directly or indirectly affiliated with the concern or a shareholder exercises a directly or indirectly controlling influence over the receiving company, and (ii) income derived from interest or royalties on the level of the receiving company are tax exempt or subject to an effective tax rate of less than 10%

Write-offs for participation in companies that are accounted as assets (presumed for a participation amount of at least 5%) are tax deductible, but must be spread over seven subsequent years. This limitation applies for domestic and foreign participations; however, write-offs in international holding participations are tax deductible only if the option according to s 10(3) of the CITA was exercised (see 'Taxation of dividend income'). Write-offs on participations in tax group members are not tax deductible since this would lead to a double utilization[17] of tax losses.

Losses and carry-forward of losses

Generally, an unlimited carry-forward of losses applies; however, tax losses may not be carried back. Limitations on the utilization of losses exist for losses that are derived from a participation if the main purpose of the participation is to obtain tax advantages. In this case, these losses may be set off against future profits derived from this participation.[18]

Corporations can compensate up to 75% of their positive income with existing tax loss carry-forwards, except if profits are derived from a reorganization of the taxpayer or insolvency proceedings, liquidation profits, profits generated from the alienation of certain assets, and profits due to recapturing losses of foreign tax group members or permanent establishments. In the latter cases, the tax losses can be offset up to 100%.

Moreover, corporate income tax law provides for loss-trafficking rules, according to which the tax loss carry-forward may no longer be used in case the company has lost its identity within the meaning of s 8(4) of the CITA. This is to be assumed if the ownership as well as the organizational and business structure has substantially changed in the course of a transfer of the shares in the company against a consideration. Apart from this, the Austrian Reorganization Tax Act provides for further loss-trafficking rules applicable to certain types of reorganizations (for example, mergers).

International business-related issues

Austrian tax law does not provide for a specific controlled-foreign-corporation (CFC) legislation. Nevertheless, general tax rules, especially the 'substance-over-form principle', the concept of beneficial ownership, and the general anti-abuse rules, are applied by Austrian tax courts when deciding on the lawfulness of actions taken by the taxpayer.

Austria has concluded more than 90 tax treaties in the areas of personal and corporate income tax as well as in the area of inheritance and gift tax. The number of tax treaties should ensure an overall low withholding-tax burden regarding interest, dividends, and royalties.

---

17 *Doppelverwertung*
18 *Wartetastenverluste*

Limited tax liability and taxable income

If a corporation does not have its statutory seat or place of effective management in Austria, it can be subject to limited income tax liability if it carries on a business in Austria through an Austrian permanent establishment or an Austrian partnership.[19] In this case, tax liability is limited to the income attributed to that permanent establishment or partnership. Further, income from Austrian real estate is subject to limited tax liability if it belongs to the business of the foreign corporation. The corporate income tax rate is 25%.

Capital gains of a non-resident corporation (or individual) resulting from the alienation of a participation in an Austrian corporation (such as a GmbH or an AG) are taxable in Austria (with a final withholding tax of 25%) if the shareholding amounts to at least 1% in the capital of the GmbH or AG, at any time during the five preceding years. Tax treaties usually prohibit Austria from taxing if they contain an OECD Model-type capital gain provision. If the capital gain was realized at the level of an Austrian permanent establishment of the non-resident seller, the gain is treated as business income of the permanent establishment and is subject to tax under the general rules.

If withholding tax has been levied (for example, on dividends and royalties), it can be credited against the final CIT liability of the permanent establishment if the respective dividends and royalties are attributable to the permanent establishment. Furthermore, if assets which are attributable to a permanent establishment are transferred from Austria to another country, hidden reserves are realized since these assets are evaluated with the fair market value.

Transfer pricing

On 1 August 2016 the Austrian Transfer Pricing Documentation Law (TPDL) was officially published in Austria. Based on the TPDL, a transfer pricing documentation must be prepared for fiscal years starting on or after 1 January 2016. Transfer pricing documentation requirements for prior fiscal years as well as for local constituent entities not covered by the TPDL are based on the FFC, taking into account the OECD Transfer Pricing Guidelines.

TPDL stipulates an obligatory, three-tiered, standardized approach to transfer pricing documentation, as proposed by the OECD, including Master File (MF), Local File (LF) and Country-by-Country Reporting (CbC) in Austria.

19 See s 21(1) CITA in conjunction with s 98 ITA

- Multinational enterprises must prepare a CbC report containing information on the worldwide distribution of its revenue, taxes, etc., if the consolidated group turnover amounted to at least EUR 750 million in the previous fiscal year
- Austrian subsidiaries of a multinational company must prepare an MF (a report about the whole company's group, its worldwide economic activity, and its transfer pricing policy) and an LF (a report about the business transactions in the Austrian company) if turnover exceeded EUR 50 million in each of the two previous fiscal years

Austrian tax law does not provide for specific rules on the determination of transfer prices, either. In general, transfer pricing issues are governed by the provisions concerning hidden profit distributions, hidden contributions, and the cross-border transfer of assets. In practice, the tax authorities generally refer to the OECD Transfer Pricing Guidelines as the main basis when examining the accuracy of transfer prices. Furthermore, the tax authorities use the non-binding Austrian Transfer Pricing Guidelines[20] of October 2010, published by the Austrian Ministry of Finance, as another reference for interpreting transfer pricing issues, and are thus of high practical relevance.

Rulings

Rulings are in general not binding except for the principles of good faith; an appeal against the ruling is correspondingly not possible. No charges are levied apart from stamp duties.

On the other hand, advanced rulings regarding reorganizations, group taxation, and transfer prices[21] are available, and binding for the tax authorities. For these issues, an appeal against the ruling is possible. The issued fees for these advanced rulings range from EUR 1,500 to EUR 20,000 depending on the turnover of the taxpayer.

Other business-related taxes

Value-added tax

Within the EU, value-added tax (VAT) is uniformly regulated according to the Council Directive on the common system of VAT.[22]

20 See Directive of the Federal Ministry of Finance (BMF) of 28 October 2010, BMF-010221/2522-IV/4/2010

21 The draft of the Annual Tax Act 2018 intends to extend the rulings to questions concerning international tax law, VAT, and tax abuse

22 See Council Directive 2006/112/EC of 28 November 2006 on the common system of value-added tax

Taxable transactions

The following taxable transactions are listed in the Value-Added Tax Act (VAT Act):

- Supply of goods and services
- Deemed supply of goods and services
- Import
- Intra-community acquisitions

The supply of goods means the transfer of the right to dispose of tangible property as owner, whereas the supply of services is any transaction which does not constitute a supply of goods.

Deemed supply of goods and services means the withdrawal of goods or the use of goods by a taxable person for his/her private use or for that of his/her staff, if the goods form part of the business assets of the taxable person, and the VAT on the goods was (partly) deductible (see 'Input VAT deduction').

The transfer of goods from a country outside the EU to Austria is subject to import VAT.

An intra-community acquisition is the acquisition of goods transported from an EU member state to Austria, provided that both the supplier and the recipient are taxable persons for VAT purposes. Special provisions exist for the acquisition of goods from an EU member state to Austria in conjunction with the temporary usage of the goods.

Place of supply

The supply of goods and services will be taxed under the VAT Act only if the place of supply is considered to be in Austria. According to the VAT Act the place of supply is determined by the following provisions.

Supply of goods

The place of supply of goods is deemed to be either (i) the place where the goods are located at the time the right to dispose of them as an owner is transferred to the recipient, or (ii) if the goods are dispatched or transported by the supplier, the recipient, or by a third person (for example, the carrier), at the place where the dispatch or transport begins. Special rules for 'distance selling' are applicable.

Supply of services

Supply of services distinguishes between the supply of services to taxable persons (B2B transactions) and supply of services to non-taxable persons (B2C transactions).

- B2B transactions: In general, the supply of services is taxable at the place where the recipient has established his/her business or has a fixed establishment to which the service is supplied. However, the VAT Act provides several particular regulations for determining the place of supply of services
- B2C transactions: In general, the supply of services provided to non-taxable persons is taxable at the place where the supplier has established his/her business. However, as well as for B2B transactions, the VAT Act stipulates several special regulations for determining the place of supply of services

Tax rates and exemptions

Tax rates

The tax rates that are applicable in Austria are shown in Table 3.2 below.

Table 3.2 Applicable tax rates

VAT RATE (%)	DESCRIPTION
20	Standard VAT rate
13	Reduced VAT rate which applies, in particular, to hospitals, childcare, and youth services, supply of services by performing artists, art objects, cultural services, and leisure facilities (for example, cinema, theatre, sport events, musical performances, museums, transportation of persons via aircraft, etc.)
10	Reduced VAT rate, which applies particularly to foodstuffs, rent for living purposes, medicines, books, newspapers, transportation of persons, collection and disposal of waste and liquids

Exemptions

Exemption from VAT can be classified in two categories, depending on whether they preclude or allow the deduction of input VAT.

The following supplies do not affect the right to deduct input VAT:

- Export of goods (goods are transported outside the EU)
- Intra-community supply of goods
- Cross-border transport of exported goods
- Cross-border transport of persons by vessels and aircraft
- Work on, and the processing of, goods to be exported outside the EU

The following exemplary VAT exemptions preclude the deduction of input VAT:

- Banking and financial transactions (for example, the transaction of shares) as well as insurance transactions
- Transfer of immovable property including buildings (the option for taxation connected with the right to deduct input VAT is available)
- Leasing or letting of immovable property for business purposes (the option for taxation connected with the right to deduct input VAT is possible under certain conditions)
- Services supplied by dentists, doctors, or psychotherapists
- A special exemption scheme for small (domestic) businesses (annual supplies below EUR 30,000)

Input VAT deduction

A taxable person is entitled to deduct input VAT issued in an invoice for the supply of goods or services carried out in Austria by another taxable person. Moreover, VAT due in connection with received supplies of goods or services where the VAT liability is shifted to the recipient (reverse-charge transactions, see below), importations, and intra-community acquisitions may be deducted if the received transaction is directly linked to a tax-exempt output supply.

VAT liability

In general, a taxable person carrying out a taxable transaction is liable for the payment of VAT and is obliged to pay the invoiced VAT to the tax authorities.

Exceptions apply for the supply of goods with installation and/or assembly and services carried out in Austria by a foreign taxable person (no seat and no fixed establishment in Austria that is involved in the supply) to another (domestic or foreign) taxable person. In this case, the VAT liability shifts from the supplier to the recipient (reverse-charge mechanism) of the goods or services.

Capital duty

As of 1 January 2016, provisions regarding capital duty were abolished. For matters up to 31 December 2015, the injection of equity capital to Austrian corporations (i.e. the AG, GmbH, and GmbH & Co. KG) by the shareholders was subject to capital duty of 1%.

Stamp duty

Stamp duty is levied on selected legal transactions that are concluded in written form (for example, protocols, official documents, easements, lease and rental agreements, guarantees, and assignment agreements). The rates are either fixed fees according to the relevant tariff item of s 14 of the Court Fee Act, or vary between 0.8% and 2% of the underlying value of the transaction. In practice, however, stamp duty-avoiding strategies are available that are frequently applied; however, detailed tax planning precautions are essential.

Customs duty

In general, all goods crossing the Austrian border are subject to customs duty. As an EU member state, Austria does not levy customs duty on the import of goods from other member states. The customs tariffs for imports from countries outside the EU are determined by the EU. In addition to the EU regulations, Austria has concluded various international agreements that provide for customs exemption or preferential customs tariffs.

Other excise duty

Excise duty is levied on tobacco, alcoholic drinks, and mineral oils. These duties are non-recurring and payable by the seller, who passes the costs on to the customer.

Environmental tax

Austrian law provides for various environmental taxes. Suppliers or users of energy are subject to electricity, natural gas, or coal contributions. A residual waste contribution is levied on landfills of garbage (waste).

Advertising duty

Advertising duty is levied at a rate of 5% on the consideration for advertising activities performed in Austria as well as advertising broadcasts in Austria from abroad. Advertising activities within the meaning of the advertising duty law are advertising insertions in newspapers or journals, commercials on radio or TV, and the leasing of billboards and banners.

Bank tax

Since 2016, the credit institutions in Austria have been obliged to pay a bank tax; as of 2017, this tax is 0.024% of their balance sheet total (0.029% of the balance sheet total exceeds EUR 20 billion).

3.2 Special areas of taxation of business-related activities

Holding structures

Austria as holding location offers several tax benefits (participation exemption, distribution of capital reserves instead of dividends, many double tax treaties, etc.) which are detailed in the following sections.

Taxation of dividend income and anti-abuse rules

Taxation of dividend income

Domestic participations

Any income (for example, dividend distribution) derived by an Austrian holding company from a participation in another Austrian corporation is exempt from corporate income tax regardless of the capital ownership percentage and the holding period. However, capital gains or losses resulting from the alienation or liquidation of the domestic participation in another Austrian corporation are tax-effective at normal rates (i.e. 25% CIT).

Foreign portfolio shareholdings

Dividend income derived by an Austrian corporation from a participation of less than 10% in the capital of a foreign corporation from the EU or from third countries is exempt under the following conditions:

- The EU subsidiary has a legal form listed in Annex 2 of the ITA
- The subsidiary is situated in a non-EU member state, has a legal form comparable to domestic corporations, and the residence state of the subsidiary has concluded an agreement providing for comprehensive administrative assistance

Capital gains or losses resulting from the alienation or liquidation of the foreign portfolio shareholdings are tax-effective.

International holding participations

An international holding participation (participation in the capital of a foreign corporation from the EU or third countries) requires the fulfillment of the following conditions:

- Direct or indirect (for example, via an intermediate transparent partnership) equity participation of at least 10% in a foreign corporation for an uninterrupted minimum period of one year
- Comparability of the legal form of the foreign subsidiary corporation to Austrian corporations or listing of the legal form in Annex 2 of the ITA

If these conditions are fulfilled, dividend income, capital gains, and capital losses from the alienation of the foreign portfolio shareholdings as well as write-offs are, in general, tax neutral. However, the parent company may exercise an option to have capital gains and losses as well as write-offs from the participation be treated as taxable or tax-deductible. The option must be exercised in the year of acquisition or founding of the subsidiary in the tax return of the holding company and is binding on any group company holding or acquiring that participation.

Anti-abuse rules

Switch-over clause regarding portfolio shareholdings in foreign portfolio corporations

Dividend income from portfolio shareholdings in foreign portfolio corporations is not tax exempt if the following conditions are met:

- The subsidiary is not subject to a tax in the foreign country that is comparable to the Austrian corporate income tax
- The level of taxation of the profits of the foreign subsidiary is not comparable to Austrian standards; this is fulfilled if the applicable foreign tax rate is lower by more than 10 percentage points than the Austrian corporate income tax rate
- The subsidiary is exempt from taxation in the foreign country

If the above-mentioned criteria are met, the dividend income is taxable at the level of the Austrian parent company and the foreign tax (if any) can be credited. If the foreign tax exceeds the Austrian tax liability it is possible to carry forward the excess amount indefinitely. However, the excess amount to be carried forward must be assessed by the tax authorities in the way of a formal assessment.

Switch-over clause regarding international holding participations

The tax exemption of dividend income and capital gains from foreign participations does not apply in the case of suspected tax avoidance or abuse of law. The switch-over clause provides that the dividend income is taxable at the level of the Austrian parent (corporate income tax 25%); however, any foreign corporate (and withholding) tax may be credited against the Austrian tax burden of the Austrian parent company.

With respect to international holding participations, tax avoidance or abuse of law is assumed if two tests as described below are cumulatively fulfilled:

- 'Passive-business test': The business of the foreign subsidiary is focused on deriving (directly or indirectly) 'passive' income, which covers interest income, royalty or lease income, and capital gains on portfolio investments.

Rental income from immovable property, dividend income, or capital gains resulting from qualified shareholdings that meet the criteria of an 'international holding participation' are not regarded as passive income. This test is met if the majority of the company's assets (or the company's staff) is used for deriving passive income and the company's income predominantly results from 'passive' sources (i.e. more than 50% of its income)[23]

- 'Low-taxation test': The income of the foreign subsidiary is not liable to taxation comparable to Austrian tax law, i.e. the foreign average tax burden is not more than 15% of the tax base determined under Austrian tax law

Hybrid shareholdings

Dividend income received from portfolio shareholdings in foreign subsidiaries and from international holding participations is not exempt from corporate income tax if the dividend is deductible as a business expense at the level of the foreign subsidiary. This could be especially the case if a participation in a foreign company is characterized from an Austrian perspective as equity and from the foreign tax law perspective as debt, i.e. a hybrid shareholding.

Excursus: Draft Annual Tax Act 2018

1. Inclusion of passive income[24]

The draft of the Annual Tax Act 2018[25] stipulates a new CFC regime to implement arts 7 and 8 of the EU Anti-Tax Avoidance Directive.[26] The new CFC rules foresee inclusion of the income of any Austrian corporation that holds a controlling participation (directly or indirectly) in a foreign subsidiary that generates low-taxed, passive income. The following list defines the type of passive income of a controlled foreign company that must be included in the tax base of the Austrian parent:

- Interest
- Royalties
- Dividends
- Income from insurance and banking
- Income from invoicing companies[27]

---

23 See CITA guidelines, point 1236

24 *Hinzurechnungsbesteuerung*

25 *Jahresteuergesetz*

26 See (EU) 2016/1164

27 *Abrechnungsunternehmen*

In contrast to the current legal situation, the new CFC regime applies also to the 'other income' from financial assets and intellectual property and from dividends and capital gains from the alienation of participations.

If the following three criteria are met cumulatively, passive income must be included in the tax base of the Austrian corporation:

- Low taxation
- Control
- The controlled foreign company does not have 'substance' (see 'Dividends' below)

Low taxation is met in cases in which the effective tax burden of the foreign subsidiary is below 12.5%. Further prerequisites must be met to trigger the new CFC rules, i.e. (i) passive income amounts to more than one third of the income of the respective subsidiary and (ii) the Austrian corporation must establish control (directly or indirectly through its associated companies) over the foreign subsidiary (i.e. more than 50% of the voting rights, or more than 50% capital participation, or entitlement of more than 50% of the profit).

The new CFC regime will be applicable to financial years that begin after 30 September 2018.

2. Amended switch-over clause

The switch-over clause, as described above, will also be amended. According to the Annual Tax Act 2018, the tax exemption of portfolio participations with a minimum capital participation of 5% and international participations will be switched to taxation with credit if the main business focus of the respective foreign companies in which the participations are held is to derive low-taxed, passive income, as defined in the new CFC rules.

Dividends derived by the foreign companies that would be tax exempt according to Austrian law are not considered for the determining of the main business focus of the foreign company.

Withholding taxes

Withholding tax on domestic payments

In general, dividends and other profit distributions to corporations made by an Austrian corporation are subject to a withholding tax of 25% (the withholding tax rate in the case of dividend payments to individuals amounts to 27.5%). If the resident corporate shareholder holds a capital participation of at least 10% of the subsidiary, no withholding tax is levied. In all other cases, the withholding tax is credited against the final tax liability of the shareholder or refunded during the annual tax assessment.

Withholding tax is not levied on royalties paid to resident companies.

Withholding tax on payments to non-resident companies

Dividends

Withholding tax is levied on dividends paid to non-resident companies at a rate of 25%. However, the domestic law in conjunction with the EU Parent-Subsidiary Directive[28] provides an exemption from the withholding tax for dividends if the following criteria are met:

- The EU parent company has a legal form listed in Annex 2 of the ITA
- The participation of the EU parent company in the subsidiary amounts to at least 10%
- The shares are held directly or indirectly for an uninterrupted period of one year

The exemption is not applicable in cases of tax avoidance and abuse of law, hidden profit distributions, or dividend distributions to shell companies. Tax avoidance or abuse of law is not assumed in a case in which the parent company derives income from active business and provides substance (for example, employment of its own staff and maintenance of business facilities) in its state of residence.

Furthermore, if the EU Parent-Subsidiary Directive is not applicable (for example, a non-EU member state), relief from withholding tax on outbound dividends may be provided by the respective tax treaties. Generally, reduction (or even exemption) of withholding tax may be granted at source[29] if the receiving non-resident corporation runs an active business and has its own staff and facilities. Otherwise, treaty relief may be granted by way of a refund procedure.[30]

Interest

Generally, the payment of interest to non-resident shareholders is not subject to withholding tax; however, regarding the deductibility of these interest payments the provisions of s 12(1)(10) of the CITA have to be considered (see 'Interest deductibility on debt financing').

28 Implemented in the Austrian tax law under s 94(2) ITA
29 *Entlastung an der Quelle*
30 *Rückerstattungsverfahren*

Royalties

Payments of royalties to non-resident shareholders are subject to withholding tax (see s 99 of the ITA) with a general rate of 20%.

Domestic provisions which implement the EU Interest and Royalties Directive[31] provide a tax exemption regarding withholding taxes for royalties paid by resident subsidiaries to their non-resident EU parent companies or their permanent establishments if the following conditions are met:

- The parent company has a form listed in the Directive (2003/49/EC)
- The parent company holds a participation of at least 25% of the capital
- The shares are held directly for an uninterrupted period of one year

The tax exemption is not applicable in cases of tax avoidance, abuse of law, and if the royalties exceed the arm's length amount. In such cases, tax must be withheld at source.

Other transactions

There is no withholding tax for management fees. However, payments for technical and commercial consulting services carried out by a non-resident are subject to withholding tax at a rate of 20%.[32] It must be ascertained on a case-by-case basis whether Austria has the right to levy withholding tax. Further types of transactions exist where withholding taxes are levied.[33]

Interest deductibility on debt financing

General provisions on the deduction of interest

Interest on debt financing and royalties are, in general, tax deductible if they comply with the arm's length principle. Specific rules on thin capitalization do not exist in Austria. Nevertheless, the adequacy of the debt-equity ratios will be assessed on a case-by-case basis. If the debt financing is not recognized for tax purposes because the equity is inadequate or has not been concluded in accordance with the arm's length principle, a loan may be (partly) regarded as hidden equity. As a result, interest payments on such loans are treated as a hidden dividend distribution and are not tax deductible.

Austrian tax law stipulates a prohibition on deduction of interest and royalties, however, if the interest-receiving corporation directly or indirectly belongs to a

31 See EU Interest and Royalties Directive (2003/49/EC)
32 See ss 99 and 100 ITA
33 See ss 30, 30a, and 98 ITA

corporate group and the received interest (royalty) at the level of the receiving corporation is:

- Not taxed at all, based on personal or objective tax exemption
- Taxed at a nominal tax rate lower than 10%
- Taxed at a tax rate effectively lower than 10% because of an envisaged tax relief

Furthermore, if the receiving company is not the beneficial owner of the interest (royalty) payments, the interest (royalty) is attributed to the beneficial owner.

Interest deduction on debt financing on the acquisition of shares

Interest on the debt financing of the acquisition of a participation in a (resident or non-resident) corporation is under some conditions tax deductible, regardless of the fact that the participation exemption provides for a tax exemption on income from the acquired participation. However, interest on the debt financing on the acquisition of shares is not tax deductible if one of the following criteria is met:

- If the participation is not part of the business assets of the shareholder
- If the participation was (i) acquired directly or indirectly from a group company or (ii) from a shareholder exerting a dominant influence ('intra-group acquisition')
- In the case of a capital increase or of contributions to a company in which the shareholding was acquired via an intra-group acquisition
- If the general limitations on interest deductibility are applicable (see above)

Group taxation

Austrian tax law provides companies with a tax planning instrument to pool profits and losses (from local or foreign group member companies) in Austria. This applies for tax purposes only and has no consequences for accounting purposes (i.e. there is no requirement to draw up consolidated balance sheets). A so-called tax group has the effect that the profit and loss of group members will be allocated at the level of the group leader for tax purposes. A tax group provides for funding benefits allowing timely utilization of losses and temporary utilization of allocated losses of foreign group members.

An Austrian corporation or a permanent establishment of an EU corporation registered in Austria can be a group leader. Group members can be the following corporations if they are affiliated (more than 50%) directly or indirectly (for example, through partnerships) with the group leader or other Austrian resident group members:

- Austrian resident corporations
- Comparable foreign corporations from the EU or from third countries that have concluded comprehensive administrative assistance with Austria

The minimum holding requirement as a group leader can also be met together with other companies (i.e. multiple group leaders) provided the shareholding of one corporation amounts to at least 40% and the shareholding of other corporations amounts to at least 15%.

The following restrictions apply for foreign tax group members:

- Foreign tax group members can attribute solely tax losses to the tax group leader, but no profits
- Losses of foreign group members may be deducted from the taxable income of the group in proportion to the amount of the direct shareholding of the group in the foreign entity
- The foreign tax losses must be determined on the basis of the Austrian tax law; however, the amount of losses to be deducted is capped with the losses determined by the foreign tax law
- The deduction of losses assigned from foreign group members with the tax group's profit is capped at 75% of the profit of all domestic group members (including the group leader). The remaining loss surplus may be carried forward by the group leader

The tax group must remain in existence for at least three years. If the tax group is terminated earlier, all benefits from the group taxation will be lost and each member of the group will be taxed on a stand-alone basis, with retroactive effect. Write-offs on participations in tax group members are not tax deductible.

In addition, it is required to conclude a tax group and tax allocation agreement[34] between the group parent company and the group companies. A key element of the agreement is a compensation clause for the allocation of the positive tax income and/or tax losses (as the case may be) between the group member company and the group parent company. These compensation payments do not, however, increase or decrease the taxable income of the companies.

Capital repatriations to shareholders

From a tax perspective the distribution of profit may be treated as either capital repayment or distribution of profit.

34 *Steuerumlage und Gruppenvertrag*

Distribution of profit

Profit distributions to individuals made by an Austrian corporation are subject to a capital gains tax of 27.5%. If the individual is tax resident in another state, the regulations under the double tax treaty between Austria and the other state are applicable.

If a company is the recipient of a distribution of profit it is generally tax exempt according to s 10 of the CITA in addition to being exempt from the obligation to withhold taxes if the criteria of s 94(2) of the ITA are met.

Capital repayments

According to s 4(12) of the ITA, from a tax perspective the distribution of profit may be treated as either (taxable) distribution of profit or tax exempt capital repayment. The distribution of profit is subject to withholding tax, while the capital repayment reduces the tax book value of the participation at shareholder level.

In the recent tax reform of 2015–2016 in conjunction with AbgÄG 2015, the tax authorities obliged companies to provide a tax equity account[35] as well as a tax internal profit account.[36] In September 2017, the Austrian Ministry of Finance published an issuance[37] that stipulates prerequisites for the applicability of capital repayments and the distribution of profits.

The legislator grants the distributing company the right to choose between a capital repayment and a distribution of profit if the tax equity account, as well as the tax internal profit account, do show a surplus respectively. If, for example, the tax equity account is negative, but the tax internal profit account shows a surplus, a distribution of only profit is viable. Furthermore, the decree of the Ministry of Finance distinguishes between available and unavailable sub-accounts of tax equity contributions (with regard to the tax equity account) and internal financing (with regard to the tax internal profit account).

The decree of the Austrian Ministry of Finance does also provide an easement for small and medium-sized companies.

Excursus: hidden profit distribution

Hidden profit distributions are pecuniary advantages granted by the company to its shareholders (or to related parties of the shareholders) and are disproportionally high. A hidden profit distribution can also be realized if the company waives receivables against its shareholders at the expense of its own revenue. Hidden profit distributions are caused by *causa societatis.*

---

35 *Einlagenevidenzkonto*

36 *Innenfinanzierungskonto*

37 See BMF-010203/0309-IV/6/2017; *Einlagenrückzahlungs- und Innenfinanzierungserlass*

For a pecuniary advantage to be qualified as hidden profit distribution, it has to meet certain criteria, particularly the subjective element[38] and the objective element.[39] If these criteria are met, the respective expenses are (partially) not tax deductible, VAT is not deductible, and WHT must be withheld.

Under certain circumstances, hidden profit distributions can be reversed in the same year within which they occurred.

Reorganization

A reorganization is a procedure in which the legal body changes but the asset remains unchanged. Regarding the tax consequences of a reorganization, a distinction must be made between form-changing conversion[40] and transferring reorganization.[41]

The form-changing conversion does not lead to a change in the identity of the legal entity or to the transfer of assets. Consequently, form-changing conversions generally do not trigger tax consequences. Such a conversion is possible for companies as well as for partnerships (for example, AG into GmbH, KG into OG, and vice versa).

The transferring reorganization transfers assets from one legal entity to another legal entity. According to the general principles of the ITA and CITA, such a transfer leads to the realization of hidden reserves, triggers real estate transfer tax and stamp duty, and has VAT consequences. As a result, the adjustment and optimization of company structures would lead to a high tax burden. To avoid tax consequences for transferring reorganizations, the Austrian Reorganization Act provides relief (for example, tax-neutral transfer of assets, transfer of loss carry-forward to the receiving entity, beneficial rules regarding real estate transfer tax, exemption from VAT, etc.) if certain conditions of the respective reorganization forms are met. As a general rule, the existing tax book values need to be continued in the course of the reorganization, otherwise the reorganization leads to a taxable event, resulting in taxation of the hidden reserves contained in the transferred assets.

The following reorganization forms are regulated by the Austrian Reorganization Act:

- Mergers (art I, *Verschmelzung*): Two or more companies (for example, GmbH, AG) merge into one company
- Conversions (art II, *Umwandlung*): The assets of companies (for example, GmbH, AG) are transferred to the main shareholder or a newly established partnership

38 *Subjektive Tatseite*
39 *Objektive Tatseite*
40 *Formwechselnde Umwandlung*
41 *Übertragende Umgründung*

- Contribution (art III, *Einbringung*): Qualified assets are contributed to a company by an individual or a legal entity
- Merger (art IV, *Zusammenschluss*): Individuals combine or merge into a partnership
- Partnership division (art V, *Realteilung*): A partnership transfers its assets to the shareholders of the partnership
- De-merger (art VI, *Spaltung*): A company (for example, GmbH, AG) transfers assets to one or more companies

Real estate investments of corporations

Income taxation

The same tax rules apply to domestic and foreign investors. Foreign investors are taxed on income derived from Austrian real estate.

Generally, the income received by a corporation that is derived from real estate activities (rentals, alienation of real estate) qualifies as business income and the respective profit is taxed at the standard corporate tax rate of 25%.

Acquisition and manufacturing costs must be capitalized. For buildings, these costs may be depreciated over the useful life of the building. According to tax law, the maximum depreciation rates for buildings[42] are:

- 2.5% per year if used for business activities
- 1.5% per year if used by lessee for living purposes
- Higher depreciation rates if supported by appraisal

Regardless of whether or not the building is used for business purposes, some maintenance costs that may not be capitalized as manufacturing costs, but that increase the value of the building significantly or increase its useful life significantly, must be allocated over a period of 15 years. Expenses (for example, on-going expenses and maintenance) are, in general, immediately tax deductible.

Real estate transfer tax

Real estate transfer tax is levied on transfers of immovable property (land, buildings, comparable rights) located in Austria. Taxable transactions include, inter alia, the sale and exchange of immovable property as well as transfers without a legal title and transfers of beneficial ownership.

Real estate transfer tax is also levied if 95% of all shares of a corporation owning Austrian immovable property are held by or taken over by one or more shareholders

42 In contrast, a plot of land is not depreciable

(one shareholder or several shareholders deemed to be one shareholder if they meet the criteria for a tax group). Real estate transfer tax is also triggered if 95% of the shares of a partnership have been transferred to new partners within the preceding five years.

The tax base is, in general, the value of the consideration (for example, purchase price and assumed liabilities) but no less than the tax value of the real estate, which can be determined by one of the following methods:

- 'Flat-rate value scheme',[43] which derives the tax value of the sum of the projected triple assessed land value plus the building value
- Derivation of an appropriate real estate price index (published by the Austrian Commercial Chamber) only if the evaluated real estate is similar to those of the real estate price index
- Lower real estate value if supported by appraisal

The applicable tax rate amounts to from 0.5% to 3.5% depending on whether real estate was acquired for (partially) valuable consideration or without any consideration (gratuitous).

Real estate tax

Real estate tax is levied on Austrian immovable property, i.e. agricultural, forestry, business, and private immovable property. The tax is assessed at a basic Federal rate (generally 0.2%) and is multiplied by a municipal coefficient (up to 500% depending on the municipality); therefore, the tax rate amounts to up to 1% of the assessed value for tax purposes of the property.

Registration duty

The registration duty of ownership rights of real estate in the real estate register is 1.1% of the purchase price. In some cases, three times the assessed or unit value[44] or, if lower, an application of the fair market value can be used (for example, transitions between family members). If shares in a company owning real estate are transferred, no registration fee is triggered since the owner of the real estate remains unchanged.

Value-added tax on real estate

The sale of real estate is VAT exempt. The seller may, however, opt for VAT liability. As such, the sale of business premises would be subject to 20% VAT. The seller is

43 *Pauschalwertmethode*
44 *Einheitswert*

entitled to deduct input VAT for services received related to the acquisition of real estate, and the acquisition costs only when he/she sells the respective real estate with the application of VAT.

The leasing out of real estate for living purposes is subject to 10% VAT. The leasing out of real estate for business purposes is, in general, VAT exempt. However, the lessor is also entitled to opt for 20% VAT liability under certain conditions. In the latter case, the lessor can deduct input VAT provided that the lessee uses the real estate almost exclusively (i.e. more than 95%) for sales/supplies which do not exclude an input VAT deduction. Hence, for example, if real estate is leased to a bank the lessor is not entitled to deduct input VAT on its incoming invoices. In practice, lease agreements contain 'VAT clauses' stipulating that the lessee must compensate the lessor for VAT damages.

Structuring of real estate investments

Asset deal

An Austrian corporation may directly acquire Austrian real estate. Austrian real estate can also be acquired through the purchase of Austrian partnership interest. Interest expenses for a debt-financed acquisition may be deducted from income from real estate if the real estate is rented out or used for the business of the corporation or partner.

Share deal

There are many share deal structuring opportunities available in order to, for example, not constitute a real estate transfer tax taxable event, inter alia, restructuring measures and the formation of a tax group.

3.3 Taxation of employees and board members

An employee (including board members) receiving income under an employment contract is deemed to derive employment income which is subject to the wage tax. The wage tax is withheld by the employer. An employee must file a tax declaration in a limited number of cases only, for example, if he/she receives other types of income or is employed by two or more employers.

During an annual tax assessment, certain expenses and allowances can be considered which the employer was not allowed to consider for the purpose of the correct wage tax calculation. These include: deductible expenses, special allowances (for example, church contributions, fees for tax advice, etc.), and extraordinary expenses (for example, expenses to compensate shock losses, costs related to the education of children away from home, etc.).

The wage tax is calculated as the standard income tax at a tax rate from 0% to 55%. An annual salary in Austria is paid in 14 equal installments; the 13th and 14th salary payments are subject to beneficial tax rates. Furthermore, the employer is obliged to withhold social security contributions from gross salaries paid to employees. However, in Austria, social security contributions are levied up to the maximum contribution base only.

If the executive director of a corporation is working based on a service contract for the company, he/she derives income from independent professional services and must file a tax return. In general, for the purpose of income tax, an employment relationship is constituted if the employee owes his/her entire manpower to the employer and if he/she works under the supervision of the employer.

If the executive director of a corporation is a substantial shareholder (participation of more than 25%), his/her remuneration is treated as 'income from (other) professional services'.

It is to be noted that a salary that exceeds EUR 500,000 is not tax deductible with its exceeding amount. This limitation does affect employees, as well as individuals who are working based on a service contract if they are fully integrated in the company (for example, members of management). Furthermore, this limitation is also applicable for severance payments and related provisions.

Specific provisions for cross-border employments

Non-residents are taxed in Austria on employment income only if the employment is executed in Austria. The Austrian tax rules for non-residents are comparable to those applicable to residents. Persons resident in the EU are subject to the provisions of European law in the area of social insurance.[45]

According to art 15(2) of the OECD Model Convention, remuneration derived by a resident of a Contracting State in respect of an employment exercised in the other Contracting State shall be taxable in the state of his/her residence only if:

- The recipient is present in the other state for a period or periods not exceeding, in the aggregate, 183 days in any 12-month period, commencing or ending in the fiscal year concerned
- The remuneration is paid by, or on behalf of, an employer who is not a resident of the other state

45 See EC Regulation 883/2004, EC Regulation 1408/71

- The remuneration is not borne by a permanent establishment which the employer has in the other state

The Supreme Administrative Court[46] held that the short-term (period not exceeding 183 days) secondment of an Austrian resident employed by an Austrian company at its foreign subsidiary triggers the foreign working state's right to tax the remuneration of the employee, since the 183-day rule in art 15(2) of the OECD Model Convention is not applicable if the subsidiary economically bears the remuneration.

Generally, income from (other) professional services is taxed in the state of residence. According to art 16 of the OECD Model Convention, directors' fees and other similar payments derived by a resident of a Contracting State, in his/her capacity as a member of the board of directors of a company which is a resident of the other Contracting State, may be taxed in that other state.

Annex: List of Double Tax Treaties Concluded by Austria[47]

LIST OF DOUBLE TAX TREATIES CONCLUDED BY AUSTRIA				
A–C	**D–J**	**K–N**	**P–S**	**T–V**
Albania	Denmark	Kazakhstan	Pakistan	Taiwan
Algeria	Egypt	Kuwait	Philippines	Tajikistan
Armenia	Estonia	Kyrgyzstan	Poland	Thailand
Australia	Finland	Latvia	Portugal	Tunisia
Azerbaijan	France	Libya[1]	Quatar	Turkey
Bahrain	Georgia	Liechtenstein	Romania	Turkmenistan
Barbados	Germany	Lithuania	Russia	Ukraine
Belarus	Greece	Luxembourg	San Marino	UAE
Belgium	Hong Kong	Macedonia	Saudi Arabia	UK
Belize	Hungary	Malaysia	Serbia	US
Bosnia and Herzegovina	Iceland	Malta	Singapore	Uzebekistan
Brazil	India	Mexico	Slovak Republic	Venezuela
Bulgaria	Indonesia	Moldova	Slovenia	Vietnam
Canada	Iran	Mongolia	South Africa	
Chile	Ireland	Montenegro	South Korea	
China	Israel	Morocco	Spain	
Croatia	Italy	Nepal	Sweden	
Cuba	Japan	Netherlands	Switzerland	
Cyprus		New Zealand	Syria[2]	
Czech Republic		Norway		

1 Signed as of 16 September 2010, but has not yet entered into effect
2 Signed as of 3 March 2009, but has not yet entered into effect

46 See VwGH 22 May 2013, 2009/13/0031
47 See website of the Austrian Federal Ministry of Finance, category Double Tax Treaties

Taxation

APPENDIX

List of abbreviations

AG	Joint stock company
BMF	Federal Ministry of Finance
CbC	Country-by-Country reporting
CFC	Controlled foreign corporation
CIT	Corporate Income Tax
CITA	Austrian Corporate Income Tax Act
DTT	Double Tax Treaty
FFC	Austrian Federal Fiscal Code
GAAP	Austrian Generally Accepted Accounting Principles
GmbH	Limited liability company
i.e.	id est
ITA	Austrian Income Tax Act
KG	Limited partnership
LF	Local File
MF	Master File
OECD	Organisation for Economic Co-operation and Development
OG	General partnership
RETT	Real Estate Transfer Tax
SEnt	Sole Entrepreneurs
TPDL	Transfer Pricing Documentation Law
UGB	Austrian Commercial Code
VAT	Value-added tax
VAT Act	Value-added Tax Act
VwGH	Supreme Administrative Court
WHT	Withholding tax

About the authors

MICHAEL PUCHER is a tax advisor and a partner at LeitnerLeitner. He advises family-owned businesses, corporate groups, domestic and international financial investors, and private equity/real estate funds on matters relating to group tax law, M&A, due diligence, transaction tax, international tax law, transfer pricing, and real estate. He also provides support to start-ups and company founders at every stage of a company's lifecycle.

MAXIMILIAN LAUSENHAMMER joined LeitnerLeitner in 2015 as an associate. Previously, he worked for the Federal Ministry of Finance as a tax auditor. His areas of expertise are corporate tax law, M&A, due diligence, international tax law, real estate, and anti-money laundering.

4 Leaving Germany: The Tax Impact

Dr. Wolf Wassermeyer, Flick Gocke Schaumburg

People have many different reasons for moving their tax domiciles away from Germany. Tax aspects frequently play a substantial or at least a secondary part in motivating one to move abroad depending on one's individual circumstances.

4.1 Tax reasons for moving to Austria

Experience has shown that until 2002, if German residents left the country for tax reasons it was chiefly income tax factors that prompted them to move abroad. Since 2002, the introduction of the half-income approach and the lowering of German income tax rates has caused the focus of people's motivation for moving abroad to shift from income tax to inheritance tax. Since Austrian inheritance tax was as a rule lower than German inheritance tax, and was abolished completely on 1 August 2008, Austria became a popular country to which German taxpayers migrate. This trend has declined slightly since 2009 owing to the German inheritance tax reform, under which business assets in Germany can now be transferred to the next generation tax-free, as in Austria, subject to certain prerequisites and the termination of the Double Inheritance and Gift Tax Treaty (Double Tax Treaty — DTT) between Germany and Austria. Nevertheless, moving to Austria can still bring tax benefits depending on one's individual circumstances.

Generally, the material tax issues arise in Germany and not in the country of destination. To achieve the desired tax effect, the tax nexi for German income tax and/or inheritance tax liability should be avoided if possible.

4.2 Income tax issues relating to moving abroad

To fully or partly avoid the income tax consequences of a move from Germany, the first points to address are the prerequisites of the various forms of German income tax liability.[1] This part covers the prerequisites for optimizing the income tax impact of moving away from Germany.[2] Lastly, exit taxation is depicted as a particular legal consequence under s 6 of the German Foreign Tax Act.[3,4]

German income tax liability

Like most countries, Germany distinguishes between unlimited and limited income tax liability. Under certain circumstances, residents moving abroad are also subject to 'extended limited income tax liability'.

Unlimited tax liability

If an individual's liability to income tax in Germany is unlimited, in principle, Germany taxes him/her on his/her worldwide income. In turn, Germany's right to tax potentially may be restricted by an applicable DTT. Unlimited tax liability arises under German income tax law if the person in question has a domicile as defined in s 8 of the AO, or a habitual abode as defined in s 8 of the AO of the German General Tax Code,[5,6] or his/her habitual abode in Germany as defined in s 9 of the AO of the German Income Tax Act.[7,8]

Limited tax liability

If an individual maintains neither his/her domicile as defined in s 8 of the AO nor his/her habitual abode as defined in s 9 of the AO in Germany, he/she is subject to German limited tax liability.[9] The legal consequence is that he/she is subject to German taxation in only the categories of German-source income listed in s 49(1) of the EStG. Germany's right to tax may in turn also become restricted by an applicable DTT.

---

1 For details, see 'German income tax liability'
2 For details, see 'Prerequisites for a tax-optimized move abroad'
3 *Außensteuergesetz* (AStG)
4 For details, see 'Specific legal consequence: Exit taxation under s 6 of the AStG'
5 *Abgabenordnun* (AO)
6 S 8 AO of the German General Tax Code (AO)
7 *Einkommensteuergesetz* (EStG)
8 S 1(1) sentence 1 EStG
9 S 1(4) EStG

Extended limited tax liability

If an individual ceases to be subject to unlimited German tax liability he/she becomes subject to extended limited tax liability[10] under the following prerequisites:

1. The emigrant has been, as a German, subject to at least five years' unlimited tax liability in the previous 10 years before such liability ended
2. The emigrant will become resident in a low-tax jurisdiction or in no state and does not owe income tax there. The income tax corresponds to less than two thirds of a German tax that would be levied if unlimited tax liability is assumed to exist
3. The emigrant still has business interests in Germany in the form of an interest exceeding 25% in a German partnership or corporation, non-foreign income exceeding EUR 52,000, or non-foreign assets exceeding EUR 154,000

The legal consequence of extended limited tax liability is that the list of taxable income is extended for the year of departure and the following 10 years to all non-foreign income under s 34c(1) of the EStG. However, as Austria is not a low-tax jurisdiction, extended limited tax liability does not, as a general rule, apply to any German taxpayer moving to Austria.

Prerequisites for a tax-optimized move abroad

In respect of income tax, two effective options exist in principle for moving from Germany to Austria. These solutions restrict German income tax liability and optimize the tax applicable to the move abroad. Either the individual seeks to avoid the income tax nexi for German income tax liability, in particular German unlimited income tax liability (Option 1), or the individual establishes a dual domicile and comes under the protection of the DTT/Austria by shifting the center of his/her vital interests to Austria (Option 2).

Option 1: Elimination of domestic nexi

Under Option 1, the emigrant gives up his/her domicile and habitual abode in Germany, and thus ends his/her unlimited German tax liability. If necessary, he/she also seeks to avoid tax nexi for (extended) limited income tax liability.

Giving up one's German domicile

A person has a domicile where he/she maintains a dwelling under circumstances which lead to the conclusion that he/she will keep and use the dwelling.[11] To establish

10 Under s 2 AStG
11 S 8 AO

unlimited tax liability in the domestic country based on a domicile, it is of significance whether the taxpayer has further domiciles at home, or abroad,[12] or where the center of his/her vital interests lie.[13] A dwelling in this sense encompasses all premises that are suited for living,[14] such as a furnished room, a second residence, a hunting lodge,[15] or a holiday home;[16] a hotel room permanently at the individual's disposal is also sufficient. It is immaterial for tax purposes under s 8 of the AO whether a principal or secondary domicile is involved.[17] 'Maintaining' a dwelling presupposes that the person in question may use the dwelling at will. The actual right of use is crucial;[18] it is therefore not absolutely decisive who the legal tenant or owner of the dwelling is. As part of an overall evaluation, all the actual circumstances[19] must be taken into account that show that the dwelling serves as a lodging, that it is used constantly or at least regularly and habitually, or is not designated solely for the purposes of temporary residence.[20] Having the intention to establish a domicile is not required;[21] nor is the permanent use of the dwelling[22] or a stay for a specific minimum period.[23] Short stays in Germany for holiday and recreational purposes do not create a domicile per se,[24] but can be sufficient for the tax authorities to assume that a dwelling exists before the

12 Federal Tax Court of 19 March 2002, BFH/NV 2002 1411, 1412; Gersch in Klein, AO, § 8 recitals 2 and 5; Heinicke in Schmidt, EStG, § 1 recital 20; Kruse in Tipke and Kruse, AO/FGO, § 8 AO recital 4 with further references

13 Federal Tax Court of 24 January 2001, BFH/NV 2001 1402, 1403; of 19 March 2002, BFH/NV 2002 1411, 1412; Heinicke in Schmidt, EStG, § 1 recital 20

14 AEAO recital 3; Heinicke in Schmidt, EStG, § 1 recital 21; Birk in Hübschmann, Hepp and Spitaler, AO/FGO, § 8 AO recital 19 et seq. with further references

15 RFH of 3 April 1941, RStBl 1941 290

16 Heinicke in Schmidt, EStG, § 1 recital 21; Gersch in Klein, AO, § 8 recital 2; Kruse in Tipke and Kruse, AO/FGO, § 8 AO recitals 5 and 8; Birk in Hübschmann, Hepp and Spitaler, AO/FGO, § 8 AO recitals 23 and 26 with further references

17 Federal Tax Court of 24 January 2001, I R 100/99, BFH/NV 2001 1402; Cologne Tax Court of 27 June 2002, 10 K 6348/97, EFG 2002 1198

18 Federal Tax Court of 23 November 1988, II R 139/87, Federal Tax Gazette Part II 1989 182, 183; Federal Tax Court of 12 January 2001, VI R 64/98 BFH/NV 2001 1231, 1232; AEAO recital 4; Heinicke in Schmidt, EStG, § 1 recital 22; Kruse in Tipke and Kruse, AO/FGO, § 8 AO recital 6; Birk in Hübschmann, Hepp and Spitaler, AO/FGO, § 8 AO recital 28

19 Federal Tax Court of 19 March 1997, I R 69/96, Federal Tax Gazette Part II 1997 447, 448; Federal Tax Court of 19 March 2002, I R 15/01, BFH/NV 2002 1411, 1412; Kruse in Tipke and Kruse, AO/FGO, § 8 AO recital 9; Gersch in Klein, AO, 9th edn 2006, § 8 recital 4

20 Heinicke in Schmidt, EStG, § 1 recital 23. Similarly, Gersch in Klein, AO, § 8 recital 4

21 AEAO recital 2 sentence 1, Kruse in Tipke and Kruse, AO/FGO, § 8 AO recital 2; Heinicke in Schmidt, EStG, § 1 recital 21

22 Heinicke in Schmidt, EStG, § 1 recital 23. Cf also Federal Tax Court of 19 March 2002, I R 15/01, BFH/NV 2002 1411, 1412

23 Federal Tax Court of 12 January 2001, VI R 64/98, BFH/NV 2001 1231, 1232

24 Federal Tax Court of 6 March 1968, I 38/65, Federal Tax Gazette Part II 1968 439 (440)

individual moves abroad that will be retained.[25] On the other hand, registering with the police in a specific place serves as an indication[26] of a domicile.[27]

It should be noted that the tax authorities will presume that spouses have a joint family domicile.[28] Accordingly, they will proceed on the assumption that one spouse also uses the dwelling in which his/her family lives and will therefore have a domicile there as well.[29] This assumption can be refuted, but only by proof in the individual case that the spouse is not expected to return to the joint domicile.[30] It will be extremely difficult, if not almost impossible to furnish such proof if one spouse continues to maintain a domicile in Germany and is not divorced or proven to be permanently separated from the spouse who emigrated. Proving this is more difficult if the offspring continue to maintain a domicile in Germany.

If the individual wishes to avoid a German domicile with legal certainty, all dwellings actually used in Germany should be given up, and ideally this should be substantiated by terminating any tenancy agreements, or selling any dwellings to a third party.

Terminating habitual abode

To avoid German unlimited income tax liability, the emigrant must give up not only his/her German domicile, but also his/her habitual abode in Germany. Habitual abode exists if a person stays in Germany under circumstances which lead to the conclusion that the person does not stay at the place only temporarily.[31] In the individual case, the objective circumstances are decisive; the personal wish of the individual is not relevant, even if it contradicts the actual circumstances.[32] 'Staying' or 'spending time' presupposes physical presence in Germany.[33] If it continues for a considerable length of time, the stay is not only temporary. It is worth noting that the law does not specify any minimum period. Habitual abode is always assumed for an ongoing stay exceeding six months.[34] In the individual case, however, the duration of a stay can also be (substantially) less than

25 Heinicke in Schmidt, EStG, § 1 recital 23. Cf also Federal Tax Court of 12 January 2001, VI R 64/98, BFH/NV 2001 1231, 1232; Tax Court of Lower Saxony of 9 September 2004, file No 10 V 302/04 (not published)

26 View taken by the tax authorities; see AEAO recital 2 sentence 3

27 Federal Tax Court of 14 November 1969, III R 95/68, Federal Tax Gazette Part II 1970 153, 155; Federal Tax Court of 12 April 1978, I R 136/77, Federal Tax Gazette Part II 1978 494, 495; Gersch in Klein, AO, § 8 recital 5; Heinicke in Schmidt, EStG, § 1 recital 23

28 Federal Tax Court of 17 May 1995, I R 8/94, Federal Tax Gazette Part II 1996 2

29 Established case law. Cf Federal Tax Court of 17 May 1995, I R 8/94, Federal Tax Gazette Part II 1996 2 with further references

30 Federal Tax Court of 29 October 1959 IV 129/58 S, Federal Tax Gazette Part II 1960 61

31 S 9 AO

32 Stapperfend in Herrmann, Heuer and Raupach, EStG, § 1 recital 76 with further references

33 Kruse in Tipke and Kruse, AO/FGO, § 9 AO recital 4

34 S 9 sentence 2 AO

six months. It is also not necessary in a particular case for the stay to take place without interruption. On the contrary, stays for visiting, recreational, spa or similar personal purposes are not detrimental.

An individual gives up his/her habitual abode within the meaning of s 9 sentence 1 of the AO if he/she ceases to stay at the place or in the region, and the external circumstances do not create the impression that he/she will return and continue to stay there. Following s 9 sentence 2 of the AO, this can be presumed if the person stays abroad for more than six months.[35] This is, however, refuted if, despite the absence, the objective circumstances indicate that the individual will return and continue to stay at the place or in the region.[36] In any case, to the extent that the person establishes his/her habitual abode abroad, the German habitual abode must be given up because establishing a new habitual abode always means that the existing one is given up.[37]

Spouses establish their habitual abode independently of each other.[38] Therefore, crediting the spouse's habitual abode — unlike the case of the domicile (see above) — is not an option.

One further criterion for the existence of a habitual abode in Germany is if the individual spends three to four days a week pursuing his/her profession in Germany. It is immaterial whether, on the remaining week days, the individual stays at the foreign family domicile that forms the center of his/her vital interests.[39]

Legal consequences of a move abroad

If the emigrant has given up his/her domicile and habitual abode in Germany, he/she has effectively moved abroad. In other words, he/she ceases to be subject to unlimited income tax liability in Germany and must pay tax only on certain German-source income, i.e. he/she is subject to German limited tax liability.[40] If he/she moves to Austria, Germany's right to tax this income will usually also be restricted by the applicable DTT/Austria. It may be advisable to avoid leaving any sources of income in Germany by restructuring German assets into foreign assets. In consequence, the restriction on Germany's right to tax becomes even more far reaching.

35 Federal Tax Court of 27 July 1962, VI 156/59, Federal Tax Gazette Part III 1962 429; Kruse in Tipke and Kruse, AO/FGO, § 9 AO recital 16; Stapperfend in Herrmann, Heuer and Raupach, EStG/KStG, § 1 EStG recital 83

36 Cf Stapperfend in Herrmann, Heuer and Raupach, EStG/KStG, § 1 EStG recital 83 with reference to the Tax Court of Baden-Württemberg of 23 September 1975, EFG 1976 13

37 Federal Tax Court of 27 April 2005, I R 112/04, BFH/NV 2005 1756

38 Cf Federal Tax Court of 14 November 1969, III R 95/68, Federal Tax Gazette Part II 1970 153

39 Federal Tax Court of 22 June 2011, BFH/NV 2011, 2001 et seqq.

40 S 49 EStG

Option 2: Triggering the protection afforded by the DTT/Austria (dual domicile)

In respect of tax, an effective move to Austria can also be achieved by retaining a German domicile and German unlimited income tax liability, but also becoming an Austrian resident under Treaty law and relocating one's permanent home (*Wohnstätte*) and center of vital interests to Austria. This would restrict Germany's right to tax to certain types of German-source income specified in the DTT/Austria.

Art 4(1) DTT/Austria provides that an individual is resident under Treaty law in the contracting state in which he/she is subject to unlimited income tax liability. Owing to the dual domicile in Germany and Austria, however, unlimited income tax liability applies in both contracting states.

Permanent home

If an individual is subject to income tax liability in both contracting states, he/she is deemed to be resident under Treaty law in the contracting country in which he/she has a permanent home.[41]

The term home (*Wohnstätte*) should not objectively differ from domicile (*Wohnsitz*), the term used in domestic law.[42] Unlike the domicile, the permanent home must be used regularly (as the term permanent (*ständig*) indicates). A permanent home in this sense is any premises frequented in a way and with a frequency that represents a point of contact integrated into the taxpayer's general rhythm of life, and not simply a place visited on occasion.[43] The Federal Tax Court determined in the above judgment that a domicile constitutes a permanent home in principle if it is used for 50 days in a year. However, it cannot be inferred according to the Federal Tax Court that a use of the domicile for less than 50 days a year does not create a permanent home. Still, the Court went on to rule that no permanent home exists if the domicile is used on only a few days per year by reason of a business activity.

A dual domicile triggering unlimited tax liability in both contracting states will regularly prompt the tax authorities to presume that a permanent home exists.

Center of vital interests

If it is assumed that the emigrant maintains a permanent home in both contracting states, he/she is deemed pursuant to art 4(2a) of the DTT/Austria to be resident under Treaty law in the state in which he/she maintains his/her center of vital

41 Art 4(2)(a) DTT/Austria

42 See 'Giving up one's German domicile'

43 Federal Tax Court of 5 June 2007, Federal Tax Gazette Part II 2007 812

Taxation

interests. The center of a person's vital interests is the place in which, according to objective criteria,[44] that person has closer personal and business relationships. The term 'personal relationships' comprises the person's entire personal lifestyle, i.e. especially familial, social, political, and cultural ties to the place in question.[45] As a rule, the key, but not only, decisive criterion is family ties.[46] Further indicators of a personal center of vital interests are actual length of stay, size of the dwellings, domestic staff, the location of personal valuables of tangible or sentimental value, club memberships, etc. A person's business relationships with a place arise particularly from local activities such as work or specific local sources of income or assets.[47] If these personal and business relationships are located in both contracting states, personal relationships do not generally take precedence over business relationships or vice versa.[48] A comprehensive analysis must be performed as to which place is more significant.[49] Length of stay can be an indicator.[50] It should be noted that, despite the general equality of personal and business relationships, court decisions give personal relationships, especially family relationships, a certain priority.[51]

In practice, an evaluation of the facts regularly determines in which of both contracting states the center of a person's vital interests is located. In light of this, Option 2 should be implemented only if, on the basis of the specific facts, the center of vital interests is clearly in Austria.

Legal consequences of a move abroad

If the emigrant establishes a permanent home in Austria (while retaining a permanent home in Germany) and shifts his/her center of vital interests to Austria, he/she has effectively moved abroad as well. That means he/she is subject to unlimited income tax liability in Germany and Austria. However, as he/she is deemed under Treaty law to be

---

44 Federal Tax Court of 31 October 1990, Federal Tax Gazette Part II 1991, 562 (563); Wassermeyer in Debatin and Wassermeyer, DBA, art 4 OECD-MA recital 67

45 Federal Tax Court of 31 October 1991, Federal Tax Gazette Part II 1991 562 (563); Tax Court of Berlin of 18 June 2002, IStR 2002 845 (847); Wassermeyer in Debatin and Wassermeyer, DBA, art 4 OECD-MA recital 68; Lehner in Vogel and Lehner, DBA, 5th edn 2008, § 4 recital 192

46 Wassermeyer in Debatin and Wassermeyer, DBA, art 4 OECD-MA recital 68; Lehner in Vogel and Lehner, DBA, 5th edn 2008, § 4 recital 193

47 Federal Tax Court of 31 October 1991, Federal Tax Gazette Part II 1991 562 (563); Tax Court of Berlin of 18 June 2002, IStR 2002 845 (847); Wassermeyer in Debatin and Wassermeyer, DBA, art 4 OECD-MA recital 69; Lehner in Vogel and Lehner, DBA, 5th edn 2008, § 4 recital 194

48 Tax Court of Berlin of 18 June 2002, IStR 2002 845 (847); Wassermeyer in Debatin and Wassermeyer, DBA, art 4 OECD-MA recital 70; Lehner in Vogel and Lehner, DBA, 5th edn 2008, § 4 recital 195

49 Federal Tax Court of 23 July 1971, Federal Tax Gazette Part II 1971, 758 (759). Cf also Federal Tax Court of 31 October 1991, Federal Tax Gazette Part II 1991 562 (563)

50 Wassermeyer in Debatin and Wassermeyer, DBA, art 4 OECD-MA recital 70

51 Federal Tax Court of 31 October 1991, Federal Tax Gazette Part II 1991 562 (563); Tax Court of Berlin of 18 June 2002, IStR 2002 845 (847)

resident in Austria, Germany may tax only the types of German-source income listed under arts 6 to 22 of the DTT/Austria. It may be advisable to avoid any German-source income by restructuring German assets into foreign assets. In consequence, the restriction on Germany's right to tax would become even more far reaching.

Specific legal consequence: exit taxation under s 6 of the AStG

If an emigrant should hold at least 1% of the shares of a German or foreign corporation as personal assets he/she, in principle, triggers 'exit taxation' under s 6 of the AStG, which can be deferred permanently and tax free without security.

Exit taxation under s 6(1) of the AStG aims essentially at taxing hidden reserves in shares held as private assets for tax purposes in domestic or foreign corporations within the meaning of s 17 of the EStG, if these are withdrawn from the German tax net by an event with a foreign nexus. 'Shares in corporations' means not only stocks or business shares but also *jouissance* certificates or similar interests and claims to such interests.[52] The shareholder within the meaning of s 17 of the EStG is the relevant beneficial owner of the shares in accordance with s 39 of the AO. In principle, s 6 of the AStG provides for a deemed capital gain if the emigrant ceased to be subject to unlimited tax liability in Germany or the applicable double tax treaty deprives Germany of its right to tax these shares because the taxpayer has shifted the center of his/her vital interests. The same applies in principle if the taxpayer gives or leaves the shares to a recipient who is resident abroad.[53]

In these cases, the deemed capital gain, i.e. the difference between the market value and the historical acquisition costs of the shares, must in principle be taxed in Germany at a rate of up to about 28.5% (taxation in accordance with the 'partial-income approach'). If the interest is sold later, Austria recognizes as acquisition costs the amount that was recognized as a capital gain under s 6 taxation.[54]

It is true that various structuring options exist in principle to avoid exit taxation completely.[55] The issue can easily be solved when moving to Austria, however, by permanently deferring payment of exit taxation under s 6(5) of the AStG. Section 6(5) sentences 1 and 2 of the AStG permits an EU member state national to apply for long-term, interest-free deferral of exit taxation without providing any security if he/she moves to a member state of the EU or the EEA, and is subject to tax liability similar to German income taxation. These prerequisites are met when

52 S 17(1) sentence 3 EStG

53 S 6(1) sentence 2 No 1 AStG

54 Art 13(6) DTT/Austria

55 Explained by Häck in Haase, AStG/DBA, § 6 AStG recital 263 et seqq.

a German individual moves to Austria.[56] In this case, an exit tax assessment notice is issued deferring payment of the resulting exit tax permanently. If the taxpayer or his/her legal successor later returns to Germany, again becoming subject to domestic unlimited tax liability, and Germany's right to tax the capital gains is re-established, its right to exit taxation lapses, and the exit tax assessment notice is annulled.[57]

It should be noted, however, that this deferral of payment must be revoked if a reason to do so exists under s 6(5) sentence 4 of the AStG. This applies, for example, (i) to a gain on the sale of shares of which the hidden contribution is into a corporation, or (ii) to a gift to a person not subject to unlimited tax liability in Germany who is not subject to taxation comparable with German unlimited income tax liability in an EU/EEA state. A further move by the shareholder or his/her legal successor to a destination outside EU/EEA territory would also cause the deferral to be revoked.[58] The same applies if the shares are given or left to a beneficiary who is not deemed to be subject to unlimited tax liability in an EU/EEA state, and is resident there within the meaning of the relevant Treaty law.[59]

During the deferral of payment, the shareholder is required to discharge certain duties to cooperate under s 6(5) sentence 1 of the AStG. Under s 6(7) sentence 4 of the AStG, he/she must notify the competent tax office[60] annually in writing, by expiry of 31 January, of his/her address at 31 December of the previous calendar year, and confirm that the shares continue to be attributable to him/her or his/her legal successor within the meaning of s 39 of the AO. If the shareholder fails to discharge his/her duties to cooperate, the local tax office may revoke the deferral of payment.[61]

In summary, exit taxation does have to be considered, but the above deferral offers a solution to the problem.

4.3 Inheritance tax issues relating to moving abroad

To fully or partly avoid in Germany the legal consequences of a move abroad in terms of gift and inheritance tax, the first points to address are the prerequisites of the various forms of German income tax liability.[62] These indicate the prerequisites for an income tax-optimized move from Germany.[63]

56 According to the rationale of the Act, the necessary informal collaboration is ensured by the EC Mutual Assistance Directive, and the EC Tax Recovery Directive. Cf BR-Drs. 542/06 of 11 August 2006 87

57 S 6(3) sentence 4 AStG

58 S 6(5) sentence 4 No 4 AStG

59 S 6(5) sentence 4 No 2 AStG

60 The competent tax office is the one that has granted the deferral of payment, because it is this tax office that must decide on any revocation of the deferral. Cf Häck in Haase, AStG/DBA, § 6 AStG recital 249

61 S 6(7) sentence 5 AStG

62 For details, see 'German income tax liability'

63 For details, see 'Prerequisites for a tax-optimized move abroad'

German inheritance tax liability

Germany distinguishes between unlimited and limited income tax liability. Extended unlimited and extended limited tax liability also exist.

Unlimited tax liability

A taxpayer is subject to German inheritance or gift tax liability if either the person with dispositional rights (i.e. the deceased or the donor) or the beneficiary in Germany (as is the case with income tax) has a domicile within the meaning of s 8 of the AO or a habitual abode within the meaning of s 9 of the AO.[64] The legal consequence is that all the taxpayer's worldwide assets transferred gratuitously are liable to inheritance or gift tax in Germany.

Extended unlimited tax liability

If the person with dispositional rights or the beneficiary is a German national, he/she is also subject in Germany to 'extended unlimited inheritance or gift tax liability' for five years after giving up a domicile or a habitual abode. The legal consequence is that all the taxpayer's worldwide assets transferred gratuitously remain liable to inheritance or gift tax in Germany during the subsequent five-year period mentioned above.

Limited tax liability

If the person with dispositional rights (deceased or donor) or the beneficiary has a domicile within the meaning of s 8 of the AO or a habitual abode within the meaning of s 9 of the AO in Germany, only the gratuitous transfers via the domestic assets held in Germany within the meaning of s 121 of the German Valuation Act[65] are subject to German gift or inheritance tax. The main cases of domestic assets to which this applies are real estate located in Germany, business assets situated in Germany, and directly or indirectly held interests in German corporations of at least 10%.

Extended limited tax liability

If a deceased person or donor were subject to extended limited income tax liability at the time of the gratuitous transfer,[66] extended limited inheritance and gift tax liability applies. Accordingly, all gratuitous transfers of extended domestic assets are taxable in Germany. Extended domestic assets exist if the income from the assets of a person subject to unlimited income tax liability represents non-foreign income within the meaning of s 34c(1) of the EStG. This results in, for example, the gratuitous transfer of debt claims against a German debtor becoming liable to inheritance or gift tax.

---

64 For details, see 'Unlimited tax liability'

65 *Bewertungsgesetz* (BewG)

66 For details, see 'Extended limited tax liability'

This definition of assets therefore goes beyond the scope of 'domestic assets' under limited tax liability. Extended limited inheritance and gift tax liability can regularly be avoided by restructuring the assets at the disposal of the potential taxpayer.

Prerequisites for a tax-optimized move abroad

As Germany terminated the Inheritance and Gift DTT/Austria with effect from 1 August 2008, only one way exists to avoid German inheritance and gift tax, and to optimize a move from Germany in terms of inheritance tax. This method presupposes that unlimited and limited inheritance and gift tax liability can be avoided in Germany.

On the one hand, this means that both the deceased or donor and the beneficiary must give up their domicile and habitual abode in Germany.[67] If the prerequisites for extended unlimited tax liability are met, the deceased, donor, and beneficiary must have had neither a domicile nor a habitual abode in Germany for over five years before the transfer in Germany. On the other hand, if only persons with dispositional rights move from Germany, and the potential beneficiaries retain a domicile or habitual abode in Germany, a transfer to an Austrian private foundation could be considered, which may avoid German tax especially if an inheritance accrues.

To avoid German limited inheritance and gift tax liability, however, no right of control over domestic assets may exist. If domestic assets are affected by the envisaged transfers, these assets should be converted into foreign assets by contribution or assignment to foreign entities.

A move abroad would be optimized for inheritance tax purposes subject to the above prerequisites. The gratuitous transfers are then not liable to any inheritance or gift tax.

Moving from Germany to Austria can have considerable benefits, particularly from the perspective of inheritance and gift tax law. To avoid tax issues, it is advisable to prove compliance with the prerequisites for a tax-optimized move abroad.

About the author

DR. WOLF WASSERMEYER is a lawyer and a certified tax advisor. He has been a partner at Flick Gocke Schaumburg, Partnergesllschaft mbH for the past 16 years, where he is an expert advisor on international tax law. He studied law in Constance and Kiel (1995 Dr. iur.). Dr. Wassermeyer is a guest lecturer at the *Bundesfinanzakademie* (German Federal Finance Academy) and a lecturer at the Fresenius University of Applied Sciences in Munich.

---

67 For details, see 'Option 1: Elimination of domestic nexi'

5 Customs Procedures

Dr. Rainer Brandl, LeitnerLeitner

Customs

It is important for those intending to relocate to Austria to familiarize themselves with the customs regulation details which are summarized in this chapter.

5.1 Customs procedures for the relocation of private individuals to Austria

As a member of the EU, Austria is part of the EU customs territory. If a person moves to Austria, customs procedures vary depending on whether one is relocating from an EU member state or a non-EU member state. The following explanations focus primarily on customs regulations for private persons relocating to Austria.

Relocation from an EU member state

If the domicile is moved from an EU country to Austria, there are generally no special procedures to be considered regarding personal property, and therefore there are no customs duties to be paid. Exceptions may apply for the relocation of motor vehicles.

The initial registration of a motor vehicle for use in Austria is subject to taxation whether the vehicle is new or used. This also includes motor vehicles that are brought to Austria during relocation and registered there for the first time.[1] For example, if a German citizen brings a car to Austria during his/her relocation,

1 NoVA-RL 2008, Rz 26

the car must be registered domestically. In this case, the Car Registration Tax (NoVA) of up to 32% must be paid, calculated based on the general value of the vehicle (purchase value or Euro-tax median value exclusive of sales tax). This process requires submission of a declaration to the local tax authorities by completing a NOVA 2 form.[2]

The private importation of a new motor vehicle to Austria from an EU member state is subject to individual vehicle tax (VAT) and requires a tax return to be filed.[3] A motor vehicle is considered new if its initial use has occurred no more than six months previously or if it has been driven for 6,000 km or less.

Relocation from a non-EU member state

Import duties (particularly customs and import VAT) apply to the import of (new or used) goods to the EU. However, in the case of relocation to Austria from a non-EU country (third country), certain goods (goods of personal property) are exempt from import duties. They do not require the payment of customs fees or import VAT. The conditions for import duty exemption are detailed in a comprehensive working directive by the Austrian Ministry of Finance. The key declarations made in this directive are summarized below under '5.2 Import duty exemption due to relocation'.

For taxation (car registration tax) on the first-time registration of motor vehicles in Austria, please refer to 'Relocation from an EU member state' above.

5.2 Import duty exemption due to relocation

Under certain circumstances, those who are moving their usual place of residence to an EU customs territory may request a tax exemption for goods of personal property. Duties must be paid on goods that do not fall within the following exemptions:

Overview of requirements[4]

- Relocation of the usual place of residence (primary residence or center of vital interests) to a place within the EU
- The usual place of residence was in a third country for at least 12 consecutive months
- (Economic) property on the relocation goods

2 *formulare.bmf.gv.at/service/formulare/inter-Steuern/pdfs/9999/NOVA2.pdf*

3 Purchase declaration for new vehicles (single-vehicle tax); see *formulare.bmf.gv.at/service/formulare/inter-Steuern/pdfd/9999/U10.pdf*

4 See *bmf.gv.at/zoll/uebersiedlung-fahrzeugeigenimport/uebersiedlung-nicht-eu-staat.html*

- Any goods being moved have been used for at least the previous six months at the previous usual place of residence in the third country
- Any goods will continue to be used for the same purposes at the new usual place of residence within the EU
- Any goods must be registered for customs processing within the 12 months following relocation of the usual place of residence to Austria
- Goods may not be sold, loaned, rented, or pawned for 12 months after customs clearance has been granted

Personal property[5]

All goods are considered personal property if they are intended for personal use or consumption or for household use (for example, household effects, bicycles, motorcycles, cars with trailers, household supplies, pets and riding animals, and any portable instruments for technical or freelance work necessary to carry out one's profession). Personal property must be used goods. New items are not counted as personal property.

The exemption excludes alcoholic products, tobacco or tobacco products, commercial vehicles, and commercially used items (except portable instruments for technical or freelance work).

Changing one's usual place of residence

The exemption of customs and taxes on goods of personal property requires that one's usual place of residence is moved to an EU customs territory and that it was maintained for at least 12 consecutive months in a third country. The previous place of residence in a third country may be maintained as a secondary residence.[6]

The usual place of residence refers to the residence of a natural person in which he/she establishes his/her domicile because of personal and professional connections. A normal stay is defined as a stay of at least 185 days spent at the residence within one year. Individuals who alternate between places inside and outside the EU are considered to have their usual residence at the place in which they maintain a personal connection if they return to this place regularly. Attendance at a university or school is not considered to be a relocation of one's usual place of residence.

5 3.1.1. Working directive on entry tax exemption

6 3.1.2. Working directive on non-tariff exemption

Declaration for free circulation

Personal property must be declared for duty-free handling. For this purpose, a completed and signed ZBefr 2 form[7] should be submitted. The form declares that one's previous sole place of residence has been moved from a third country to Austria. In addition, it may be necessary to submit a ZBefr 2a form[8] before the planned import of personal property (especially if such goods include motorcycles or cars, if residence was once established in the EU, or if a secondary residence outside the EU is to be maintained after relocation).[9]

If the customs clearance — without representatives — is to be successfully completed, the goods of personal property that are brought with the individual must be registered with the border customs office for clearance. It is often helpful to make use of an international logistics company[10] to handle the transport of the goods as well as the customs formalities.

An exemption is granted for goods of personal property that are submitted for customs clearance (release for free circulation) within 12 months of the usual place of residence having been established (this describes the point in time at which residence is formally established). Within this period, goods of personal property may also be released for free circulation through multiple partial shipments.[11] However, these goods may not be transferred to a third person within 12 months of customs clearance, which means that they may not be sold, loaned, rented, or pawned during this time.

Other documents for verification[12]

Within 12 months of customs clearance, registration or deregistration confirmation, a rental agreement, work or service contract, or child's school enrolment form can be submitted as evidence of normal residence in a domestic context for at least 12 months of normal residence in a third country and the maintenance of the prohibition of disposals. These verification documents must be retained and submitted in case of follow-up checks by the customs agency.

---

7 Explanation of customs exemption for goods of personal property *(formulare.bmf.gv.at/service/formulare/inter-Zoll/pdfs/9999/ZBefr2.pdf)*

8 Application for assessment of customs exemption for goods of personal property; *(formulare.bmf.gv.at/service/formulare/inter-Zoll/pdfs/9999/ZBefr2a.pdf)*

9 See *bmf.gv.at/zoll/uebersiedlung-fahrzeugeigenimport/uebersiedlung-nicht-eu-staat.html*

10 Refer to, for example, Zentralverband Spedition & Logistik, Austria's central association for shipping and logistics *(spediteure-logistik.at/)*

11 3.1.3. Working directive for import duty exemptions

12 See *bmf.gv.at/zoll/uebersiedlung-fahrzeugeigenimport/uebersiedlung-nicht-eu-staat.html*; 3.1.8.4. and 3.1.4. Working directive for non-tariff exemptions

Documented proof is required for used personal property. If certain objects cannot be easily recognized as having been used because of their condition or appearance, customs authorities may request proof (for example, invoice, delivery slip, warranty card) to verify that the goods were already in use before relocation to Austria.

5.3 Import prohibitions and import restrictions

Not all goods may be imported to Austria. Goods of personal property may also be subject to travel prohibitions or restrictions. This particularly includes restrictions on animals by veterinarian authorities, security restrictions for weapons, restrictions based on species protection laws for animals and plants, and restrictions based on plant protection laws.

5.4 Cash transactions[13]

General prerequisites

In general, cash may be carried in unlimited amounts without approval. In the context of relocation, certain registrations may apply as part of so-called border-crossing cash transactions if cash to the value of EUR 10,000 or more is brought across the border. Cash funds include both currency and means of payment equal to cash.

Cash includes banknotes and coins that are a valid means of payment or may be exchanged for a valid means of payment. For coins of which the output value significantly exceeds the nominal value, the actual value must be considered for calculations within the EUR 10,000 threshold.

Means of payment equal to cash[14] include gold and other precious metals, as well as transferable bearer instruments such as travelers' checks, savings bank books, stock, etc. Jewelry and other products made of precious metals are not considered to be means of payment equal to cash and therefore do not require declaration.

13 See also Bader and Zimnig, *Cash transaction in the tri-state area Germany – Austria – Switzerland,* (PStR 2010), 298, particularly some of the differences in Austrian law compared to German law and Swiss law

14 See § 17b Abs 1 ZollR-DG

Cash transactions beyond the external borders of the EU

Cash (currency and/or equal means of payment) brought by a natural person from or through the EC must be declared if at least EUR 10,000 in cash is carried.

For example, if a Swiss person brings cash funds of EUR 10,000 across the border to Austria as part of his/her relocation, he/she must declare the cash funds upon crossing the border to Austria. In Austria this declaration is often completed verbally, but can also be made by completing a Za 292 form.[15]

Cash declarations must include the following information:[16]

- Name of the person who is declaring the cash
- Travel route and means of transportation
- Amount and type of cash funds
- Origin of cash funds
- Intended use
- Owner and recipient of cash funds

Intra-community cash transactions

While cash transactions with third countries require declaration, intra-community transactions require declaration upon request only.

As part of his/her relocation, a German citizen must declare cash funds of EUR 10,000 brought with him/her only if asked by an official to do so during a check.

If requested, information must be provided on whether cash funds or equal means of payment of EUR 10,000 or more are carried. In this case, information about the origin, economic value, and purpose of the funds must also be provided upon request.[17]

Penalties in the event of failure to declare

If the obligatory customs declaration is breached or if incorrect or incomplete information is provided during the declaration, it constitutes an offense and may be punishable by a fine of up to EUR 100,000 in the case of intent or up to EUR 10,000 in the case of negligence. The cash could also be detained or seized.

15 *formulare.bmf.gv.at/service/formulare/inter-Zoll/pdfs/9999/Za292.pdf*
16 See art 3 s 2 VO (EG) 1889/2005
17 See § 17b s 2 ZollR-DG

Links to useful online resources and addresses

- *bmf.gv.at/zoll/_start.htm*
  The Austrian Federal Ministry of Finance provides interesting information on customs in Austria, particularly regulations on travel and relocation
- *findok.bmf.gv.at/findok*
  Financial Documentation (Findok) provides useful information on BMF work guidelines and UFS/BFG customs laws
- *spediteure-logistik.at/*
  The central association for shipping and logistics provides a useful overview of shipping and logistics companies that serve Austria
- The Central Customs Information Office provides information about general customs matters and handles specific questions on customs rates and queries about prohibitions and restrictions. It operates from Monday to Friday, from 06:00 a.m. to 10:00 p.m. The address and contact details are:
  Zollamt Klagenfurt Villach
  Ackerweg 19
  A-9500 Villach
  Phone: +43 50 233 740
  Fax: +43 (0)1 51433 5964053
  Email: zollinfo@bmf.gv.at

About the author

DR. RAINER BRANDL is a tax advisor and has been a partner at LeitnerLeitner since 2010. His main areas of focus are criminal tax law, tax litigation, general Austrian tax law, and tariff law. His expertise includes extensive knowledge of the avoidance and mitigation of the fiscal risks of businesses and individuals, as well as the handling of company audits, and the defense in criminal proceedings concerning financial offences.

Dr. Brandl has authored many publications, particularly within his specialist fields of criminal tax law, and tax litigation. He is the co-editor of *Zeitschrift für Wirtschafts- und Finanzstrafrecht*, a professional journal that focuses on criminal business law and criminal tax law. Dr. Brandl is a highly regarded speaker and a part-time lecturer at the Institute for Financial Law, Tax Law, and Tax Policy at Johannes Kepler University in Linz.

6 The Law of Residence and Settlement in Austria

Mag. Gottfried Schmutzer LL.M., Schmutzer & Ott Sander

This chapter will deal with the Austrian Law of Residence, which is based on EU Law and the Settlement and Residence Act (NAG).[1] These cover the issuance, denial, and withdrawal of residence titles for foreigners residing or wishing to reside in the Federal Territory for more than six months and the documentation of right of residence under EU law.

Citizens of the EU and their family members have the right to move and reside freely within the territory of the EU subject to certain conditions. Because of their special legal status these requirements will be explained separately.

Foreigners from third countries are required to hold a residence title if they intend to stay for more than six months. The extent of the permissions depends on the type of residence title held and will therefore be discussed by dividing them into time-limited and time-unlimited Right of Residence. The general requirements are applied to both and will consequently be discussed before contemplating the specifics.

To complete the portrayal of the law of residence and settlement in Austria the chapter will be concluded by depicting the responsible authorities, their procedures, and the required German language skills for first time permits and extension applications.

1 *Niederlassungs- und Aufenthaltsgesetz*

6.1 Right of residence for EU citizens

EU/EEA citizens

EU/European Economic Area (EEA) citizens and citizens of Switzerland are exempted from visa requirements. They are not required to hold any residence titles for Austria and have the right to reside in Austria for a period of three months, irrespective of any economic activity.

If they are fulfilling one of the following requirements they have the right to reside in Austria for more than three months:

- Citizens who work as employees or who are self-employed
- Citizens who have sufficient means of subsistence and a sufficient health insurance[2]
- Citizens who attend an Austrian school or a recognized education facility as the main purpose of their stay, earn a secure living, and have sufficient health insurance coverage

If the length of residence of EU/EEA citizens and Swiss nationals extends to more than three months, the only step required is to apply for a Registration Certificate.[3]

EU/EEA citizens and Swiss nationals have the right to obtain a permanent residence in Austria after a five-year period of legal and uninterrupted residence in Austria's Federal Territory. In this case, they will be issued a Certificate of Permanent Residence.[4]

Dependents

A distinction must be made between dependents who are EU/EEA or Swiss citizens and dependents from third countries.

Dependents from EU/EEA countries or Switzerland

Dependents from EU/EEA countries or Switzerland who are themselves citizens of the EU/EEA or Switzerland are exempted from the visa requirements, and have the right to reside in Austria for a period of three months irrespective of any economic activity.

---

2 Sufficient means of subsistence are given if the EU citizen is in receipt of an income which exceeds the standard rate of the national minimum collateral. Since 2017, the standard rate of the national minimum collateral is regulated by the Federal States. To verify if sufficient means of subsistence is given, the following website enlists the standard rate of each Federal State: *arbeiterkammer.at/beratung/arbeitundrecht/Arbeitslosigkeit/Mindestsicherung_Wer_bekommt_wie_viel.html*

3 *Anmeldebescheinigung*

4 *Bescheinigung des Daueraufenthalts*

They are entitled to reside by themselves in Austria for more than three months if they fulfill the requirements listed above. Otherwise, they have the right to reside in Austria for more than three months in any of the following circumstances:

- Spouses or registered same-sex partners
- Relatives of an EU/EEA citizen or citizen of Switzerland as well as relatives of the spouse or registered same-sex partner of an EU/EEA citizen or citizen of Switzerland in the directly descending line until the age of 21. For those over the age of 21, this applies only if they have been granted child support from him/her
- Relatives of an EU/EEA citizen or citizen of Switzerland as well as relatives of the spouse or registered same-sex partner of an EU/EEA citizen or citizen of Switzerland in the directly ascending line if they have been granted maintenance from him/her
- Other relatives of an EU/EEA citizen or citizen of Switzerland if compelling health reasons require that they are given care by the EU/EEA citizen or citizen of Switzerland, or if they lived in a common household with the EU/EEA citizen or citizen of Switzerland in the country of origin, or if they have been granted maintenance from him/her

It is necessary to apply for a Registration Certificate within the first four months of arrival. After a five-year period of legal and uninterrupted residence in Austria's Federal Territory, they will then be issued with a Certificate of Permanent Residence.

Dependents from third countries

Dependents of EU/EEA citizens or citizens of Switzerland who are third country nationals themselves are entitled to reside in Austria if they accompanied them there or moved there later. In addition, one of the following cases must be applicable:

- Spouses or registered same-sex partners
- Relatives of an EU/EEA citizen or citizen of Switzerland as well as relatives of the spouse or registered same-sex partner of an EU/EEA citizen or citizen of Switzerland in the directly descending line until the age of 21. For those over the age of 21, this applies only if they have been granted child support from him/her
- Relatives of an EU/EEA citizen or citizen of Switzerland as well as relatives of the spouse or registered same-sex partner of an EU/EEA citizen or citizen of Switzerland in the directly ascending line if they have been granted maintenance by him/her

After a five-year period of legal and uninterrupted residence in Austria's Federal Territory they can apply for a Permanent Residence Card.[5]

5 *Daueraufenthaltskarte*

6.2 Residence titles

General requirements

If a stay in Austria for a period longer than six months is intended, an application for a residence permit and not for an entry permit (visa) must be submitted. Residence titles are issued by the authorities in Austria.[6] They are issued solely for stays that exceed six months. There are general requirements which must be fulfilled to be eligible for a residence title:

- Adequate means of subsistence[7]
- Adequate local customary accommodation
- Sufficient health insurance that covers all risks
- The stay should not be in contradiction with the public's benefit

The following documents are required:

- A valid travel document (for example, a passport)
- A birth certificate
- A biometric passport photo (size: 45 mm x 35 mm) not more than six months old
- If applicable, a marriage certificate, or a registered partnership certificate, or an adoption certificate
- Proof of local accommodation (for example, rental agreement), sufficient health insurance, and secured maintenance (for example, pay slips, employment contracts, a confirmation of pension, other social payments, or proof of other sufficient assets)

Obstacles to the issuance of a residence title are listed as follows:

1. If travel bans are violated according to § 53 of the *Fremdenpolizeigesetz* (FPG) or § 67 of the FPG
2. If there is a repatriation decision from another EEA state or Switzerland
3. If there is an enforceable repatriation decision and not more than 18 months have passed since the departure
4. If the permitted stay has been exceeded
5. In the case of an unconsummated marriage, an unconsummated registered partnership, or a quasi-adoption
6. If the applicant was punished within the previous 12 months for violating border controls

---

6 For more information regarding the authorities in Austria see chapter 4

7 In 2017, adequate means of subsistence required an income of EUR 1,334.17 for spouses and registered partners, EUR 889.48 for a single person, and EUR 137.30 for each child. According to § 292/3 ASVG, the amount of EUR 284.32 must be available after the deduction of current costs (for example, rent, loan rates)

The obstacles listed in points 1, 2, and 5 are absolute obstacles for the issuance of a residence title. In all other cases, a residence permit can be granted for maintenance of family life in accordance with art 8 of the European Convention on Human rights (ECHR).

The application for a residence permit must be filed before leaving for Austria at the Austrian Embassy or Consulate General. It is not permitted to enter Austria if the application has not been approved and is still pending. The period of validity is usually not longer than one year. Generally, an extension is possible.

The residence titles in particular

Time-limited Right of Residence without access to the labor market[8]

Other dependents of EU/EEA citizens or citizens of Switzerland who are third country nationals are eligible to apply for the residence title 'Settlement Permit — Dependent' under the following conditions:

- The general granting requirements are fulfilled
- The sponsor to whom the applicant refers has issued a liability declaration

Other dependents in this category are relatives of EU/EEA citizens or citizens of Switzerland, relatives of the spouse or registered same-sex partner of an EU/EEA citizen or citizen of Switzerland in direct ascending line, if they receive maintenance from the sponsor, as well as life partners providing evidence of a long-term relationship in their country of origin and receiving maintenance from the sponsor or other relatives under certain circumstances. These dependents must prove German skills at the time of the application. Persons who have been granted a Settlement Permit — Dependent do not have access to the labor market.

Time-limited Right of Residence with restricted access to the labor market

Red-White-Red Card[9]

The Red-White-Red Card (RWR Card) is issued for one year and entitles the holder to a fixed-term settlement and employment by a specific employer. If an extension is granted, the resident might be eligible for a Red-White-Red Card plus (RWR Card plus) and as a result of changes to the Aliens Law Amendment Act[10] (FrÄG) the validity of the RWR Card has been extended to two years. If the effective period of the employment contract is less than two years, the RWR Card will be issued for the time of the employment contract plus three months, but for no longer than two years. The FrÄG was legally implemented on 1 October 2017.

8 *Niederlassungsbewilligung Angehöriger*

9 *Rot-Weiß-Rot Karte*

10 *Fremdenrechtsänderungsgesetz*

The following persons are eligible for an RWR Card:
- Very highly qualified workers
- Skilled workers for occupations in which there is a shortage
- Other key workers
- Graduates of Austrian universities and colleges of higher education
- Self-employed key workers

To verify if one of the above cases is applicable, a points system is used which can be found at the following link:
- *migration.gv.at/en/types-of-immigration/permanent-immigration-red-white-red-card.html*

The points system has undergone a change as a consequence of the above-mentioned changes to the FrÄG, making it easier for employees working in occupations in which there are shortages to fulfill the criteria for language skills and work experience.

If all requirements are met, the Austrian Public Employment Service (AMS)[11] will send confirmation to the residence authority, which will then issue the RWR Card. If the application is successful, the residence authority will inform the applicant. Applicants who need a visa to enter Austria must apply for a 'D Visa'[12] to enter Austria and collect the residence title.

EU Blue Card[13]

The EU Blue Card entitles the holder to a fixed-term settlement and employment with a specific employer. It is valid for two years. If an extension is granted, the resident could be eligible for an RWR Card plus. Third country nationals may be granted an EU Blue Card if they:
- Have completed university or other tertiary education with a minimum duration of three years
- Have been employed (in line with the applicant's education) for at least one year in Austria
- Will earn a gross annual income of at least one and a half times the average gross annual income of full time employees (in 2017 this amount was a minimum of EUR 59,718 made up of approximately EUR 4,266 gross monthly income plus special payments)

11 *Arbeitsmarktservice*
12 *Visum D*
13 *Blaue Karte EU*

- The labor market test[14] shows there is no equally qualified jobseeker registered at AMS and available for the job

Moreover, they need to fulfill the general requirements discussed earlier (except for proof of adequate local accommodation and proof of adequate means of subsistence). The points system is not used for the EU Blue Card.

If all requirements are fulfilled, the AMS will send confirmation to the residence authority, which will then issue the EU Blue Card. If the application is successful, the residence authority will inform the applicant. Applicants who need a visa to enter Austria must apply for a D Visa to enter Austria and collect the residence title. The collection of the residence title is possible only on presentation of a valid city registration.

Settlement Permit[15]

The Settlement Permit grants a time-limited right of settlement and previously entitled the holder to self-employment for a maximum of one year. Consequent to the changes in the FrÄG, the length of validity has been extended to two years.

A Settlement Permit can be granted in the following cases:

1. In the case of an extension of the RWR Card:
   - The holder of the RWR Card for self-employed key workers must have carried out the stipulated activities within the previous 12 months and must be continuing with them
2. In cases of Family Reunification for third country nationals:
   - If they are family members of a holder of a Settlement Permit or a Settlement Permit — Dependent and if a quota space is available
   - If they are family members of a holder of the residence title 'Long-term Resident — European Union'[16], if the third country national who is being reunited with his/her family will hold a Settlement Permit thenceforth
3. In other cases of third country nationals:
   - Persons having the right of establishment by reason of the European Union Act
   - Persons holding a Long-term Resident — European Union permit from other member states if a quota space is available
   - If a case of § 43/3 of the Residence and Settlement Act (NAG)[17] is applicable

14 *Arbeitsmarktprüfung*

15 *Niederlassungsbewilligung*

16 *Daueraufenthalt EU*

17 *Niederlassungs- und Aufenthaltsgesetz*

Time-limited Right of Residence with unrestricted access to the labor market

Red-White-Red Card plus[18]

Holders of the RWR Card plus are entitled to a fixed-term settlement and unlimited labor market access (self-employment and gainful employment not limited to a specific employer). It was previously generally granted for 12 months. After a two-year period of legal and uninterrupted residence in Austria a person can be granted an RWR Card plus for three years if he/she fulfills Module 1 of the Integration Agreement.[19]

On account of the changes to the FrÄG that were implemented on 1 October 2017, the length of validity has been extended to two years.

The following persons who seek to renew their RWR Card or EU Blue Card are eligible with certain provisos for the RWR Card plus:

- Holders of an RWR Card plus if they have been employed in accordance with the requirements for receiving the RWR Card for at least 10 months within the past 12 months. Therefore, a confirmation of the AMS is needed
- Holders of an EU Blue Card if they have been employed in accordance with the requirements for receiving the EU Blue Card for at least 21 months within the past 24 months. Therefore, a confirmation of the AMS is needed

Family members can apply for an RWR Card plus in the following cases:

- Spouses, registered same-sex partners, and minor unmarried children including adopted children and stepchildren of RWR Card holders or EU Blue Card holders
- Spouses, registered same-sex partners, and minor unmarried children including adopted children and stepchildren of foreign citizens permanently settled in Austria

In addition, the RWR Card plus can be issued to:

1. Scientists who have held the residence title 'Residence Permit — Researcher' for at least 24 months
2. Holders of a Settlement Permit or a Settlement Permit — Dependent if they:
   - Have been lawfully settled in Austria for two years and are progressively integrated (for example, have previously been lawfully employed, have close social and family ties to Austria)
   - Hold a valid work permit or a valid exemption certificate

18 *Rot-Weiß-Rot Karte Plus*
19 *Integrationsvereinbarung*

   - Are family members of a third country national who falls within the scope of either of the above two items, provided they have been residing in Austria for 12 months
3. Persons who previously held the residence title 'Long-term Resident — European Union' whose title has expired because of their prolonged residence outside the EEA
4. Holders of a residence title based on the grounds of the Asylum Act [20] may change in certain cases

Residence title Family Member [21]

A third country national who is the spouse, registered same-sex partner, or minor unmarried child of an EEA/EU citizen or Swiss citizen can obtain the residence title 'Family Member', if his/her sponsor does not have a right of residence according to EU law or is a family member of an Austrian who did not exercise his/her right of residence according to EU law. The sponsor must live in Austria permanently. Spouses or registered same-sex partners must have reached the minimum age of 21 years on the date of filing the application. German language skills must be proved at the time of application.

Residence titles limited to a certain purpose

Residence title Employee Sent on Temporary Duty [22]

A temporary duty assignment refers to an employee being sent to work in an Austrian location other than the employee's permanent duty station for more than six months. He/she is eligible for the residence title 'Employee Sent on Temporary Duty', if he/she fulfills the following conditions:

1. Being sent on temporary duty:
   - By employers from third countries without an operating headquarters in Austria
   - To an Austrian employer to fulfill contractual agreements
2. Being a resident of the foreign employer in Austria during his/her temporary duty
3. Having a Confirmation of Employment [23] or Employment Permit as an Employee Sent on Temporary Duty [24]

---

20 *Asylgesetz*
21 *Aufenthaltstitel Familienangehöriger*
22 *Aufenthaltsbewilligung — Betriebsentsandter*
23 *Sicherungsbescheinigung*
24 *Bewilligungsbescheinigung als Betriebsentsandte/Betriebsentsandter*

Henceforth, § 18 of the Act Governing the Employment of Foreign Nationals (AuslBG)[25] shall regulate not only the classical temporary duty assignments, but also the transboundary assignment of EU and EEA citizens.

Residence title Rotational Employee[26] and residence title Intra-corporate Transferee (ICT)[27]

The section on Rotational Employees was amended by the changes that were made to the FrÄG in October 2017. The following part of the chapter is therefore divided into discussing first, the current legal situation and second, the changes as a result of the amendments to the FrÄG.

Rotational Employee

The AMS will approve applications of employees who are obligated to a change of employment within an international company. Rotational Employees are required to be in possession of a Confirmation of Employment[28] or an Employment Permit as a Rotational Employee.[29]

Members of a company's management, executive staff, and representatives of a company's interests are eligible for the residence title 'Rotational Employee'.

Intra-corporate Transferee (ICT)

The above-mentioned changes to the FrÄG converted the ICT Council Directive to national law. The hitherto existing definition of Rotational Employee has been replaced by ICT. For the admission of intra-corporate employees within the EU for a short time (a maximum of 90 days within 180 days) the provisions of the EU Posting of Workers Certificate[30] are still applicable if the employees hold an ICT title from another member state, and are sent to another location within the company. It is therefore not necessary for short-term intra-corporate employees to hold an additional Austrian residence title.

Third country nationals will be eligible to obtain the residence title 'Intra-corporate Employee' under the following conditions according to the AuslBG:[31]

25 *Ausländerbeschäftigungsgesetz*

26 *Aufenthaltsbewilligung — Rotationsarbeitskraft*

27 *Aufenthaltsbewilligung — Unternehmensintern transferierte Arbeitnehmer*

28 *Sicherungsbescheinigung*

29 *Bewilligungsbescheinigung als Rotationsarbeitskraft*

30 *EU-Entsenderichtlinie*

31 § 18a/1

- Members of the company's management and executive staff who have worked for the company continuously for over nine months, and trainees who have been employed by the company for six months
- An existing contract of employment and a transferring agreement
- The company adheres to Austrian wage regulations and working conditions
- The company has not violated the provisions of the AuslBG within the previous 12 months
- The company is not insolvent and has actual business operations in Austria

The Federal Minister for Labor and Social Affairs will be able to determine a certain quota for intra-corporate employees in Austria.

Third country nationals who already hold a valid residence title 'ICT' from another member state of the EU can obtain the residence title 'Mobile Intra-corporate Transferee' if they fulfill the following conditions in addition to the general requirements:

- A written notice from the AMS
- The total length of stay does not exceed the maximum of three years for executive staff and the maximum of one year for trainees

The decision about the issuance of the residence title 'Mobile Intra-corporate Transferee' should be made within eight weeks by the responsible Austrian authorities.

Residence title Self-employed Individual[32]

The residence title 'Self-employed Individual' can be granted if the foreign citizen has contracted to perform certain services and the contract covers a period of more than six months without the intention to settle in Austria. If doubt arises, the AMS can verify whether self-employment exists or not.

Residence title Researcher[33]

Prior to the amendments to the FrÄG, researchers could obtain the residence title 'Researcher'. According to § 43c of the FrÄG, the law since 1 October 2017, researchers can obtain a 'Settlement Permit — Researcher' instead of the residence title 'Researcher'; the conditions remain the same. It is not necessary to file the application in advance; applicants and their dependents can file the application in Austria.

32 *Aufenthaltsbewilligung — Selbstständiger*

33 *Aufenthaltsbewilligung — Forscher*

In addition to the general requirements, researchers must provide a hosting agreement with a certified research facility that must indicate the monthly salary or another corresponding income. The occupation of the researcher must be excluded from the AuslBG.

Residence title Artist[34]

Prior to the amendments to the FrÄG, self-employed or employed artists could obtain the residence title 'Artist'. Since 1 October 2017, the FrÄG has entitled artists to hold a 'Settlement Permit — Artist'. The conditions will remain the same. In the case of employment, an approval by the AMS is required. An Employer's Certificate[35] is therefore needed. Self-employed artists are required to hold a contract for an artistic activity lasting longer than six months.

To be eligible for the Settlement Permit — Artist, the activity must be primarily of an artistic nature and the income earned must be sufficient to cover his/her livelihood. A liability declaration is permissible.

Residence title Specific Cases of Gainful Employment[36]

Prior to the amendments to the FrÄG, if one's employment was exempted from the AuslB one could apply for the residence title 'Specific Cases of Gainful Employment'. According to § 43b of the FrÄG, which has been law since 1 October 2017, those who previously qualified for the residence title 'Specific Cases of Gainful Employment' can obtain a 'Settlement Permit — Specific Cases of Gainful Employment'. The conditions remain the same. An explanation of the exemption circumstances is required.

Some examples of cases in which the Settlement Permit — Specific Cases of Gainful Employment is applicable are au pairs, scientists, executive staff, and media staff.

Residence title Student attending college/university and residence title Pupil attending primary or secondary school (grades 1–12)[37]

Students are granted a residence title for regular and extraordinary studies at a public university, a polytechnic institute, an accredited private university, a public or an accredited teachers' college, an accredited private study program, or an accredited private university course.

---

34 *Aufenthaltsbewilligung — Künstler*

35 *Arbeitgebererklärung*

36 *Aufenthaltsbewilligung — Sonderfälle unselbständig Erwerbstätiger*

37 *Aufenthaltsbewilligung — Studierender; — Aufenthaltsbewilligung Schüler*

Regular pupils attending a public school, a private school under public law or a statutory school under public law, or a certified non-academic educational institution and extraordinary pupils attending a public school or a private school under public law in cases where a first residence permit has been issued, can be granted the residence title 'Pupil'.

Unaccompanied minors must have proof that an adult with a main residence in Austria is responsible for them.

Regarding the general requirement of adequate means of subsistence, it is necessary to mention that a liability declaration is permissible.

Any gainful employment can be engaged in under the following conditions:

- The provisions of the AuslBG are respected
- The employment does not interfere with the studies

Students attending college or university must provide proof of success in their studies to extend their residence titles. Holders of the residence title 'Student' can obtain an RWR Card after successfully completing their master's studies or the second period of their diploma studies.

Henceforward, bachelor's and doctoral students will also be eligible to apply for an RWR Card owing to the above-mentioned changes to the FrÄG.

Residence title Family Community[38]

Family members of sponsors holding the following residence permits can obtain the residence title 'Family Community':

- Rotational Employee[39]
- Artist
- Special Cases of Gainful Employment
- Student
- Researcher

Family members are spouses, registered partners, or unmarried minors including adopted children and stepchildren. Spouses and registered partners must be 21 years of age or older when applying.

A family reunification is not permissible if the intended sponsor is a pupil attending primary or secondary school (grades 1–12), a self-employed person, or an employee sent on temporary duty.

38 *Aufenthaltsbewilligung — Familiengemeinschaft*

39 Henceforth ICTs according to § 20f/4 AuslBG

Unlimited right of settlement and unrestricted access to the labor market
Resident title Long-term Resident — European Union[40]

Holders of the residence title 'Long-term Resident — European Union' have an indefinite right of residence and full access to the Austrian labor market. It is issued for a period of five years for third country nationals. When it expires, it is necessary to re-apply and the residence title will be reissued unless the residence permit has become invalid or unnecessary or has lapsed.

The Long-term Resident — European Union residence permit can be granted to third country nationals if the following conditions are fulfilled:

- A legal and continuous main residence in Austria for five years immediately prior to the application
- A valid residence title
- Module II of the Integration Agreement is completed

Concerning the five-year period, the consideration of prior times is possible. For instance, prior times can be imputed to holders of an EU Blue Card for a minimum period of two years.

6.3 Authorities

Austrian diplomatic representations abroad, such as embassies and consulates, support the national authorities by receiving applications and forwarding them to the national authorities in Austria. They can reject the application because of formal reasons or give an improvement notice to the applicant.

The provincial governors[41] are responsible for legal acts concerning settlement, but they usually delegate their competencies to the District Administrative Authorities,[42] such as the district commission[43] or the Municipal Authorities in statutory cities.[44] The place of residence determines to which authority the application must be submitted.

At the second level of jurisdiction, the administrative courts[45] are responsible if the application is rejected because of formal reasons. If the decision is made with regards to content, the revision must be submitted to the Minister of the Federal Ministry of the Interior of Austria.

---

40 *Calt EU*
41 *Landeshauptmann*
42 *Bezirksverwaltungsbehörden*
43 *Bezirkshauptmannschaft*
44 *Magistrat*
45 *Landesverwaltungsgerichte*

At the third and last level of jurisdiction, the Higher Administrative Court is responsible,[46] or if the constitutional law has presumably been violated, the Constitutional Court of Justice[47] is responsible.

6.4 Procedures

First time permits

Applications for first time permits must be filed from abroad with the responsible diplomatic representatives of Austria, and only under certain conditions can they be filed in Austria. All applications for permits and visas for stays of up to six months must be submitted at the official Austrian diplomatic representations abroad, such as embassies and consulates.

Submitting one's application from abroad

The place of current residence determines at which Austrian diplomatic representation the applicant must submit his/her application. It is necessary that he/she appears in person. The application will be forwarded to the competent authority in Austria.

In the case of approval, the next step is to submit a separate application for an entry visa which enables the applicant to go to Austria, where the residence permit must be collected from the competent authority in Austria within six months of notification.

Submitting one's application in Austria

The application can be submitted in person at the responsible authority in Austria in the following cases:

1. Foreign nationals who do not require a permit under the Residence and Settlement Act (must submit their application within the first six months of their arrival)
2. Persons who do not need to hold a visa during the permitted visa-free stay
3. Foreign nationals who have lost their nationality but were previously Austrian or EEA nationals
4. Spouses, registered same-sex partners, and unmarried minor children, including adopted children and stepchildren of Austrian, EEA, or Swiss nationals who reside in Austria and have not exceeded the permissible duration of three months

46 *Verwaltungsgerichtshof*

47 *Verfassungsgerichtshof*

5. Infants within six months of their birth if their mother is a legal resident of Austria[48]
6. Foreign nationals applying for the residence title 'Researcher' and their family members after their legal arrival and settlement in Austria
7. Very highly qualified third country nationals applying for an RWR Card during their legal stay in Austria with a visa pursuant to Art 24a FPG
8. Third country nationals applying for an RWR Card on the grounds of graduating from an Austrian university during their legal stay in Austria with a confirmation pursuant to Art 64(4) of the Residence and Settlement Act
9. Third country nationals[49] who are applying for the residence title student or specific cases of gainful employment, after their legal arrival and legal stay in Austria

If one files an application in Austria this does not permit one to stay in Austria beyond the visa-free period.

Application for an extension

To extend a residence title, the applicant must file his/her application on time. If not, he/she must await the response abroad. The application is considered as filed in due time if the residence title is still valid, however at the earliest it can be submitted three months before expiration. Depending on one's residence title, German language skills could be necessary for an extension to be granted.

6.5 German language skills

Learning German before immigrating[50]

Third country nationals must possess German language skills at A1 level according to the Common European Framework of Reference for Languages: Learning, Teaching, Assessment (CEFRL) before immigrating to Austria when applying for one of the following residence titles:

- RWR Card plus
- Settlement Permit
- Settlement Permit — Gainful Employment Excepted
- Settlement Permit — Dependent
- Family Member

48 This point has been changed by the FrÄG, which has been law since 1 October 2017: Infants can submit their application in Austria within six months of their birth in the case of family reunification, if the sponsor, to whom the applicant refers, is responsible for the child and legally residing in Austria
49 In accordance with § 1(1) lit i or lit j AuslBG; § 1 Nos 5, 7, or 9 AuslBVO; or § 1 No 4 PersGV 2014; *Personengruppenverordnung* 2014
50 *Deutsch vor Zuwanderung*

The requisite German language skills can be proven in one of the following ways:

1. Obtaining a generally acknowledged certificate of adequate German language skills, particularly from one of the following institutions:
   - Österreich Schweiz Deutschland (ÖSD) (Austrian German Language Diploma)[51]
   - Goethe-Institut e.V.
   - Telc GmbH
2. Obtaining a generally acknowledged certificate from an institute determined by the decree of the foreign minister for local sphere of influence of a professional representation authority[51] abroad
3. Completing Module 1 or 2 of the Integration Agreement

The following persons are exempted from the requirement to possess German language skills at A1 level:

1. Minors at the time of filing the application (up to the age of 14)
2. Foreigners in bad health from whom it may not reasonably be expected to provide evidence (the bad mental or physical health condition must be proven by a medical report from a public health officer)
3. Family members of RWR Card holders if the sponsor is a very highly qualified employee, EU Blue Card holders, or Long-term Resident — European Union permit holders (if they initially held an EU Blue Card)

Integration Agreement

General information

To ensure the integration of third country nationals lawfully settled in Austria, the Integration Agreement obliges them to acquire German language skills, particularly regarding writing and reading. The aim is the social, economic, and cultural assimilation of the Austrian lifestyle.

The Integration Agreement is divided into Module 1, which is mandatory for certain residence titles and Module 2, which is required for obtaining a long-term residence title (Long-term Resident — European Union) as well as for obtaining citizenship.

Module 1

Module 1 usually needs to be fulfilled when a residence title is granted for the first time and must be completed within two years. To complete Module 1, language skills at A2 level according to the CEFRL need to be obtained.

51 *Berufsvertretungsbehörde*

The following methods are available:

1. Attending German Integration classes and providing evidence from the Austrian Integration Fund (ÖIF)[52] that such classes were completed successfully
2. Obtaining a generally acknowledged certificate of adequate German language skills; particularly from one of the following institutions:
   - ÖSD
   - Goethe-Institut e.V.
   - Telc GmbH
3. Obtaining a school-leaving qualification with general eligibility for admission to university,[53] or completing a medium-level vocational school
4. Completing Module 2 of the Integration Agreement

For certain family members, the Federal Government will refund 50% of the costs of German integration classes up to a maximum amount of EUR 750 if such classes were successfully completed within 18 months of the start of the compliance obligation.

Third country nationals are obliged to complete Module 1 if one of the following residence titles was granted for the first time:

- RWR Card
- RWR Card plus
- Settlement Permit
- Settlement Permit — Gainful Employment Excepted
- Settlement Permit — Dependent
- Family Member

The following persons are exempted from the requirement to achieve Module 1:

1. Minors at the time of compliance obligation (up to the age of 14, who will still be under the age of 14)
2. Foreigners in bad health from whom it may not reasonably be expected to provide evidence (the bad mental or physical health condition must be proven by a medical report from a public health officer)
3. Foreigners who have declared in writing that they will not stay in Austria for more than 12 months within a 24-month period. By such a declaration they also renounce the right to file an application for an extension

52 *Österreichischen Integrationsfonds*

53 Pursuant to s 64(1)

Module 2

Third country nationals applying for the residence title 'Long-term Resident — European Union' or citizenship applicants must have completed Module 2 of the Integration Agreement when filing an application. German language skills at B1 level according to the CERFL need to be acquired.

Module 2 can be fulfilled in the following ways:

1. Attending German Integration classes and providing evidence from the ÖIF that such classes were completed successfully
2. Obtaining a generally acknowledged certificate of adequate German language skills, particularly from one of the following institutions:
   - ÖSD
   - Goethe-Institut e.V.
   - Telc GmbH
3. Being underage and attending primary school[54] according to the requirements of compulsory education
4. Being underage, attending secondary school,[55] and having successfully completed German language classes in a previous term's school report
5. Providing evidence of having successfully completed German language classes at ninth-grade level or having attended a compulsory school in Austria for a minimum of five years and having successfully completed German language classes
6. Providing evidence of having successfully completed German language classes at a school abroad where German is taught at the equivalent level of at least the ninth grade of an Austrian compulsory school
7. Passing a final apprenticeship examination[56] according to the Vocational Training Act

The following persons are exempted from the requirement to achieve Module 2:

1. Minors who are not yet subject to compulsory education when applying. Compulsory general education starts on 1 September of the year following the applicant's sixth birthday
2. Foreigners in bad health from whom it may not reasonably be expected to provide evidence (the bad mental or physical health condition must be proven by a medical report from a public health officer)

Citizenship Law

54 *Volksschule*

55 For example, *Hauptschule* — (AHS)

56 *Lehrabschlussprüfung*

References

Sources of law

Law of nations

Bilateral Agreement between Switzerland and the EU of 21 July 1999.

EEA Agreement of 2 May 1992.

EU law

Council Directive 2003/86/EC of the European Council of 22 September 2003 on the right to family reunification.

Council Directive 2003/109/EC of the European Council of 25 November 2003 concerning the status of third country nationals who are long-term residents.

Council Directive 2004/38/EC of the European Parliament and Council of 29 April 2004 on the right of citizens of the Union and their family members to move and reside freely within the territory of the member states amending Regulation.

Council Directive 2014/66/EU of the European Parliament and of the Council of 15 May 2014 on the conditions of entry and residence of third country nationals in the framework of an intra-corporate transfer.

National laws

Act Governing the Employment of Foreign Nationals (AuslBG), Federal Law Gazette No 218/1975, in valid wording.

Fremdenpolizeigesetz (FPG), Federal Law Gazette I No 100/2005, in valid wording.

Fremdenrechtänderungsgesetz (FrÄG), Federal Law Gazette I No 84/2017, in valid wording.

The Residence and Settlement Act (*Niederlassungs- und Aufenthaltsgesetz*, NAG), Federal Law Gazette (*Bundesgesetzblatt*) I No 100/2005, in valid wording.

Personengruppenverordnung 2014 (PersGV 2014), Federal Law Gazette II No 340/2013, in valid wording.

National regulations

Integration Agreement Regulation (IV–V), Federal Law Gazette II No 449/2005, in valid wording.

The Residence and Settlement Act Ordinance (*Niederlassungs- und Aufenthaltsgesetz-Durführungsverordnung*, NAG-DV), Federal Law Gazette II No 451/2005, in valid wording.

Niederlassungsverordnung 2011 (NLV 2011), Federal Law Gazette II No 482/2010, in valid wording.

Bibliography

Literature

P. Jessner, 'Grundzüge des österreichischen Aufenthaltsrechts', in Steffen (Hrsg.), *Die Wohnsitzverlegung nach Österreich, Einführung für vermögende Personen und Unternehmer*, (Wien, 2011).

E. Rath, 'Änderung des AuslBG: Schaffung von Regelungen für unternehmensintern transferierte drittstaatsangehörige Arbeitnehmer', in ASoK (2017) 147.

Links to useful online resources

- *bmi.gv.at/cms/bmi_niederlassung/*
  The Federal Ministry of the Interior of Austria (BM.I) provides general information
- *help.gv.at/Portal.Node/hlpd/public/content/12/Seite.120217.html*
  The Federal Chancellery of the Republic of Austria provides general information
- *bmi.gv.at/cms/BMI_Niederlassung/2017_Arbeitsexemplar_Unterhaltsbroschuere.pdf*
  BM.I's information brochure for the calculation of maintenance
- *migration.gv.at/en/types-of-immigration/permanent-immigration/eubluecard/#c2869*
  BM.I provides useful information about the EU Blue Card
- *migration.gv.at/en/types-of-immigration/permanent-immigration-red-white-red-card.html*
  BM.I provides useful information about permanent immigration and the Red-White-Red Card
- *help.gv.at/Portal.Node/hlpd/public/content/12/Seite.120260.html*
  The Federal Ministry of the Interior of Austria, BM.I, Proof of knowledge of German ('German before immigration') Nachweis von Deutschkenntnissen provides helpful information
- *migration.gv.at/en/living-and-working-in-austria/integration-and-citizenship/integrationagreement/*
  BM.I provides information about the Integration Agreement
- *help.gv.at/Portal.Node/hlpd/public/content/12/Seite.120310.html iederlassungsbewilligung*
  BM.I help service for foreign citizens retrieved from:
  help.gv.at/Portal.Node/hlpd/public/content/12/Seite.120310.html
- *migration.gv.at/en/types-of-immigration/temporary-residence/*
  BM.I provides useful information about temporary residence
- *migration.gv.at/en/types-of-immigration/permanent-immigration/redwhiteredcardplus/*
  BM.I provides useful information about the Red-White-Red Plus Card

- *bmi.gv.at/cms/BMI_Niederlassung/english/files/Family_Reunification_2014.pdf*
  BM.I provides useful information about Family Reunification
- *wien.gv.at/english/e-government/documents/residence/indefinite-leave/long-term-resident-ec.html*
  The Public Relations (Municipal Department 35) provides useful information about indefinite leave to remain and the Long-term Resident — European Union application
- *wien.gv.at/english/administration/civilstatus/immigration/residence/responsibility.html*
  The Public Relations (Municipal Department 35) provides useful information about filing applications for residence permits in Austria and from abroad

About the author

MAG. GOTTFRIED SCHMUTZER LL.M., is a partner in the law firm Schmutzer & Ott Sander. His areas of focus and expertise are labor law, data privacy, and representation in court and government agencies. He lectures and publishes widely in his areas of special interest. He is the author of *Product Safety and Liability*.

7 Austrian Citizenship Law

Dr. Sonja Kerschbaum, Kerschbaum Partner

In classical political theory, a state consists of three elements: citizens, national territory, and government. Following this view, every state must legally regulate its framework of conditions for acquiring, holding, and losing citizenship.

The substance of citizenship is determined by a series of rights and obligations (for example, basic rights and freedoms, protection abroad, the right to vote, compulsory military service, and jury duty) that are exclusively afforded to or imposed upon the citizen with respect to the state to which he/she belongs. There is therefore a justified interest in obtaining or receiving a citizenship that is favorable to the citizen.

International circumstances and greater mobility among people increasingly prompt the key question of which law should be applied to a particular legal relationship. Here there exist two jurisdictional principles: the law relating to citizenship and the law relating to residence. Particularly as a result of EU regulations, the citizenship principle has been increasingly superseded by the residence principle in Central Europe, and therefore also in Austria; most recently perhaps in succession law (EU Regulation on Succession Law). In the EU, citizenship law is no longer afforded the importance it once had; however, because of increasing nationalist tendencies, citizenship could regain greater significance in the EU in the future.

7.1 Basic principles of Austrian citizenship law

Current Austrian citizenship law is based on the citizenship law of 1985, which underwent a comprehensive amendment in 2013. The following principles are stipulated:

Jus sanguinis
In principle, citizenship in Austria is acquired by descent from Austrian nationals and not by birth.

Avoidance of dual or multiple citizenship and prevention of statelessness
Personal autonomy
The will of the individual largely determines the procedure; the discretion of the authorities and the dependence of family members must not be given too much weight.

Family unit
Where possible, all family members living in one household should hold the same citizenship.

7.2 Acquiring Austrian citizenship

Austrian citizenship can be acquired by descent, award, or declaration.

Acquisition of citizenship by descent
The principle of *jus sanguinis* (right of blood) means that a child automatically becomes a citizen at birth if one parent is a citizen at the time of the child's birth or was a citizen until his/her (the parent's) death. Unlike other countries (for example, the US), Austria attaches no significance to one's place of birth.

Descent is equated to legitimation. A minor therefore acquires citizenship through a legitimizing act (the parents marrying or the child being declared legitimate) if the father is an Austrian national or was an Austrian national at the time of his death. It must be noted that citizenship is not automatically acquired through adoption. However, there is a claim for acquiring citizenship in this case provided certain conditions are met (in particular, for minors).

Acquisition of citizenship by award

To acquire Austrian citizenship by award, the general requirements for naturalization must be met in all cases, and a corresponding application must be filed. Only then is it possible to acquire citizenship on the basis of a legal claim or at the authority's discretion. Further requirements for the award of citizenship will then determine whether citizenship will be awarded on the basis of a legal claim or whether the decision lies at the discretion of the competent authority.

If the decision is made at the discretion of the authority, for example, if awarding citizenship is in the interest of the Republic because of past or prospective extraordinary achievement/s in the fields of science, business, arts, or sport, exceptions can be made to the general requirements for naturalization.

General requirements for naturalization

- At least 10 years of uninterrupted and lawful residence in Austria, during which a minimum of five years with possession of a residence permit is required; deviations from this requirement exist in the case of an award due to a legal claim
- Integrity:
  - No court convictions or imprisonments for a premeditated act either in Austria or abroad
  - No court convictions or imprisonments for a fiscal offence
  - No pending criminal proceedings for a premeditated act or fiscal offence punishable by imprisonment
  - No serious administrative offences with a special degree of unlawfulness
- Sufficient means of subsistence: proof of one's own fixed and regular income through acquisition, income, judicial claim to maintenance, or insurance benefits over an average period of 36 months within the last six years prior to the date of application. The last six months claimed must immediately precede the date of application
  Note: A sum of EUR 1,000 per person is usually sufficient
- Knowledge of the German language and having basic knowledge of the democratic system, of the history of Austria, and of the respective federal state: this is proved by means of a written examination, provided there are no exempting circumstances (for example, German being the native language, being a minor, attending school and achieving a positive grade in the subject German)
- Positive attitude towards the Republic of Austria and providing assurance that one does not pose a risk to public peace, order, or security

- No current prohibition of residence and no pending proceedings regarding the termination of residence
- No return decision
- No expulsion decision issued by another EEA state or by Switzerland
- No eviction order within the last 18 months
- No close connection to any extremist or terrorist group
- In principle, loss of previous citizenship
- By being awarded citizenship
  - The international relations of the Republic of Austria must not be significantly impaired
  - The interests of the Republic of Austria must not be harmed

Since the most recent amendment to citizenship law, it is possible, upon the fulfillment of certain prerequisites, to claim citizenship after six years of uninterrupted residence in Austria.[1] Among other things, this step is possible if, in accordance with the Austrian Citizenship Act,[2] "awarding citizenship is in the interest of the Republic due to extraordinary achievements previously rendered or to be rendered in future by foreign nationals in the fields of science, business, arts or sport." (Please also see 'Awarding citizenship in the interest of the Republic' with regard to extraordinary achievements.) In such cases, the applicant must nonetheless comply with all other general conditions.

Required documents

The documents currently required for individual applications can be determined based only on personal details. In principle, the following documents must be submitted with the application for Austrian citizenship, as a minimum:

- Persons over the age of 14: comprehensive and signed curriculum vitae, particularly places of residence and addresses from birth to the present date, school education, professional training and career, internships and employments outside Austria, as well as personal circumstances
- Valid travel document
- Valid biometric passport photo
- Documents indicating civil status
  - Birth certificate
  - If applicable, marriage certificate — also proof of previous marriages
  - If applicable, document registering the partnership

1 Art 11a s 4 Austrian Citizenship Act (StbG)
2 Art 11a s 4 Z 4 StbG

  - If applicable, divorce certificate with notice of legal validity or document confirming the dissolution of the partnership
  - If applicable, death certificate of spouse/registered partner
- Proof of citizenship (through valid travel pass, certificate of nationality)
- Proof of residence in Austria: valid proof of registration in Austria issued by the Federal Ministry for European and International Affairs for holders of a *Legitimationskarte*
- Certificate or confirmation of registration
- Current extract from the register of convictions from the applicant's home country as well as from all countries in which he/she has spent more than eight months from the age of 14; these must be no older than six months
- Income tax assessment from the last three years; for married couples living in the same household where the family income is considerable, a declaration by one spouse that he/she pays for the subsistence of the other is sufficient, and in this case the other spouse need not provide his/her own evidence
- Social security statement
- Final declarations
- If applicable, proof of an academic degree attained in Austria or abroad
- If applicable, official ruling of name change, proof of reacceptance of a former family name
- If applicable, all residence titles, documentation, or photo ID for holders of privileges and immunities since entry into Austria (including documents proving the date since which one has been resident)

Documents and certificates in a foreign language must be presented in the original together with a translation certified in Austria. If a foreign-language document in the original needs to be presented with a certified translation, the translation must as a rule be undertaken by a sworn and court-certified translator only. Whether or not certified translations from other countries are recognized depends on the respective procedural rules. For example, an *apostille* may be required in order to certify the documents. In addition, court rulings and decisions (including from abroad) require confirmation of legal validity.

Note: Since awarding citizenship is a matter for individual states, there are differences in the documents required. For this reason, the applicant should contact the relevant authority in advance.

Awarding citizenship in the interests of the Republic

In the event that the Federal Government unanimously confirms that awarding citizenship is in the particular interest of the Republic by reason of the applicant's past or prospective extraordinary achievements, the general conditions for awarding citizenship no longer apply (with the exception of the condition that granting citizenship must not significantly impair the international relationships of the Republic of Austria or harm the interests of the Republic of Austria). In such a case, proof of sufficient German language skills as well as basic knowledge about the democratic system and history are not required.

Extraordinary achievements are classed as those that are far above average and cannot be attained by any other person of the same level of education and training. These achievements must either have been performed in the past, or will be performed in the future. Services in business as well as services in social or humanitarian work can be rewarded, as can extraordinary achievements in art, culture, sport, and science.

Note: Austrian citizenship cannot be 'bought', as is often claimed. A single investment is not sufficient, as this does not constitute an extraordinary achievement and is not a measure of prospective extraordinary achievements.

Extension of the award

Following the family unit principle, the acquisition of citizenship can be extended to family members. To extend the award to spouses, applicants must fulfill the same conditions of residence and marriage that apply to the foreign spouses of Austrian nationals (i.e. six years of residence and five years of marriage). Furthermore, it is possible to extend the award to legitimate and illegitimate children. The general conditions for awarding citizenship must be met, and the extension must be applied for separately.

Acquisition of citizenship by declaration

Acquisition by declaration applies to so-called putative Austrians. This is understood to mean people who have been erroneously treated as Austrians by the Austrian authorities for at least 15 years. However, the acquisition of citizenship is ruled out if the person concerned is responsible for this error. According to official explanations, this particularly refers to such cases in which the person concerned has deceived the authorities by submitting incorrect facts or by withholding essential facts. A different case of application concerns reparation for former Austrian citizens who have been the victims of National Socialism. In these cases, it is not necessary to have a main residence in Austria, means of subsistence do not need to be proved, administrative offences have no negative impact on the process, and foreign citizenship can be retained if necessary. However, the remaining general conditions must all be fulfilled.

7.3 Losing Austrian citizenship

Certain actions can lead to the loss of citizenship. In the same manner as in acquisition, the loss of citizenship also has an effect on minors. The loss of citizenship extends to children if the other parent is not, or does not remain, a citizen.

Loss by acquisition of a foreign citizenship

If an Austrian citizen is not granted permission to retain his/her citizenship while acquiring the citizenship of a foreign country, he/she will automatically lose it. To avoid dual citizenship and possible conflicts in civic duties (a particular example of this is compulsory military service) the chance of retaining citizenship in such a case is very limited. First, the foreign state must give consent, and second, the Republic must have an interest in retaining the Austrian citizenship as a result of past or prospective achievements, or a particular reason worth considering. The essential conditions for awarding citizenship must moreover be fulfilled.

Loss by entrance into military service in a foreign country

Those who voluntarily enter the military service of a foreign country forfeit their Austrian citizenship.

Loss by renunciation

In a written statement filed with individual autonomy, a citizen may renounce his/her Austrian citizenship. As a rule, this is the case if an Austrian citizen wishes to acquire a different citizenship. To do so, proof of foreign citizenship must be shown. Renunciation of citizenship is not possible if there are pending criminal proceedings based on a crime punishable by more than six months of imprisonment, or if the execution of such a sentence is pending. Male citizens, if of military service age, must have completed their military or civilian service, or must have been declared unfit to do so.

7.4 Sanctions

Transgressions against Citizenship Law, for example, providing false information, are considered administrative offences, and carry fines of EUR 1,000–EUR 5,000.

References

Bachmann in Bachmann, Baumgartner, Feik, Fuchs, Giese, Jahnel, and Lienbacher, *Besonderes Verwaltungsrecht*

Baumgartner, *Jahrbuch Öffentliches Recht* (2014)

Braga, *Staatsangehörigkeitsprinzip oder Wohnsitzprinzip?* Erlanger Forschungen (1954)

Deixler-Hübner, *Handbuch Familienrecht* (2015)

Fessler, Keller, Pommerening-Schober, and Szymanski, *Das neue österreichische Staatsbürgerschaftsrecht*

Hailbronner, Renner, and Maaßen, *Staatsangehörigkeitsrecht* (2010)

Kutscher and Wildpert, *Das österreichische Personenstandsrecht* (2016)

Mayer, Kucsko-Stadlmayer, and Stöger, *Bundesverfassungsrecht* (2015)

Plunger, Esztegar, and Eberwein, *Kommentar zum StbG* (2017)

Unterweger, *Staatsbürgerschaftsrecht* (2007)

About the author

DR. SONJA KERSCHBAUM is the founder of the law firm Kerschbaum Partner Rechtsanwälte GmbH. She specializes in international inheritance law, general civil law, and is an advisor to wealthy families. She is a correspondent of the *Fuchsbriefe* and publishes regularly on her topics of special interest.

8 Statutory Health Insurance in Austria

Mag. Manfred Pöltl, Austrian Ministry of Labor, Social Affairs, Health, and Consumer Protection

It is important for those intending to relocate to Austria to familiarize themselves with the statutory health insurance details which are summarized in this chapter.

8.1 The insurance relationship

General

Statutory health insurance in Austria is founded on the principle of compulsory insurance; those in the pursuit of gainful employment are generally subject to compulsory insurance. By law, compulsory insurance commences when earned income, i.e. monthly income, exceeds a certain minimum threshold. Opting out of compulsory insurance is possible only for certain groups of self-employed individuals, who must then demonstrate proof of comparable coverage acquired through voluntary insurance.

Receiving an Austrian pension is necessarily linked with health insurance in all cases. In Austria, the German term *Pension* is used for benefits claimed under old-age insurance, while *Rente* is used for benefits claimed under accident insurance.

Since other vulnerable groups are covered by health insurance in a non-contributory capacity, for example, recipients of childcare allowance or guaranteed minimum resources *(Mindestsicherung)*, approximately 99% of Austria's inhabitants have statutory health insurance.

Unlike Switzerland, in Austria there is not a basic insurance scheme, with extended insurance coverage above this basic level that is open only to a restricted group of people. Austrian health insurance offers, in principle, the same entitlement to benefits in kind and cash benefits to all those holding health insurance in his/her respective scheme (regarding benefits in kind, there may be restrictions for contractors). To receive benefits beyond this, one must take out private supplementary insurance; the legal system does not offer this possibility. In principle, Austrian health insurance can be said to be a high-quality system that does not, however, offer policyholders the same leeway as the schemes to be found in other states.

Organization

There are legal schemes for:

1. Workers and employees: General Social Insurance Act (ASVG)[1]
2. Self-employed persons: Social Insurance Act for Self-Employed Persons in Trade and Industry (GSVG)[2]
3. Farmers and foresters: Farmers' Social Security Act (BSVG)[3]
4. Civil servants and contract staff: Civil Service Health and Accident Insurance Act (BKUVG)[4]
5. Members of certain independent professions: Social Insurance Act for the Liberal Professions (FSVG)[5]

It is not possible to choose a provider, as is done in Switzerland or Germany. Rather, the responsible institution is stipulated by law. In each of the nine federal states, there is a Regional Health Insurance Fund[6] that is responsible for insuring employees from the general scheme. A person's affiliation to a fund is linked either to his/her place of employment or — for pensioners — his/her place of residence. The Austrian Insurance Fund for Miners and Persons Employed with the Federal Railways (VAEB)[7] insures the corresponding companies. The Austrian Insurance Fund for Civil or Public Servants (BVA)[8] insures civil servants.

---

1 *Allgemeines Sozialversicherungsgesetz*
2 *Gewerbliches Sozialversicherungsgesetz*
3 *Bauern-Sozialversicherungsgesetz*
4 *Beamten-Kranken- und Unfallversicherungsgesetz*
5 *Freiberufliches Sozialversicherungsgesetz*
6 *Gebietskrankenkasse*
7 *Versicherungsanstalt für Eisenbahnen und Bergbau Arbeitnehmer*
8 *Versicherungsanstalt der Beamten*

For self-employed individuals, there are two institutions: the Insurance Fund for Trade and Industry (SVA)[9] for contractors and so-called 'newly self-employed persons'[10] and the Insurance Fund for Farmers (SVB)[11] for farmers and foresters.

The Main Association of Austrian Social Security Institutions[12] is the umbrella organization. Austrian social security is organized according to the principle of self-administration; for this reason, the catalog of services covered by individual institutions may vary when it comes to statutory supplementary benefits.

The principle of multiple insurance applies if the person concerned pursues several occupations simultaneously or receives a pension at the same time. If an individual is insured with several different insurance institutions, the policyholder may choose which institution he/she wishes to use for benefits in kind. This also applies to eligible family members, who, if need be, can choose between their father's or their mother's insurance.

Low income threshold and maximum contributions

Compulsory insurance comes into effect for employees only when the monthly income or the sum of monthly incomes earned from professional activities exceeds EUR 438.05 (valid in 2018).

The minimum income threshold of EUR 438.05 per month also applies to contractors and 'newly self-employed persons' (valid in 2018). Newly self-employed persons are those who receive income from independent work. In principle, the term encompasses all those who are not already covered by any other provisions within the scope of a social security act on the basis of their employment pursuits (for example, as an employee, freelancer, or contractor).

The general contribution basis must not exceed the monthly maximum contribution base. In 2018, the maximum contribution basis is EUR 5,130 per month for employed individuals and EUR 5,985 for self-employed individuals. If the policyholder pursues multiple jobs at the same time, the maximum contribution basis must be taken into account for each job. As this can lead to the annual maximum contribution basis being exceeded, health insurance contributions can be partially refunded the following year on request.

It is possible for contributions to be refunded when the sum of all contribution bases for compulsory insurance, including special payments, as a result of the

9 *Sozialversicherungsanstalt der gewerblichen Wirtschaft*

10 *Neue Selbständige*

11 *Sozialversicherungsanstalt der Bauern*

12 *Hauptverband der österreichischen Sozialversicherungsträger*

pursuit of gainful employment exceeds the daily maximum contribution basis by 35 times for the months in the calendar year in which compulsory insurance is to be paid in the respective contribution year. A month of compulsory insurance refers to all calendar months in which the policyholder was compulsorily insured for at least one day. Overlapping months are counted only once. In health insurance, 4% is refunded from the excess amount; 7.4% is refunded if an additional contribution was made for family members. For pension recipients who also pursue gainful employment that justifies compulsory insurance, it is possible for health insurance contributions to be refunded if the sum of all contribution bases and received pension exceeds the daily maximum contribution basis by 35 times for the months in the calendar year in which compulsory insurance is to be paid in the respective contribution year.

Contribution rates in health insurance (2018)

Table 8.1 A comparison of health insurance rates

	EMPLOYEE %	EMPLOYER %	TOTAL %	MONTHLY MAXIMUM CONTRIBUTION BASIS (EUR)
Employees	3.87	3.78	7.65	4,980
Workers	3.87	3.78	7.65	4,980
Pensioners			5.10	4,980
Self-employed (GSVG)			7.65	5,810
Farmers and foresters			7.65	5,810

A difference is seen in the monthly maximum contribution basis for employees and/or pensioners compared to self-employed persons because employees receive 14 salaries per year (additional payments are known as 'special payments', i.e. a holiday bonus and a Christmas bonus). For self-employed individuals, the annual maximum contribution basis is organized around 12 calendar months.

Family members' entitlement

As co-insured persons, family members are in principle entitled to receive benefits in the same way as the policyholder. Essentially, family members are deemed to be the spouse, the registered partner, and the children (including adopted children and foster children), provided that their main residence is in Austria and they do not hold health insurance in their own name. The requirement for residence inside the country is irrelevant within the framework of the freedom of movement agreement with Switzerland. Children usually lose their status as a family member when they reach the age of 18; however, this can be extended to the age of 27 if they are undergoing education or training.

Life partners (including same-sex life partners) who have lived in the same household as the policyholder for at least 10 years and run the household for him/her free of charge are considered to be family members. Other relatives can also be deemed to be family members under these conditions.

A person is not considered a family member if he/she is gainfully employed abroad in a capacity that would subject him/her to compulsory health insurance in Austria if practiced domestically or if he/she receives a pension on the basis of this employment.[13] This requirement was introduced to accommodate systems in other countries and to prevent, for example, insurance-exempt pensioners from Germany who were voluntarily insured during their working lives from being co-insured as family members despite a possibly high pension in Austria. In this context, information in article 32 of Regulation (EC) no. 987/2009 appears helpful: "When a person or a group of persons are exempted upon request from compulsory sickness insurance in a Member State, and are thus not covered by a sickness insurance scheme to which the basic Regulation (EC) no. 883/2004 applies, the institution of another Member State shall not, solely because of this exemption, become responsible for bearing the costs of benefits in kind or in cash provided to such persons or to a member of their family."[14] This regulation also applies to Switzerland as a result of the freedom of movement agreement.

For family members, an additional contribution must be paid by the policyholder amounting to 3.4% of the contribution basis. The additional contribution is not applicable for children, for family members who dedicate themselves to raising one or several children living in the same household (or who have dedicated themselves to the same for at least four years straight), or for family members who receive a minimum level-3 care allowance.

13 Art 123 s 10 ASVG
14 Art 32 of Regulation (EC) no. 987/2009

Voluntary insurance

For those who are not compulsorily insured by statutory health insurance, there is an option in the legal system to take out voluntary self-insurance. The person must be resident in Austria. In this case too, EU law, i.e. the freedom of movement agreement with Switzerland, stipulates regulations that would allow this residence requirement to be abandoned if the person concerned was employed or self-employed in Austria at some point in the past.[15]

Self-insurance begins directly after exiting statutory compulsory insurance if the application is filed within six weeks. In 2018, the monthly contribution is EUR 418.69 (for students: EUR 58.39). If any claims arise, a waiting period of three to six months usually applies, to prevent speculation. However, there is no waiting period if the policyholder was compulsorily insured for at least 26 weeks within the 12 months prior to the self-insurance commencing, or was insured by the health insurance scheme for at least six weeks immediately before application. As a result of the freedom of movement agreement between the EU and Switzerland, compulsory insurance in Switzerland is to be equated with Austrian compulsory insurance.

8.2 Health insurance benefits

Compulsory benefits and voluntary benefits

A distinction is made between compulsory benefits based on a claim by the policyholder and voluntary benefits, which are granted without obligation on the basis of legal or statutory provisions. The range of benefits and services is determined in the statutes of each respective insurer and may differ from institution to institution. However, the Main Association of Austrian Social Security Institutions issues a standard statute specifying binding content. In principle, benefits are issued as benefits in kind and settled directly between the healthcare supplier and the responsible institution (exception: assistance from a *Wahlarzt* — a private doctor of choice).

Panel doctors (*Vertragsarzt*) and doctors of choice (*Wahlarzt*)

Health insurance benefits in kind are rendered primarily by contracting parties operated by the responsible health insurance institution. Proof of insurance comes

15 Art 14 s 4 Regulation no. 883/04

in the form of an electronic chip card called an e-card. Family members receive their own e-cards. If the e-card cannot be produced upon visiting a doctor, it can be supplied later upon leaving a security deposit.

Alongside this, there is the option of using a *Wahlarzt* (or a hospital of choice), who has no contract with the responsible institution. In such cases, the patient must pay for the service at the agreed rates as a private patient and can consequently apply for reimbursement from his/her institution. It is possible to claim reimbursement of costs for treatments stipulated in the catalog of services issued by the responsible institution, and in the amount that the responsible institution would have had to pay a panel doctor according to the fee structure, less 20% (this deduction is to compensate for the additional administrative expense). Because of the considerably higher rates of receiving treatment as a private patient, reimbursement will absorb only a small fraction of the costs. The legal conditions for using a *Wahlarzt* also apply to using a doctor or hospital abroad. Approval from the relevant Austrian institution is not required here, insofar as the service is provided in Austria. Naturally, the reimbursement of costs is always limited to the actual costs incurred. Supplementing this, entitlements also exist pursuant to the EU's Patient Mobility directive.[16]

Scope of medical treatment

The policyholder is entitled to the benefits listed in the catalog of services issued by the competent institution; they are to be sufficient and appropriate but must not exceed what is necessary. Cosmetic treatment is considered medical treatment if it serves to remedy an anatomical or functional medical condition, is advantageous for restoring the capacity to work, or is necessary for occupational reasons. Medical assistance is equated to psychotherapy, physiotherapy, and ergo-therapy treatments, among others.

Medical treatment is guaranteed for as long as is medically necessary, with no time limit, i.e. when the insurance ends. Under certain conditions, a person may be entitled to benefits in insurance claims that emerge only after the end of the insurance.

In accordance with the GSVG, only those contractors and shareholders whose income from employment covered by compulsory insurance does not exceed the benefit-in-kind threshold of EUR 71,819.99 (valid in 2018) in the three preceding calendar years (plus the contributions to health insurance and pension insurance

16 2011/24/EU

required in the current year) are entitled to benefits in kind. Those earning a relatively high income are entitled to cash payments. In such a case, visits to the doctor must first be pre-financed by the patient as a private patient; subsequently, the patient may claim a reimbursement of costs at *Wahlarzt* fees less 20% for administrative expenses. Those entitled to benefits in kind can take out additional insurance in order to acquire entitlement to cash benefits (sickness benefit, daily allowance). Furthermore, according to the GSVG, it is possible to take out voluntary family insurance for certain persons who do not fall within the bracket of family members.

Patient personal contributions

In the general scheme for employees, policyholders do not as a rule have to pay their own contribution (excess) for medical treatment. Civil servants, self-employed individuals, and farmers pay a 20% excess for every treatment. In principle, however, policyholders entitled to benefits in kind can use health insurance services with contract partners without any prior expenses. The 20% excess is applied retroactively, i.e. deducted from the pension.

No costs are levied for benefits in kind that are associated with particularly high costs or do not justify an excess for socio-political reasons. This includes, for example, hospital stays in the general fee class (apart from the daily hospital charge, which is to be paid directly to the hospital), medical home nursing care, and dialysis treatment attributable to kidney disease.

Individual services

Services for the early detection of illness and to maintain health are rendered in the form of examinations of young persons and preventative medical check-ups. In the event of illness, medical assistance, home medical care, and hospital care are offered.

Patients within the general fee class of a hospital are admitted provided that the type of illness necessitates this. A daily hospital charge of EUR 12.15 (valid in 2018 for Vienna) must be paid for a maximum of 28 days. There is no time limit placed on the duration of treatment at the hospital. For family members, in the scheme for employees, 10% of the hospitalization charge is required in the first four weeks of the person's stay in hospital. The insured person must pay only a small daily contribution for each day of his/her stay in hospital (maximum 28 calendar days per year). From the fifth week, hospital treatment is free for policyholders and family members. The Health Insurance Fund[17] also covers the costs of patient transport.

Since financing hospital care is the biggest cost factor for statutory health insurance, home medical care is provided instead of hospital care as far as possible. This encompasses services of an exclusively medical nature as prescribed by a doctor that are performed by qualified nurses (for example, administering injections, artificial feeding, surgical dressings, etc.).

Medical assistance comprises the dispensing of medicine and health aids. Medicine comprises the drugs and other remedies necessary to overcome or ease illnesses. Drugs are dispensed in pharmacies upon presentation of a prescription issued by the attending physician. The competent institution settles the costs directly with the pharmacy, but a prescription fee of EUR 6.00 (2018) must be paid by the policyholder for each drug prescription. Policyholders are obliged, however, to continue to pay the prescription fee only until they reach an amount of 2% of their net annual income in a current calendar year. Having reached the 2% figure, the policyholder is exempted from paying a prescription fee for the rest of the calendar year. The social security system creates a prescription fee account for each policyholder As soon as the charges reach the upper limit of 2% of the person's net income, the prescribing doctor will be notified via the e-card. The exemption from the prescription charge is then marked on the prescription and the pharmacy charge is not applied. Policyholders not wholly exempt from the prescription charge must, however, have paid for at least 37 prescription charges before being exempted from further prescription charges for the remainder of the calendar year after reaching the 2% upper limit of the prescription charge.

Costs for health aids are covered by the insurer only if they exceed 20% of the maximum contribution basis (for glasses and contact lenses: 60%). The policyholder must cover 10% of the costs, but at least 20% of the maximum contribution basis (glasses and contact lenses: 60%).

In the case of incapacity to work because of illness, sickness benefit is payable from the third day of the loss of earnings for a period lasting up to 26 weeks. The maximum period can be extended to 78 weeks under the statutes of the insurer. Sickness benefit is guaranteed as a statutory minimum benefit amounting to 50% of the assessment basis and increases to 60% from the 43rd day of the inability to work.

17 *Krankenkasse*

In the case of pregnancy and after childbirth there is an entitlement to attendance by a doctor, midwife, qualified nurse, or maternity nurse. In the eight weeks before and after the expected delivery date (12 weeks for multiple births), there is an entitlement to maternity allowance, the only benefit in Austria's social security system that compensates in full for the loss of earnings (average earnings of the final 13 weeks of employment).

With respect to dental treatment and dentures, health insurance provides for conservative and surgical dental treatment, orthodontic regulation (orthodontic treatments), and necessary dentures. Denture costs and orthodontic regulation are covered only in part, however; the policyholder must pay a personal contribution.

For mutilations, disfigurements, and physical defects that significantly impair a person's health, working capacity, or ability to provide for essential personal needs, the statute can stipulate benefits for the procurement and use of the necessary aids. Physical defects that are the result of age alone do not fall within the protective scope of statutory health insurance.

In order to ensure the success of the health treatment or to ease the consequences of the illness, health insurers also perform medical rehabilitation measures with the aim of restoring the health of the policyholder and his/her family members so far as to be able to take a suitable place in the community for as long as possible and without supervision or aid.

Health stabilization measures include stays in the country and accommodation in health spas or sanatoriums in order to prevent the onset of illness as well as to prevent an existing illness from worsening. A daily contribution must be paid by the policyholder for this; the amount depends on the monthly gross earned income. Insurers also perform health promotion measures by providing clarification and advice on health hazards and ways to prevent illnesses and accidents.

Benefits for people in need of care

Pursuant to the Austrian system, long-term care allowance is not a health insurance benefit but a *sui generis* benefit for all Austrian residents who meet the eligibility requirements. It seeks to compensate as a lump sum for care-related additional expenses in order to ensure that persons in need of care are provided with the necessary support and assistance as far as possible, and to improve their chances of leading a self-determined and need-oriented life. Persons entitled to benefits are those who receive a pension from the statutory pension insurance and are in need of care. Other persons requiring care are, however, also entitled. A person is in need of care if he/she requires constant support and assistance because of a physical, mental, or psychological disability or a sensory impairment and this circumstance is anticipated to last for at least six months. There are seven categories of care needs:

Table 8.2 Categories of care requirements

CARE CATEGORY	MONTHLY CARE NEEDS	MONTHLY AMOUNT (VALID IN 2017) (EUR)
1	More than 60 hours	157.30
2	More than 85 hours	290.00
3	More than 120 hours	451.80
4	More than 160 hours	677.60
5	More than 180 hours + other requirements	920.30
6	More than 180 hours + other requirements	1,285.20
7	More than 180 hours + other requirements	1,688.90

The European Court of Justice has determined that Austrian long-term care allowance constitutes a sickness benefit pursuant to Regulation (EC) No. 883/2004 and that the regulations on coordinating sickness benefits shall apply.[18] For this reason, Austria is obliged to render the service if Austria is the responsible country for the health insurance of the person concerned. If a recipient of an Austrian and Swiss pension lives in Austria, Austria is responsible for the health insurance and the person is entitled to care allowance — upon meeting the other eligibility requirements. If, on the other hand, a recipient of only a Swiss pension lives in Austria, then Switzerland is responsible for the health insurance and renders an equivalent service to the pensioner.

18 Decision dated 8 March 2003, Rs C-215/99, Jauch

8.3 Aspects to consider regarding the freedom of movement agreement with Switzerland

Because of the freedom of movement agreement with Switzerland, Regulation (EC) No. 883/2004 applies to the relationship between Austria and Switzerland. It stipulates that persons with cross-border earnings are covered by the legislation of one country only. For the working population this will be the country of employment. If gainful employment is pursued in several countries simultaneously this will be dependent on the circumstances, the country of residence, or the country in which the (single) employer has its registered office.

In principle, those not in employment fall under the regulations of the country of residence. The relevant country determines whether, and under what conditions, health insurance protection shall be applied in accordance with its national legislation.

There are special provisions relating to health insurance for pensioners. If a person receives a pension from one country only, for which the regulation is applicable, and if health insurance coverage is linked to the receipt of this pension, this country alone bears the costs of services rendered to the pensioner in the country of residence or a different country. At the same time, this country can levy the contributions stipulated according to its law. If, therefore, a medically insured recipient of just one Swiss pension relocates to Austria, from this point forward the Swiss institution is responsible for his/her health insurance. If the pensioner receives in addition (and at the same time) a pension from Austria, then upon the transfer of residence, the responsibility switches to the Austrian insurer and the obligation of the Swiss insurer ends.

Since Regulation No. 883/2004 came into effect on 1 May 2010, it is possible for the responsible institution to collect in addition the contributions stipulated in its law from the foreign pension. The contributions calculated on the basis of Swiss pension are deducted from the Austrian pension, and — if this is not sufficient — by a supplementary fee notice towards the pensioner.

If a recipient has just one Swiss pension in Austria, the so-called temporary execution of benefits system is required to render the service in Austria. The Swiss pensioner receives a Form S1 from the responsible Swiss institution and registers with the Regional Health Insurance Fund in his/her place of residence in Austria. He/she receives an Austrian e-card, and with this is treated as an Austrian insurance policyholder in Austria. The Austrian catalog of services must be consulted to ascertain the scope of entitlement to benefits in kind. It is irrelevant which services are stipulated according to the law of the responsible Swiss institution. Services are settled directly between Austrian and Swiss institutions through the intermediation of liaison offices. Any personal contributions and excesses must be paid by the Swiss insurance policyholder, as they are paid by Austrian insurance policyholders.

Links to useful online resources and addresses

- *sozialministerium.at*
  Federal Ministry for Labour, Social Affairs, Health and Consumer Protection (*Bundesministerium für Arbeit, Sociales, Gesundheit und Konsumentenschutz*)
  Stubenring 1, 1010 Vienna
- *sozialversicherung.at* (link to all funds)
  Main Association of Austrian Social Security Institutions (*Hauptverband der österreichischen Sozialversicherungsträger*)
  Kundmanngasse 21, 1030 Vienna

Regional Health Insurance Funds:
GKK Vorarlberg, Jahngasse 4, 6850 Dornbirn
GKK Tirol, Klara-Pölt-Weg 2, 6020 Innsbruck
GKK Salzburg, Engelbert-Weiß-Weg 10, 5020 Salzburg
GKK Wien, Wienerbergstraße 15–19, 1100 Vienna
GKK Oberösterreich, Gruberstraße 77, 4021 Linz
GKK Kärnten, Kempfstraße 8, 9021 Klagenfurt am Wörthersee
GKK Niederösterreich, Kremser Landstraße 3, 3100 St. Pölten
GKK Burgenland, Esterhazyplatz 3, 7000 Eisenstadt
GKK Steiermark, Josef-Pongratz-Platz 1, 8010 Graz
Insurance Fund for Trade and Industry (*Sozialversicherungsanstalt der Gewerblichen Wirtschaft*; SVA), Wiedner Hauptstraße 84–86, 1051 Vienna

Insurance Fund for Civil or Public Servants (*Versicherungsanstalt öffentlich Bediensteter;* BVA), Josefstädter Straße 80, 1080 Vienna
Insurance Fund for Farmers (*Sozialversicherungsanstalt der Bauern;* SVB), Ghegastraße 1, 1030 Vienna

About the author

MAG. MANFRED PÖLTL is deputy head of the Department of International Social Security in the Austrian Ministry of Labor, Social Affairs, Health, and Consumer Protection. He is a member of various committees of the EU dealing with the application and amendment of European law, including the Administrative Commission for the Coordination of Social Security Systems and the Council Working Party on Social Questions. Mag. Pöltl delivers numerous presentations and publishes extensively on matters of European social law.

9 Private Health Insurance

Ulrike Braumüller, Independent Consultant

Health Insurance

It is important for those intending to relocate to Austria to familiarize themselves with the details regarding private health insurance which are summarized in this chapter.

9.1 General overview

There are two complementary options for health insurance in Austria; compulsory statutory social insurance and voluntary private health insurance.

Statutory social insurance provides a compulsory insurance policy for almost all occupational groups, irrespective of their income level. Almost 99% of the population is covered by statutory health insurance provided by a social insurance institution. In Austria, private medical insurance is taken out as supplementary insurance.

There are, however, a few exceptions to this for some professions which have no compulsory insurance. Vetted freelance professionals have the right to choose between statutory social insurance and private health insurance (known as opting out).

Certain people who are not covered by the statutory health insurance can take out their own private health insurance which means that they can choose between the two types. These include students who are not covered by statutory health insurance, low-income employees, private individuals, and non-working persons.

A prerequisite for taking out this type of insurance is that the person must be an Austrian resident.

Cross-border commuters are another exception to this rule, i.e. employees or self-employed individuals who pursue their professional activity in Switzerland or Liechtenstein but continue to live in Austria. Cross-border commuters employed in these two countries have compulsory insurance in these countries but they can be exempted from compulsory health insurance there if they take out the equivalent health insurance in Austria; in accordance with the ASVG, they can choose between either statutory health insurance or private health insurance. However, if the commuter chooses private insurance, it is not possible for him/her to change to statutory health insurance at a later date during the same period of employment.

In Austria there are more than 1.2 million specially insured individuals who make up about 14% of the population. Another half a million residents, approximately 6%–7% of the population, have limited insurance cover, which means, for example, that hospital insurance cover after an accident is limited.[1]

Private health insurance is also a type of indemnity insurance, i.e. the insurance company reimburses the actual costs of medical treatment. It can also be taken out as a 'fixed sum insurance' whereby it reimburses the agreed sums, irrespective of the actual costs incurred for treatment.

The most popular form of private health insurance is the supplementary hospital cost insurance, which covers the costs of in-patient treatment in public hospitals or sanatoriums. With this option, hospital treatment costs for patients[2] are fully reimbursed. The patient receives a higher level of comfort in the hospital and can enjoy the treatment and care given by a doctor of his/her choice. In return, the doctors receive a special doctor's fee. In public hospitals, the chief physicians and subordinate physicians make a substantial portion of their income in this way. These doctors benefit the general public too, and this arrangement ensures the retention of highly qualified doctors at public hospitals.

The reimbursement of costs is paid out in full in accordance with the contract agreement, and is billed directly to the hospital by the insurer, provided that the appropriate agreements have been made with the hospitals and doctors. Private health insurers issue a list of hospitals on a regular (usually annual) basis, for which the full guarantee of cost recovery applies. The earliest this cost coverage commitment can be canceled is by the date specified in the commitment.

---

1 See VVO, Annual report 2016 Tab 3.3

2 See also Steiner, *Doctor's fee in a special class* (2004)

In addition, insurance cover for purely outpatient services, care services, and other more specific health insurance contracts (for example, those that offer daily allowances) are also available. Insurance cover for outpatient services is gradually increasing because of the noticeable reduction in the treatments covered by the statutory health insurance.

Private health insurance is also provided as a sickness benefit insurance, care insurance, and as a kind of short-term health insurance (for example, travel insurance), in addition to the two main types of insurance (hospital treatment insurance and daily allowance) mentioned above. The services depend on the individual policy.

The health insurer must take steps to balance out premium rates for the ageing population, as the elderly have a higher risk of illness and often have lower incomes. The premiums paid by younger policyholders are therefore on average 10% higher than their risk exposure.

These provisions, made over a number of years, have created a cushion which, together with the other premiums, can compensate for the rising costs of illness. If healthcare costs were to remain the same (which is not the case), there would be no age-related premium increases.

Health insurance covers mainly the treatment of illnesses that have arisen during the term of the insurance contract. With the exception of agreements to the contrary, a waiting period is usually specified, starting from the beginning of the contract. This means there is no insurance cover for any illnesses treated during this period until the treatment is concluded. The waiting period is usually not necessary in the event of accidents and for certain infectious diseases. The insurance cover therefore becomes fully effective only after the end of the waiting period (at least three months, although waiting periods of six months or 12 months do exist).

Some policies allow premium refunds to be made, usually to provide for policyholders who have not made use of insurance benefits for a certain amount of time.

There are eight insurance companies headquartered in Austria that provide health insurance, of which seven offer hospital insurance, eight offer hospital daily allowance insurance, five offer sickness benefit insurance, five offer dental insurance, four offer daily allowance insurance, and three offer caring insurance.

Table 9.1 Market shares in health insurance 2009 and 2010 (direct domestic business)

2016			2017		
Position	**Company**	**Market share (%)**	**Position**	**Company**	**Market share (%)**
1	UNIQA Österreich Versicherungen AG	46.61	**1**	UNIQA Österreich Versicherungen AG	46.02
2	WIENER STÄDTISCHE Versicherung AG Vienna Insurance Group	18.75	**2**	WIENER STÄDTISCHE Versicherung AG Vienna Insurance Group	18.48
3	Merkur Versicherung AG	16.49	**3**	Merkur Versicherung AG	17.01
4	Generali Versicherung AG	13.29	**4**	Generali Versicherung AG	13.48
5	Allianz Elementar Versicherungs-AG	3.34	**5**	Allianz Elementar Versicherungs-AG	3.47
6	MuKi Versicherungs-verein a.G.	0.76	**6**	MuKi Versicherungs-verein a.G.	0.74
7	DONAU Versicherung AG Vienna Insurance Group	0.50	**7**	DONAU Versicherung AG Vienna Insurance Group	0.55
8	Wüstenrot Versicherungs-AG	0.26	**8**	Wüstenrot Versicherungs-AG	0.25
Premiums (EUR million)		2,051	Premiums (EUR million)		2,128

9.2 Features of and differences between statutory health insurance and private health insurance

As already discussed, in most cases private health insurance supplements the basic insurance cover of the statutory health insurance. The most important differences are explained in the following sections.[3]

Compulsory insurance versus optional insurance

Statutory health insurance is a compulsory insurance and acceptance of all employed individuals is mandatory; private health insurance is taken out voluntarily on the basis of free agreements with those who wish to take out insurance.

Group insurance/allocation procedure/contribution calculation according to social aspects versus individual insurance/funded schemes/principle of equivalence

Privately insured individuals form a risk community who are responsible for managing that risk. It is only members of this community who are entitled to receive the benefits of private treatment. The premiums finance not only current treatments but also help build up reserves to cover future treatment, a system known as the capital cover system.

Private insurance cover is taken out by means of voluntary insurance contracts. Premiums are calculated according to various criteria, depending on an individual's risk of illness, age, health, and gender.

Private health insurance is based on the principle of equivalence and no premium subsidies are permitted. In this system, the treatments are financed exclusively by the premium payments. This means that there must always be a balance between premiums and treatments. Risks that can be ascertained from the outset are taken into account when calculating the premiums. Comparable risks must always be treated equally, and varied risks must be treated on a case-by-case basis. Individuals must be healthy when signing the contract.

In contrast, statutory health insurance is financed according to a pay-as-you-go system by which today's contributions finance today's treatments.

3 Cf detailed BÖV, Versicherungshandbuch 34 ff; Leonhartsberger, Skriptum PKV in Ö 3 et seq.

No risk selection/automatic co-insurance versus risk selection/ individual insurance cover

Before one signs a private health insurance contract, one has to answer a number of health-related questions. This ensures that the correct insurance coverage is provided and the risk of illness is estimated correctly. In some cases, additional insurance premiums may have to be charged; alternatively, only a limited insurance coverage can be offered excluding certain diseases. In a very few cases, taking out the insurance is not possible at all.

Statutory health insurance is a form of compulsory insurance which is available to all employed persons and their relatives. The assessment of social insurance contributions is based on social factors and the contributions depend on the insured person's income, although there is an upper cap in place. Social policy provides a fair system regarding subsidies, taxes, and income, irrespective of the insurance.

Law-based services versus contractual services

The statutory health insurance is obliged to cover treatment for illnesses and accidents of any kind and must also provide benefits in kind as well as cash benefits.

In view of the high proportion of socially insured people in Austria, private health insurance providers have the responsibility of addressing the demands of doctors who have no contractual relationship with the responsible statutory insurance provider. They are also responsible for covering the costs of add-on options in listed public hospitals or during a stay in a private hospital and for the medical fees incurred for the increased care expenses. While the treating physician in any private hospital signs a treatment contract directly with the patient, for all services incurred during a stay in any public hospital (including the medical treatment), all payments are made directly to the hospital.

There are some instances in which private health insurers fully insure those who are not covered by social insurance. This takes place when the so-called social insurance replacement tariffs come into play.

Differing objectives

While statutory health insurance provides cover for the broadest possible segment of the population, private health insurance primarily serves individuals to help secure their individual interests. Private health insurance also serves companies since their share of group health insurance contributes significantly to the occupational healthcare of their employees.

Entitlement to treatment for existing conditions

With private health insurance an individual is not entitled to treatment for conditions that existed at the time the insurance was taken out other than in the exceptional cases in which private health insurance replaces the statutory health insurance (see 'General overview'). With statutory insurance, however, an individual is entitled to receive treatment for existing conditions.

9.3 Legal foundations of private health insurance

The legal framework for private health insurance is based on the general provisions of the ABGB, KSchG, DSG, etc.: the special provisions of the Insurance Supervision Act (VAG) of 18 October 1978,[4] including the ordinances of the Insurance Supervision Act; the Insurance Contract Act (VersVG) 1958;[5] the General Terms and Conditions of Insurance (AVB); the Special Terms and Conditions (BVB); the special provisions of the Insurance Supervision Act (VAG 2016) of 1 January 2016, and the insurance contract. The VersVG included its own section[6] on private health insurance in 1994 only.

9.4 Features of private health insurance

Business operations

In accordance with the provisions of the VAG for private health insurance, business operations require a concession from the Financial Market Authority, valid in all states. For foreign insurance companies the concession granted by the home state authority is valid, while VAG 2016[7] regulates the criteria for the operation of health insurance. Health insurance is provided in the same way as life insurance plans. Companies must submit a technical business plan to the Financial Market Authority, set up a provision for future policy benefits (provision ageing), and calculate the premiums. For this purpose companies must also appoint a responsible actuary and deputy to draw up the technical components of the business plan and to monitor compliance.[8] The actuary in charge must also provide the details of the reserves and confirm the accuracy of the results in the annual balance sheet. A separate insurance

4 BGBl 1978/569 idF der Novelle BGBl I 2010/58 (IRÄG-BG)
5 BGBl 1959/2 idF BGBl I 2010/58 (IRÄ-BG)
6 Fourth section, §§ 178a–178n
7 §§ 101 c ff
8 § 1114 ff VAG 2016

coverage fund must be created to address the coverage requirement and ensure supervision by an insurance coverage trustee.[9]

The application for a license must be submitted to the Financial Market Authority together with the basic actuarial information used to draw up the tariffs and calculate the provisions.

Risk assessment

When concluding the insurance contract, the health questions on the application form have to be answered correctly and completely.[10] The answers are required to calculate the premium correctly and to assess the risk correctly. In some cases, this means that additional premiums have to be charged or that only limited insurance coverage (which excludes a particular illness) can be offered. In some cases no contract can be offered at all. During the application process, medical results, medical reports, and medical records can be drawn upon to check the information.

The risk assessment depends on the diagnosis of a disease and the type and scope of the treatment needed. Unless otherwise stated in the insurance policy, any illnesses specified in the application are included in the insurance cover.

Misleading answers to health issues on the application can lead to the insurer withdrawing the insurance contract in accordance with VersVG.[11] This right of withdrawal exists for three years from the signing of the contract. In the event of withdrawal, the insurance cover expires.

If insurers were to accept all customers indiscriminately, more and more customers with a higher risk of illness would insure themselves, and the necessary risk equalization would no longer function properly since lower risk individuals are equally needed to balance out the costs. For higher risk cases, premiums are calculated in detail, possibly leading to premium increases or restrictions on insurance coverage.

The assessment of risk is very important because in accordance with VersVG[12] health insurance cannot be terminated by the insurer, with the exception of group insurance policies, sickness benefit insurance, and short term health insurance policies limited to less than one year. This is irrespective of age or deteriorating health.

---

9 §§ 152 ff VAG 2016
10 BGBl. I 34/2015 Insurance Supervision Act 2016, VAG 2016
11 § 16
12 § 178i

Types of insurance, treatment, and scope of insurance cover

VersVG[13] differentiates among four types of health insurance contracts.[14]

Hospital insurance

The contracts concluded within the scope of private health insurance generally include hospital cost insurance. With this form of insurance, the accommodation costs are charged to the patient while the costs of treatment and material expenses are reimbursed.[15]

This type of health insurance is generally used as a supplementary insurance. It reimburses the additional costs of a stay in listed hospitals and offers additional benefits (for example, free choice of doctors, more comfortably furnished wards, fewer beds in the wards, free visiting hours, choice of food, etc.). With the general fee class for treatment in a public hospital, the agreed amount is paid as an allowance per day of the hospital stay. If there is no statutory health insurance in place, it is also possible to take out insurance specifically for a hospital stay in the general fee class (see above).

This form of insurance covers the expenses for necessary medical treatment as a result of illness or accident and other forms of treatment including treatment required during pregnancy and childbirth.

Since the individual statutory insurance providers provide different coverage plans for inpatient hospital stays, and since hospital costs vary from region to region, premiums differ regionally and for each occupational group.

The treatment cost covered by the insurance is not paid to the individual, but directly to the hospital/physician, provided that a cost guarantee was issued.

For hospitals with which provided have a contractual agreement, the insurance provider guarantees to pay the full additional costs of a stay in a listed hospital. These costs and fees are charged directly to the contract partner based on an agreement submitted prior to admission to the hospital, calculated on what the patient owes to the contract partner of the private health insurer (hospital and/or doctor) and what is covered by the insurance in accordance with the specific insurance contract.

A full cost coverage guarantee is available to all hospitals and day clinics with which a contract has been concluded. The insurance providers regularly issue lists of all hospitals and day clinics to which this applies.

This form of insurance is also offered as group insurance.

---

13 § 178b

14 Cf Dopplinger in Schrammel 112 f; BÖV, Versicherangshandbuch 35 ff

15 BÖV, Versicherangshandbuch 35 ff

Daily hospital allowance insurance

Daily hospital allowance insurance is a fixed-sum insurance. The contract covers a certain amount paid for each day spent in hospital and does not require proof of cost.

Daily hospital allowance insurance is taken for stays in listed hospitals, in the general fee class. This form of insurance can also be taken out on its own or in addition to other forms of health insurance.

Insurance for outpatient medical treatment

This type of insurance can be taken out in conjunction with hospital insurance or as a stand-alone option. It is taken by individuals who do not have statutory health insurance or by those who seek treatment by doctors whose fees and treatments are not covered by statutory health insurance.

In some states private health insurance providers offer agreements with the medical associations for doctors in private practice for the direct settlement of doctor's fees for outpatient operations.

Sickness benefit insurance

The sickness benefit insurance is a fixed-sum insurance. After the qualifying period of being fully (100%) unable to work due to illness has passed, a certain sum is paid out.

Care insurance

With care insurance, care costs are reimbursed as agreed. Here, too, the legal definitions of the different types of health insurance offer two categories of coverage provided by the insurer: nursing expenses insurance, for which the insurer is responsible for reimbursing care costs; and daily care benefits insurance, for which the insurer provides the agreed care allowance.[16] Life insurance policies also offer long-term care pension insurance.

Dental cost insurance

Dental cost insurance cover includes outpatient dental treatment as well as dental prostheses, although upper cost caps are in place and excess payments are the norm.

16 Fenyves, Kronsteiner, and Schauer, VersVG-Novellen VersVG 287

Spa subsidies

Spa subsidies are paid out for treatments approved by social insurance providers for post-hospital spa and recreational and rehabilitation treatments.

Travel insurance

Travel insurance is valid for a specific time and covers a certain percentage of out- or in-patient treatments for acute illnesses abroad up to a certain maximum.

Often, the transport costs of a patient who is ill or injured during his/her trip are covered by the insurance policy, while the recovery costs after accidents are covered by the insurance contract.

Medicines

Private health insurance policyholders pay for prescribed medicines themselves, and then submit the receipt to the insurance provider for reimbursment. This is then refunded in line with the agreed tariff.

Group insurance

Group insurance contracts are very common. They offer the individual the benefits of full insurance cover at a rate that is favorable in comparison to individual insurance contracts, since the group is a manageable risk community, and the acquisition and administration costs are lower.[17] The contract is closed by the employer or the works council for a group of employees and must apply to all employees.[18]

The insurance cover for the insured person ends when his/her employment contract comes to an end. Since 1994, however, the individual and his/her co-insured relatives have the right to apply to extend the contract without the need for a health check, via an individual insurance plan. The premium to continue the individual insurance is calculated according to the individual's age and state of health when he/she entered the group insurance contract.[19]

The final insurance contract

The insurance contract is concluded for an indefinite time. It begins on the date specified in the insurance policy. The insurance cover commences at the time specified, but not before the agreed waiting period has elapsed (see 'Waiting times'), and only after this can claims be made.

---

17 Fenyves, Kronsteiner, and Schauer, VersVG-Novellen VersVG 400

18 See also '9.5 Tax on private health insurance'

19 Fenyves, Kronsteiner, and Schauer, VersVG-Novellen VersVG 400

Waiting times

VersVG[20,21] stipulates that waiting periods can be individually agreed in certain cases although the statutory provisions stipulate maximum limits. The purpose of waiting periods is to ensure that the insurance provider can exclude insurance cover for those illnesses that are already acute or latent when the contract is concluded. Above all, waiting periods are intended to prevent individuals from taking out insurance as a last-minute, unplanned measure in the event of imminent illness. If, however, an illness occurs before the end of the waiting period, the insurer is still obliged to pay compensation if the policyholder proves that the illness was not recognizable until after the contract was signed.

Obligation for children not covered by statutory insurance

Freedom of contract applies to private health insurance contracts, i.e. the insurance provider is not obliged to accept an application. This principle is inconsistent with VersVG,[22] which stipulates that an individual who is not covered by statutory health insurance and who has a newborn child is obliged to extend his/her cover to the child. The policyholder must submit the request to the insurer no later than two months after the birth of the child.[23] If the child has an increased risk of illness, there may be an increase in the premium. Insurance cover begins with the child's birth.

Cost guarantee

Since the 1960s, hospital fees for in-patient treatment have been managed directly between the hospitals and the insurance providers, replacing direct reimbursement by the patient.

Invoicing is based upon direct settlement agreements that regulate the payment costs for hospital expenses and medical fees. As a result, these binding price regulations make hospital treatment costs, doctors' fees, etc., more predictable. The prerequisite for direct settlement and cost guarantee is continual price adjustment to effectively mirror the current cost situation.[24]

If, however, the treatment does not take place in a specified hospital, the insurer will be charged for the individual services according to the tariff. This means that if there is appropriate insurance for a stay in a listed hospital or a private hospital, both care and treatment costs including doctor's fees will be covered. These costs

20 S 178d para 1
21 Vgl Fenyves, Kronsteiner, and Schauer, VersVG-Novellen VersVG 310
22 § 178e
23 Vgl Fenyves, Kronsteiner, and Schauer, VersVG-Novellen VersVG 324; Leonhartsberger, (ecolex 1994) 607
24 BÖV, Versicherangshandbuch 55; Leonhartsberger, Skriptum PKV in Ö 23

and fees are settled directly by the private health insurer, and the patient does not have to pay anything. As mentioned above, private health insurers provide lists on an annual basis of all hospitals that have a direct settlement agreement.

The full cost recovery guarantee applies only to those hospitals of the federal state for which the list has been drawn up, as the tariffs and insurance terms are valid only in the state in which they were issued. There are insurance policies that offer nationwide tariffs, valid for all hospitals listed in all federal states across Austria.

When a patient is admitted to hospital, the insurance provider receives a request to cover the costs. After an examination of a specific claim, the insurance provider submits a declaration to assume costs either for a specific time or without restrictions. Before submitting the declaration, the insurer will have checked the relevant insurance plan to see whether there are exclusions for specific treatments or any other factors to consider.

Revocation of cost recovery commitments

The Direct Settlement Convention ensures that the insurer offers the policyholder a cost recovery commitment guaranteeing the full coverage of the costs for accommodation and treatment in specified contract hospitals.[25]

Direct Settlement Agreements are valid for a specific time and can be terminated. If the insurer no longer wishes to be bound by the cost recovery commitment, it must be officially revoked. In accordance with VersVG,[26] a contract must specify the earliest possible time for revocation of a cost recovery commitment, which in accordance with paragraph 2 sentence 1 comes into effect three weeks[27] after the request is submitted. The revocation does not apply to in-patient treatments that began before the notification comes into effect, or to cost recovery commitments that do not contain any details of the earliest possible revocation date (in which case the earliest possible expiry date is after two years and three weeks).

Adjustment of insurance contracts[28]

Private health insurance contracts are agreed upon for life. The premium is calculated taking into account possible future treatments. Since it is not possible to predict future developments, the law specifies instances when a premium adjustment can be made in light of certain changes. Costs in the healthcare system do not remain

25 Cf in detail Fenyves, Kronsteiner, and Schauer, VersVG-Noveilen VersVG to § 178 c 298 ff; Dopplinger in Schrammel, 'Medical treatment' 116,121

26 § 178 c

27 See also Leonhartsberger, (ecolex 1994) 606

28 Fenyves, Kronsteiner, and Schauer, VersVG-Novellen VersVG 329ff and 352 ff

the same; they rise far above inflationary trends, in part due to the development of new diagnostic and therapeutic methods, and in part due to rising life expectancy (see 'Continuation of insurance contracts').

The reasons for premium increases are set out in the VersVG.[29]

The particular instances when a premium adjustment can be made are listed below:

- Index, safeguarding the value of the premium by agreeing an index
- Change in average life expectancy
- Change in the frequency or complexity of treatments needed
- Change in the relationship between the agreed treatments and the corresponding social insurance contributions
- Change in charges for using healthcare facilities
- Changes in the healthcare system or the relevant statutory provisions

Duration of insurance

The insurance contract cannot be terminated by the insurance provider, thereby essentially making it a lifelong policy. This does not apply to sickness benefit insurance, group insurance contracts, or short-term insurance contracts (valid for under one year). The insurer can only terminate the contract if the policyholder knowingly answered the questions regarding his/her state of health incorrectly, if the premium is not paid punctually, or if contractual obligations have not been met.

The policyholder is entitled to terminate the contract within the contractual period of notice at the end of each insurance year during the entire term of the contract[30] unless special binding periods have been agreed.

Termination of insurance contracts

The reasons for termination are set out in the General Conditions of Insurance. The insurance contract comes to an end on a specific date if a completion date has been agreed upon. In principle, however, most health insurance contracts may be concluded for an indefinite period only, with the exception of short-term health insurance contracts that are limited to less than one year.

---

29 § 178l

30 BÖV, Versicherungshandbuch 39 ff

The policyholder has the right to terminate a contract within the period of notice that is specified in the insurance conditions. In general, the insurer may not terminate the contract unless a situation arises as specified in VersVG.[31] Termination on the part of the insurer is possible only for group insurance policies and sickness benefit insurance contracts. Termination is possible, however, if there are extraordinary grounds for termination, such as a breach of contractual obligation by the policyholder,[32] a default in payment of the premium,[33] or a non-culpable breach of the obligation to notify.[34]

The insurance provider's withdrawal of the contract is given when the individual does not comply with his/her pre-contractual obligation to notify. Providing incorrect information about health issues on the application form may lead the insurer to withdraw the insurance contract in accordance with VersVG.[35] This right is in accordance with VersVG[36] and lasts up to three years after conclusion of the contract. In this case the insurance cover expires.

VersVG[37] does not, however, apply if the policyholder purposely breaches his/her obligation to notify. In this case, the insurer can terminate the contract indefinitely. Other reasons for termination are the death of the policyholder or the transfer of the individual's residence abroad (see general terms and conditions of the individual insurance companies).

Continuation of insurance contracts

According to VersVG[38,39] an individual may apply to continue his/her insurance policy within two months of it being terminated, except if it was withdrawn because of an intentional breach of the obligation to notify, a payment default of the first premium payment,[40] or a breach of an obligation. The latter is relevant to a family insurance policy, for example, in which a divorce and the subsequent insurance termination is initiated by the policyholder.

31 § 178i paras 2 and 3
32 § 6 of the Insurance Contract Act
33 39 of the Insurance Contract Act
34 § 41 of the Insurance Contract Act; Cf Fenyves, Kronsteiner, and Schauer, VersVG-Noveilen VersVG 365 ff
35 § 16
36 § 178k
37 § 178k
38 § 178j
39 Fenyves, Kronsteiner, and Schauer, VersVG-Novellen VersVG 373 ff
40 § 38 VersVG

Premiums[41]

Premiums depend on the age of the individual at the time the contract is signed, his/her state of health, any statutory health insurance coverage he/she may have, and his/her chosen tariff.

Premiums are calculated in such a way that they can remain the same throughout the duration of the insurance policy, provided that the prices for medical treatment remain the same. However, insurance providers make provision for the fact that the cost of healthcare increases with advancing age.

This means that younger people pay higher premiums than their risk assessments warrant to help build up reserves for rising costs that are incurred with increasing age. This allows premiums essentially to stay stable, and not be adjusted as the individual gets older, provided that costs in the healthcare system remain constant (see 'Revocation of cost recovery commitments').

Important provisions regarding general terms and conditions

Insurance claim

The regulations governing insurance claims are outlined in the general terms and conditions of the contract. See also the standard conditions for hospital cost insurance published by the Association of Austrian Insurance Companies (VVO) (2016). A claim is valid if treatment is deemed necessary as a result of illness or an accident, but pregnancy examinations and deliveries also fall into this category.

Unless otherwise agreed, cosmetic treatments or geriatric-related treatments are not deemed to be valid claims.

Patients have a free choice of doctor. The costs for home visits are usually dependent on the state of health of the individual in question.

If hospital treatment is required, the patient must go to a hospital with all the adequate facilities, as opposed to centers that are geared towards rehabilitation (for example, alcohol or drug rehabilitation centers).

Curative treatments, medicines, or physical treatments are also covered if this is specified in the general terms and conditions of the policy. Any exemptions are listed here.

The EU Directive 2004/113/EC concerning equality in the treatment of men and women with regard to access to and supply of goods and services legally ensured

41 BÖV, Versicherangshandbuch 62; Leonhartsberger, Skriptum PKV in Ö 23

that different premium structures could be offered, provided such differences could be justified. Premiums could be based on the assessment of the individual's risk of illness, although the costs of pregnancy, maternity treatment, and childbirth had to be borne jointly by women and men. To an extent, Austria implemented this directive in VersRÄG 2007. The changes came into force in January 2012 for new contracts, although for existing contracts premiums could, as before, still differ based on gender. For new contracts, this change meant that premiums for women were lower and premiums for men were higher than before.

In 2011 an ECJ ruling stated that the above-mentioned directive was inadmissible. Consequently, since 21 December 2012, different premiums and treatment plans for men and women in the insurance sector may not be offered. There are no exceptions to this rule.

Insurability

In general, healthy individuals within the prescribed age bracket[42] and residing in Austria can be insured. Insurance cover can also be taken out for trips abroad by those with a permanent residence in Austria (international travel health insurance).

Individuals who reside abroad can obtain health and accident insurance cover for Austria when traveling to Austria. This type of insurance cover is particularly important for those whose stay requires a visa, because they must prove adequate insurance cover to obtain the visa.

Adjustment clauses

Insurance contracts usually contain adjustment clauses intended to protect the policyholder from underinsurance. The policyholder can object to an adjustment, which in some cases can involve a premium adjustment, but this would mean that they would remain underinsured.

9.5 Tax on private health insurance

Premiums for private health insurance are calculated using actuarial methods. They depend on the agreed cover plan and the individual's age. They are subject to insurance tax at the rate of 1%. Only existing contracts signed before 1 January 2016 can be deducted from income tax (amount, income of the taxpayer) until 2020.

42 Leonhartsberger, Skriptum PKV in Ö

Treatments covered by private health insurance are generally exempt from income tax, irrespective of whether they are treatments covered by hospital cost insurance or hospital daily allowance insurance plans.

In certain instances, employer contributions to group insurance plans are exempt from tax up to an annual contribution of EUR 300.[43] However, other employer contributions, such as life or accident insurance, must be credited against this amount.

References

BÖV, Skriptum Krankenversicherung (March 2010).

BÖV, Versieherungshandbueh, Lieferung (April 2009) 11.

Dopplinger, 'Die Funktion der Privatversicherung' in Schrammel, *Rechtsfragen der ärztlichen Behandlung* (1992).

Fenyves, Kronsteiner, and Schauer, VersVG-Novellen VersVG, Novellen 1992, 1994, and 1996, Kommentar.

FN VVO, Jahresbericht (2016).

Leonhartsberger, 'Lebens- und Krankenversicherung' in the VersVG, Novellen 1994, (ecolex 1994) 605.

Leonhartsberger, Skriptum PKV in Österreich.

Steiner, *Arzthonorar in der Sonderklasse* (2004).

WO, Jahresbericht (2010), Datenteil, Krankenversicherung.

About the author

DR. ULRIKE BRAUMÜLLER worked in a law firm after completing her studies at Vienna University. In 1982 she joined the Association of Insurance Companies (VVO) where she engaged in the fields of transport insurance, international affairs, and life, health, and accident insurance, and in 1995 she became the managing director for personal insurance. Dr. Braumüller left VVO in 2016 and now works as a consultant.

43 In accordance with § 3 para 1 No 15a EStG

10 International Aspects of Health Insurance

Marco Gantenbein, Swiss Insurance Partners

When one moves abroad it is vitally important to consider making some provision for international health insurance cover but, unfortunately, this crucial aspect of the move usually does not receive enough attention, and is frequently barely addressed. It is furthermore not incumbent on a lawyer who specializes in international real estate and/or inheritance law, an international tax advisor, or even the private banks to be in possession of particular knowledge pertaining to insurance issues or international health insurance. Worldwide, there are very few consultancy firms that specialize in this field, particularly on behalf of individual clients and families, and it complicates matters further that there is relatively little professional competence to be had in this specialist field.

Finding the ideal health insurance plan to fulfill all one's needs is not an easy task even when one is not changing domicile to a foreign country such as Austria. To avoid any unpleasant surprises regarding health matters it is essential, whether one spends long periods abroad or whether one definitively relocates, to hold comprehensive international cover against sickness and accidents. It is also important when choosing an insurance provider to take certain key criteria into account *vis-à-vis* the availability of a wide range of insurance solutions and products.

Anyone who lives, works, manages a business, or enjoys his/her retirement abroad ought to be covered by an insurance that is as comprehensive as possible and universally available. Health insurance in particular ought to include as few restrictions as possible — or better yet none — in terms of guaranteeing an unrestricted choice of doctors and/or hospitals. Ideally, making provision for unlimited options when one is choosing a medical service provider should be applied at a global level to ensure that insured persons can utilize the services of the best doctors and hospitals that any country has to offer.

10.1 A matter of residence

If one is making a temporary stay abroad that does not include the transfer of domicile then, within the EU and sometimes further afield, the basic state insurance usually secures a minimum insurance coverage. Furthermore, almost all the national health insurance schemes offer one the option of taking out a comprehensive cover against illness and accident via private, supplementary insurance, particularly for a temporary stay abroad. It is, however, advisable to inform oneself thoroughly regarding all the potential insurance options before conclusively transferring one's residence to any foreign country — from the unrestricted choice of doctor and hospital to complete cover for medication — because private health insurance protection usually ends when one moves one's domicile abroad. It is moreover important to make sure that the insurance cover is not interrupted during the period of relocation when one is, so to speak, between countries.

As a rule, comprehensive cover with free choice of doctor and/or hospital globally is highly recommended. This, bearing in mind that many countries — including within the EU — have a public health system that meets only minimum requirements, and that private hospitals should usually be sought out for competent medical treatment, i.e. to receive treatment as a private patient at a university hospital. If, after residing in Austria, there is a chance one may relocate again at a later stage to another country, for example outside the EU, then comprehensive insurance cover becomes even more imperative — and this aspect may influence one's decision to move if one does not make the appropriate provisions early enough.

In Austria, as in many countries, there are good local, private health insurance schemes that offer international cover with the freedom to choose one's doctor and/or hospital, and this type of local insurance is often cost effective. It is nevertheless seldom the optimum solution since practically all local national health insurance companies accept only the residents of the country in which they are operating, and this is generally the case in Austria. If one relocates again at some point in the future the insurance cover will usually fall into expiry which can, under some circumstances, become an insurmountable obstacle as one grows older because of the minor ailments often associated with aging. In many places it is furthermore difficult if one takes out local health insurance to choose one's doctor and/or hospital freely, in a truly unconditional way. For example, access to treatment in the US — despite it being a global leader in state-of-the-art medicine — is often limited and sometimes impossible to obtain. Insurance cover that is independent of one's domicile and length of stay in a country and that guarantees as comprehensive a cover as possible, and is recognized by the relevant country of residence (such as Austria) when it comes to benefits and services, is therefore the best option. Most local national health insurance companies offer no solutions, or only unsatisfactory ones in this regard, and very few offer private health insurance that can be taken out when traveling abroad or retained when residing abroad. It is essential to check these crucial aspects with great care to avoid the unwelcome discovery that one has no cover in the event of illness or another relocation in the future.

10.2 Global cover and unrestricted choice of doctor and/or hospital

There is an extensive range of international private health insurance schemes available around the world, yet, interestingly, very few providers from this wide range of options are recommended. When comparing the different health insurance plans it is important to look at not only the relevant insurance product but also at the financial standing and reputation of the insurance company, and its experience in the fields of international health insurance, in claims handling, and in reinsurance cover. In each case, it must be established which insurance product best fulfills the individual requirements of the policyholder and his/her country of residence.

Another aspect to consider is that private health insurance schemes, like insurance companies, are not obligated to accept everyone who applies to them for cover. Policyholders over the age of 60, and sometimes even those over the age of 50, or 55, or those who do not have a clean bill of health, encounter difficulties when taking out private health insurance, particularly comprehensive private insurance with international cover. For this reason, confirming one's insurance options as early in the relocation process as possible is strongly recommended, and preferably before one moves abroad. In certain circumstances it may be advisable to switch to an international health insurance plan several years before one's planned or possible relocation in order to safeguard the necessary flexibility.

If one does not intend to transfer residence to a foreign country but would nevertheless like to be covered optimally against sickness and accident, it is worth considering taking out international private health insurance because this can be greatly to one's advantage. Those who travel frequently and stay abroad occasionally, and those who plan to move abroad at a later date, ought to be insured so that they can retain their desired cover independently of their place of residence and/or the duration of their stay abroad — i.e. if there should be further changes of domicile abroad. Ideally, the insurance cover should include unlimited global choice of doctor and/or hospital.

The guaranteed lifelong renewability of an insurance policy including in cases of change of domicile or long-term illness, etc., is also very important. Most providers (private national health insurance providers included) stipulate that they can unilaterally terminate a contract with a policyholder in the event of long-term illness, or even without specific cause. They also stipulate that they are within their rights to drastically increase insurance premiums as a policyholder grows older. Although this is incongruous with the concept of health insurance because one depends on insurance precisely when one falls ill, such conditions — for example, that one's contract can be unilaterally terminated in the event of a big claim — are often to be found in insurance contracts and these should be avoided at all costs, irrespective of whether one takes out local or national health insurance or international health insurance.

10.3 Checklist for choosing an international health insurance

The following points should be explored and compared when one selects a suitable private health insurance provider. For instance, does the provider offer:

- Global cover with attractive premiums? It is important to compare premiums for older age groups too, to enable one to plan ahead
- A free and global choice of doctor and/or hospital, with no restrictions?
- No restrictions in respect of the insurance policyholder's country of residence and length of stay, even upon a return to one's homeland in the event of a later relocation?
- The guaranteed, lifelong renewability of the insurance policy, even upon a change of domicile at some later date or in the event of any long-term illness, etc.?
- The efficient handling of claims, including either simple claim forms to complete, or none?
- A multilingual emergency call center in operation 24 hours a day, preferably for 365 days a year?
- An internationally recognized name and an excellent reputation, and experience in the field of international health insurance (including private clinics)?
- Full cover for inpatient and outpatient treatments, including insurance services for prescription drugs?
- Letters of guarantee pertaining to insurance cover that are issued in German, for Austria?

About the author

MARCO GANTENBEIN is a private client specialist in international health insurance. He is the Chairman of Swiss Insurance Partners, and for nearly 20 years individuals and families as well as their advisors and employers have trusted in his expertise, which is backed by his extensive professional knowledge and comprehensive international experience. A frequent speaker on the topic of international health insurance at conferences worldwide, Marco Gantenbein is fluent in English, German, and French. He has for many years been a member of the Society of Trust and Estate Practitioners and holds a license from the Swiss Financial Market Supervisory Authority. He is a member of the Investment Migration Council and the founder of the Professional Cycling Team Sauerland NRW, p/b SKS Germany.

11 Acquisition and Rental of Real Estate in Austria

Mag. Anton Holzapfel, Österreichischer Verband der Immobilienwirtschaft

Real Estate

Whether one intends to acquire real estate, establish a residence, or rent an apartment in Austria, all these activities are largely governed by national law. Hence, despite having EU membership, Austria has specific national regulations relating to real estate. Austrian tenancy law in particular contains a broad range of national specifications.

Austrian regulations may thus differ greatly from those with which prospective foreign buyers or tenants might be familiar in their home countries. EU legislation has influenced Austrian real estate law only to the extent that prospective EU real estate buyers in Austria are not at a disadvantage compared to Austrian nationals.

11.1 Purchase of residential property in Austria

A prospective buyer will usually seek professional support when looking for residential space: advice regarding choices of property and property prices, conditions, advantages, and disadvantages is best obtained from a licensed real estate broker.[1] Certified appraisers[2] may also be requested to determine the market value of a property. A lawyer or notary will then ensure the smooth handling of the purchase agreement to ensure that the new owner is recorded in the land register and the seller concurrently receives the purchase price that has previously been deposited in an escrow account by the buyer.

1 Österreichischer Verband der Immobilienwirtschaft (ÖVI) is the Austrian Real Estate Association — an association for quality assurance in real estate. It's membership is voluntary. For a list of ÖVI members please visit *ovi.at*

2 *immozert.at*

Legal provisions restricting the acquisition of real estate

Subject to certain conditions, the acquisition of real estate in Austria is contingent upon approval by the Land Transfer Authority.[3] This primarily applies to the following transactions:

- The transfer of agricultural land and forests ('green' land transfer)
- The acquisition of secondary (holiday) residences ('grey' land transfer)
- The acquisition of a property by 'foreign nationals' (i.e., nationals of non-EU and non-EEA states)

Parts of the respective provisions vary greatly between Austria's nine provinces.

Austrians, EU citizens, and foreign nationals are equally subject to the restrictions regarding agricultural and silvicultural (forestry) estate. The rules governing the acquisition of property by those deemed foreign nationals apply only to third country citizens, i.e. those who are not citizens of Austria, the EU, or EEA countries.

Property acquisition by foreign nationals as a primary place of residence

The acquisition of property is governed by provincial land transfer legislation that varies greatly in certain aspects. However, what the provinces have in common is that citizens of the EEA are always treated as equal to Austrians, for example, German nationals are subject to the same provisions as Austrians. Thus, the acquisition of a property to be used as a primary residence is usually straightforward. In those provinces where it is required, the responsible Land Transfer Authority will issue a so-called negative confirmation (*Negativbestätigung*), testifying that the subject acquisition is exempt from the obligation to obtain approval for the transaction.

The approval of a property acquisition by nationals from non-EEA member countries principally requires that Austria has a cultural, social, or economic interest in the transaction, and that the transaction does not infringe upon any interests of the Austrian state. The same principle applies to companies that are not based in Austria or the EEA — they are also subject to the land transfer provisions.

Swiss nationals do not principally receive the same treatment as EU/EEA citizens; there is, however, a bilateral Free Movement Treaty between Austria and Switzerland, which provides that equal treatment is granted if the purchaser has the right of residence and primary residence in Austria, or if the desired property is required for commercial activities.[4]

---

3 Pachler and Uhl, *Grundverkehrsrecht* (*Land Transfer Law*) 11

4 Pachler and Uhl, *Land Transfer Law* 173 cont'd

Property acquisition as a secondary place of residence in Austria

Because of the scarcity of land and the intention to avoid speculation and create affordable year-round living space for the local population, almost all Austrian provinces — except Vienna and Lower Austria — restrict the acquisition of property for secondary residence to a greater or lesser extent. The trend is that land transfer provisions are less frequently applied, and restrictions imposed under regional planning legislation are gradually gaining importance.

In Vienna, there are no regulations covering the transfer of 'green' or 'grey' land. Thus, for instance, music lovers (provided they are EU citizens or citizens of equivalent status) do not require approval for their investment if they want to acquire a downtown penthouse in Vienna as a permanent secondary residence. In contrast, the situation is very different in the extremely popular holiday home areas of the Tyrol. Depending on the legal nature of the restrictions (land transfer or spatial planning), the principles discussed below are prevalent.

The land transfer legislation in the provinces of Burgenland,[5] Upper Austria,[6] and Styria[7] provide that in certain communities or areas (the so-called *Vorbehaltsgemeinde* or *Vorbehaltsgebiet*) the acquisition of secondary homes is restricted to those with a distinct holiday-residence designation. In other words, such acquisition is not possible in certain areas. There, buyers have to declare that the property will not be used as a holiday residence, either by themselves or others.

The Tyrolean land transfer legislation generally prohibits the acquisition or establishment of holiday residences. An exemption to this ruling is the acquisition or rental of buildings and parts of buildings (apartments) which are recorded in a listing of holiday residences, pursuant to s 13 of the Tyrolean Spatial Planning Act of 2006, as well as undeveloped land with a zoning designation explicitly permitting the erection of holiday residences.[8]

In Salzburg and Vorarlberg the restrictions regarding holiday residences are laid down in respective designations in the Spatial Planning Acts.[9] The use of a property as a secondary residence is permissible only if it has the appropriate designation. Carinthia also requires such designations; however, it appears that there have been no major problems in obtaining this designation for many years. Neither Vienna nor Lower Austria have any restrictions on the use of a property as a secondary residence.

5 Pachler and Uhl, *Land Transfer Law* 88f

6 Pachler and Uhl, *Land Transfer Law* 125

7 Pachler and Uhl, *Land Transfer Law* 105

8 Pachler and Uhl, *Land Transfer Law* 150

9 On 1 January 2018, additional, stricter regulations for holiday homes came into force in the province of Salzburg

Concluding a purchase agreement — proposal and acceptance

A purchase agreement is concluded by the acceptance of a proposal (offer). This means that a prospective buyer who has submitted a signed purchase proposal may be sued by the seller (once the seller has accepted it), if he/she consequently fails to fulfill it. Thus, a signed proposal has a binding effect on the signatories, and withdrawal is usually not possible.

Formal requirements of the purchase agreement

There are generally no particular formal requirements of the purchase agreement, i.e. a purchase contract may be concluded in writing, orally, or in some instances even by non-verbal conduct ('implied in fact'). This principle also applies to purchase agreements in relation to property. However, inscription in the land register requires a written purchase agreement. Thus, an oral purchase agreement also requires an ex-post deed, set up by a lawyer or a notary. This deed must be notarized to be recorded in the land register. A notary's deed is also required for purchase agreements between spouses, regardless of whether they are for an entire property or only parts thereof.

Object of the purchase

The cadaster, which is maintained by the competent land surveying office, shows the exact boundaries of a given lot. In the event that the actual on-site boundaries differ from the boundaries recorded in the cadaster, the boundaries in the cadaster will prevail. If a property is recorded in the cadaster, it is covered by the same legal protection as the records in the land register (and its records can be trusted to be valid). A parcel of land can be recorded in the cadaster only if all neighbors have agreed on the position of its boundaries on site and if its limiting points were surveyed in accurate relation to the provincial coordinates and are documented by public deed. A cadaster community is a spatial unit under which several plots of land are comprised with a name and a number. Boundaries between cadaster communities, political communities, and regional competencies of district courts may not overlap.

Acquiring ownership by inscription in the land register

After agreement has been reached between the seller and the buyer on the object and the price under the law of obligations (i.e. the purchase agreement), the legal handover is required. This is put into effect by inscription in the (electronic) land register that is maintained by the district courts, and where all rights in rem concerning the property are recorded. The land register is a public register to which brokers, lawyers, and notaries generally have full online access, and from which they can retrieve all relevant data for their clients. The lawyer who drew up the agreement acts as a trustee for the contractual document (as qualification for inscription) and the purchase price. Further documents, deeds, or permits may be required in addition. In the event of the property being released from encumbrances (mortgage), the trustee must transfer the respective amount to the bank. The (remaining) purchase price is paid to the seller once the inscription of ownership is secured in the land register.[10]

The potential transaction costs for the buyer include the following:

- 3.5% land transfer tax (reduction or exemption possible in certain cases)
- 1.1% land register fee
- Costs for drawing up the agreement and effecting the inscription in the land register (according to the Compensation Scheme for Lawyers)
- Costs of proceedings by the Land Transfer Authority and related administrative costs
- Potential communal costs for access to the property and its connection to utilities (power, gas, water, sewer)
- Up to 3% brokerage fee (for properties exceeding a value of EUR 48,448.51)

Acquisition of a condominium unit

In everyday language there is often no distinction made between the different types of ownership. While an apartment may be referred to as a condominium, it may not necessarily be one. If one intends to buy an apartment, it is advisable to be aware of the differences.

If immovable property (real estate) belongs to a single (i.e. one) natural person or legal entity, it is a sole ownership. The sole owner has the unrestricted right to use and dispose of that property and the buildings on it.

This is in contrast to co-ownership, where several persons or entities share a property, each of them owning a fraction — for instance three owners each owning one third. The share is only imaginary since the parts of the property that may be used by each co-owner are not identifiable. The allocation of shares requires distinct provision specifying which apartment, parking space, or other premises may be used by each of the owners respectively, or jointly with the other owners.

10 Details in Gartner, *Immobilienerwerb* (Acquisition of Real Estate) 64 cont'd

Condominium ownership is a specially defined type of co-ownership. Each co-owner (i.e. a natural person, legal entity, or owning partnership) is entitled to the exclusive use and disposition of a specific unit.[11] The binding statutory provisions are laid down in the Condominium Ownership Act 2002 (WEG), which also stipulates details concerning the building management and the decision-making process by the community of owners. Each owner has a pro-rata voting right in owner resolutions; voting rights correspond to the respective owner's share in the condominium property. There are distinct minority and proposition rights to secure the legal position of individual owners *vis-à-vis* the community of owners and their representative (the building manager).

The so-called *Mindestanteil*[12] is the co-ownership share required to acquire ownership of a condominium unit within a property. It represents the share of the respective unit in relation to the entire property (i.e. total shares), measured in terms of value.

When purchasing a condominium unit, it is advisable to take into account whether (and in what amount) a reserve fund for maintenance and repair has been accrued, as well as, respectively, if renovation work has been decided upon or is due within the next few years.

If the annotation of condominium ownership has not yet been inscribed for the property in the land register, it is absolutely necessary to secure the purchaser's rights through annotation in the register.

11.2 Renting apartments in Austria

Renting an apartment in Austria is at once both simple and complicated. In the event of the property being found through an agent (a broker or a building management company), the prospective lessee submits a proposal that is accepted by the lessor (owner) or the lessor's representative (building manager). After agreement has been reached in principle, a draft lease agreement is sent to both parties for signature. Thereafter, the keys to the apartment can be exchanged.

Tenants should expect the following transaction costs:

- Provision of the safety deposit (refundable)
- Lawyer's fee for drawing up the lease, as agreed (unless fully covered by the Tenancy Act (MRG)

11 Legal definition of s 2(2) WEG

12 S 2(9), as well as ss 3, 11, and 12 WEG

- Brokerage commission:
  - Rentals of indefinite duration or fixed-term rentals exceeding three years: equivalent to two times the gross monthly rental
  - Rentals for a fixed three-year period: equivalent to one gross monthly rental
  - Rentals for shorter fixed periods (only possible for one- and two-family homes: equivalent to one half of the gross monthly rental

The statutory provisions protecting the tenant depend on various factors:

- The date of the building permit for the subject property
- The type of property (single-family home, building with several apartments)
- The legal context (for example, has condominium ownership been established?)
- The agreed type of use (residential, business)
- The date the agreement was concluded[13]

Austria's MRG provides comprehensive protection in favor of the tenant, in particular with regard to termination regulations and restrictions on the rental amount. If a property is subject to the MRG, the pertinent provisions are binding and cannot be modified by agreement to the tenant's disadvantage. In other words: in the event of a dispute, only the statutory provisions are valid, and not what the tenant has actually signed.

There is a difference in the scope of applicability: lease agreements may be fully subject to the MRG provisions or subject only in parts (partial exemptions from the law). In those circumstances where the MRG is not applicable, the general provisions governing lease agreements in the Civil Code (ABGB) apply. These provisions, in turn, may be altered by the agreement of both parties, with only a few exceptions.

Subject to the MRG are the rentals:

- Of apartments or parts of apartments
- Of retail areas (however, not parts thereof)
- Of garages and other accessory areas — but only if they are part of a rental agreement
- Regarding agreements with cooperatives[14] — to the extent that s 20 of the WGG (non-profit status of property owner) applies

13 Dirnbacher, MRG 31 cont'd

14 See s 1(3) of MRG

Tenancy Act — full applicability

If the Tenancy Act is fully applicable, all provisions are effective, and may not be modified by any agreement between the lessor and the lessee (tenant) if such modification is going to be to the tenant's disadvantage. The law is based upon three pillars: protection against termination of the lease agreement, rental caps (restrictions with regard to the amount), and the lessor's obligation to maintain the rented property.

Partial exemptions from the Tenancy Act

If the Tenancy Act applies only partially, the following provisions still apply: succession of title in the event of death, duration of the tenancy, and protection against termination of the lease. The provisions concerning restrictions of the rental (amount) and the protection of the rented property itself are not, however, embraced. In these matters the general provisions of the Civil Code (on lease agreements) are applicable and may be modified by agreement between the lessor and the lessee. Constraints defined by the Consumer Protection Act, however, must also be taken into account.

The following are partly exempt from the Tenancy Act:[15]

- Rental properties in buildings that were erected without public grant after 30 June 1953 (the date of the building permit is relevant)
- Rental properties newly created by attic conversion (if the building permit and the lease agreement are dated after 31 December 2001), or through the addition of new stories (if the building permit is dated after 31 December 2001 and the lease agreement is dated after 30 September 2006)
- Unimproved attic space rented on the basis that an apartment or business premises will be created in the attic space or on an additionally erected floor level if the lease agreement was concluded after 31 December 2001. The conversion and fit-out may be partly or fully undertaken by the tenant
- Rental properties newly created by extension after 30 September 2006 (the date of the building permit is relevant)
- Leased condominium units in buildings which were newly erected after 8 May 1945 (the date of the building permit is relevant)

Rental property in a business park qualifies for a special type of partial exemption. A business park is a commercial unit used exclusively for business purposes and not primarily for retail and trade; for example, a shopping center, by definition, is not a business park.

15 See ss 1(4) and (5) MRG

Full exemptions from the Tenancy Act

The following are fully exempted from the provisions of the Tenancy Act:[16]

- Rentals falling within the scope of certain businesses, such as hotels, operators of parking garages and airports, transport companies, freight forwarding agencies, and warehousing businesses
- Apartments or rooms whose lessors are charities or humanitarian organizations if such are intended for assisted, socio-pedagogical living
- Company flats
- Business premises rented for a period not exceeding six months
- Apartments classified as category A or B that are used as a secondary residence as a result of a temporary job-related stay for a period not exceeding six months
- The rent of secondary residences for the purpose of recreation or in connection with leisure activities
- Rented property in a building containing no more than two independent apartments or retail/business units. This exemption applies only to agreements concluded after 31 December 2001 and is one of the most frequent full exemptions in rental practice. For agreements concluded before 31 December 2001, the provisions on partial exemptions from the Tenancy Act are applicable; otherwise, depending on the age of the building and date of the building permit, they are fully subject to the MRG

The general provisions on lease agreements in the Civil Code are applicable and may be modified by agreement between the lessor and the lessee, but only within the limits of the Consumer Protection Act.

Purchase of a rented property

If a rented property is sold, all rents which are fully or partly subject to the MRG remain fully valid.[17] If a rental property is not subject to the MRG, the new owner may terminate all lease agreements of indefinite duration if he/she complies with the statutory notice periods. This is particularly significant when one-family or two-family homes are sold (note: only agreements concluded after 2001 are treated as full exemptions). The only effective protection for tenants is to agree on a definite lease term and a unilateral termination right for the tenant.

16 Also see s 1(2) MRG

17 See s 30(2) para 5 MRG

Fixed-term lease agreements and termination provisions

For tenancies that are fully or partially subject to MRG, each fixed-term agreement must be made in writing and signed by all persons involved in the agreement.[18] The end date must be clearly defined. Unless explicitly agreed in the lease, early termination (prior to the end date) is possible in only a few, specific instances, and is particularly restrictive to the lessor.

Fixed-term leases of apartments must be for a minimum of three years and may be for any other term in excess of this. The tenancy period for business premises may be chosen freely. Fixed-term leases may be renewed as often as desired; however, fixed-term leases for apartments must always be for at least three years. Extensions of leases must be agreed in writing.[19]

A tenant may decide upon the early termination of a fixed-term lease, but not within the first year. In any such instance the tenant must give notice by the end of the respective month and observe a three-month notice period. The notification of termination must be in writing (since 1 October 2006, but no longer through court action); the tenant does not have to state reasons.

Tenants of business premises have no right to early termination.

In the event that the tenant does not leave the rental property at the end of the lease term, the lessor must file an action of eviction with the court within 14 days upon its expiration. If the lessor fails to file the action within this period, the lease shall automatically extend by a further period of three years, regardless of whether it is the first lease or its written renewal. During this period the tenant may terminate the lease at any time by observing the three-month notice period.

The automatic renewal applies to apartments and business premises regardless of the originally agreed fixed term. In the event the lessor again fails to file an action of eviction after the automatic three-year extension has expired, or if no valid extension is agreed in writing, the fixed-term agreement automatically converts to an agreement of indefinite duration.

If a rental property is not subject to the MRG, there are no particular regulations regarding the duration of the lease. An agreement may be concluded for any period of time and the expiration date may be freely chosen. Early termination is possible for cause only (by both the lessor and the lessee). If the tenancy continues beyond the expiration date by tacit agreement, it will automatically extend by one rental period, upon the expiry of which it may be terminated by both parties.

---

18 Also see s 29(1) para 3

19 Also see s 29(4) MRG

Indefinite rental agreements and termination provisions

If the MRG is fully or partially applicable, the lessor may terminate a lease agreement of indefinite duration only for cause (i.e. an important reason). Such reason must be stated in the termination notice and claimed instantly. Termination must be made through a court. An 'important reason' in legal practice is particularly if the tenant has been in arrears with the rental payment by at least eight days, despite having been sent a reminder.

The tenant, in turn, may terminate a rental agreement of indefinite duration at any time in writing, without stating causes; however, the notice period must be adhered to. Termination through court is not required, albeit possible.

If a rented property is not subject to the MRG (for example, a single-family home, agreement dated after 2001), both parties may terminate an indefinite tenancy at any time in compliance with the notice period, without stating cause. Termination through court is not required, albeit possible.

The lessor's maintenance obligation

If a rental property is only partially subject or not subject to the Tenancy Act, the lessor must adhere to strict maintenance obligations pursuant to the Civil Code. These obligations may, however, be changed by agreement between the lessor and the tenant. Unless otherwise agreed, the lessor must hand over the rented property in a usable condition, and such shall be at the lessor's expense; furthermore, the lessor must maintain this usable condition, and may not disturb the agreed tenant's use or enjoyment. If the Tenancy Act[20] is fully applicable, the lessor is obliged to provide maintenance only to the following extent: serious damages, the elimination of significant hazards to health, and the maintenance of the common areas in the building. There is one major exception to this rule: The Amendment to the Right of Residence Act 2015 allocates certain maintenance expenses to the lessor (if the Tenancy Act is fully applicable), such as for gas heaters and other heating devices. There are some aspects of the Consumer Protection Act which partly overlap with the Tenancy Act. Future amendments are expected to clarify the many open questions still under dispute.[21]

20 Also see s 3 MRG

21 Kothbauer, *Erhaltung und Wartung im Mietrecht* (Maintenance and Service under the Tenancy Act) 12 cont'd

Rental including service charge and value-added tax

The rental is composed of the following:

- The rent
- Service charges, public fees, and other special expenditures on a pro-rata basis
- Reasonable remuneration for the lease of furniture or for other services
- VAT

The rental is due by the fifth of each calendar month. Other agreements with the lessor are possible. It is also permissible to agree on a fixed, flat rent.

Reasonable rent (*Angemessener mietzins*)[22]

As mentioned above, the rent is regulated and subject to control, primarily in buildings erected before 1945. The law distinguishes between reasonable rent and the so-called *Richtwertmietzins* which is based on a fixed amount. In contrast to unrestricted rent, a tenant may request ex-post review and reduction of the reasonable rent by an arbitration office or by a court. The criteria applied to determine whether the rent is reasonable are the size, type, condition, location, furnishings, and state of repair of the rental property.

Reasonable rent is applied mostly to:

- The rent of business or retail premises in older buildings
- Rental property created after 8 May 1945 by conversion, extension, or addition (the date of the building permit is relevant, for example, for pre-2001 roof conversions in an older building)
- Rental property in listed historical buildings if the lessor has invested substantial equity in its maintenance after 8 May 1945
- Apartments classified as category A or B exceeding a usable area of 130 m^2

Reasonable rent with fixed basic value (*Richtwertmietzins*)[23]

The *Richtwertmietzins* is a reasonable rent, but with a fixed basic value. It was laid down for a standard apartment and differs per each province. To determine the appropriate rental under the *Richtwertmietzins* system, mark-ups and mark-downs are used. The *Richtwertmietzins* must be applied for the rent of apartments classified as category A, B, or C in buildings erected before 9 May 1945 (i.e. when reasonable or unrestricted rentals are not permitted).

22 Also see s 16(1) MRG
23 Also see s 16(2) MRG

Service charges[24]

Each tenant must pay a share of the total service charges (operating costs) corresponding to the usable floor space of the respective property. This share reflects the ratio between the usable floor space of the rented property and the total usable floor space of all apartments in that building. The calculation of the usable floor space is based on the as-built situation and equals the floor space of a rental property less the space covered by walls. It does not include cellar and attic compartments, staircases, balconies, and terraces. If the usable floor space within a rental property changes because of tenant improvements, such a change will not be taken into account prior to the termination of the lease agreement.

If the lease is fully subject to the Tenancy Act, only the following costs may be charged to the tenant, on a pro rata basis:

- Water supply and waste water costs including maintenance fees
- Costs of the calibration and maintenance of meters and meter readings to determine the tenant's consumption
- Costs of chimney sweeping
- Costs of sewage disposal
- Waste collection
- Costs of pest control
- Lighting of the common areas of the building
- Fire insurance, liability insurance, and insurance covering water damage caused by burst pipes. Insurance covering storm damage and broken glass, but only if the majority of tenants agree
- Property management fees
- Caretaking (external caretaker or resident caretaker pursuant to the 'old' Caretaker Act)

There is an option to allocate certain expenses in accordance with user shares. Service charges are usually charged at a flat rate; however, monthly invoices are possible. In the event of flat rates, tenants are charged equal monthly rates during the current year. The final annual accounting must be finalized by the lessor no later than 30 June of the following year and it must be made available for review by all tenants at a suitable on-site location. Accounting must be clear and possible to be understood by 'average' tenants. It is not required to send accounts to each tenant; however,

24 Also see s 21 MRG

tenants may inspect invoices and request copies at their own expense. The new monthly invoices are calculated on the basis of the preceding annual accounting and may not exceed that amount by more than 10%. If the annual accounting reveals a credit, the surplus must be refunded to tenants before the second next rental due date (for example, if the annual accounting is dated 30 June, repayment must be made by 1 August). Similarly, if the annual accounts reveal a debit, such must be charged within the same period.

References

Bienert and Funk, *Immobilienbewertung Österreich* (Property Valuation in Austria) (Edition ÖVI 2014)

Dirnbacher, *MRG idF des ZVG 2013* (Tenancy Act) (Edition ÖVI 2013)

Dirnbacher, *WEG idF der WRN 2015* (Condominium Ownership Act) (Edition ÖVI 2017)

Gartner and Manz, *Erfolgreicher Immobilienerwerb* (Successful Acquisition of Real Estate) (2009)

Hackl-Miheljak, Kohlmaier, and Holzapfel, *Liegenschaftskauf* (Property Acquisition) (Edition ÖVI 2004)

Kothbauer, *Erhaltung und Wartung im Mietrecht* (Maintenance and Service under the Tenancy Act) (WRN 2015, Edition ÖVI 2015)

Pachler and Uhl, *Grundverkehrsrecht für die Praxis* (Land Transfer Regulations in Legal Practice) (LexisNexis 2011)

About the author

MAG. ANTON HOLZAPFEL has been the CEO of Österreichischer Verband der Immobilienwirtschaft (ÖVI) — the Austrian Real Estate Association, the biggest voluntary organization in the Austrian real estate sector with over 550 company members — since 1997. He is also the CEO of the ÖVI Immobilienakademie Betriebs GmbH, dedicated to the training and education of real estate professionals and the ImmoZert GmbH, a company responsible for the ISO-based certification of real estate valuers. He represents ÖVI at meetings of CEPI, NAR, and TEGoVA, among others, at national and international levels. Mag. Holzapfel is a speaker at the Technische Universität Wien, the University of Vienna, and the Donau University Krems. He has published several books in his fields of expertise.

(Tr: Mag. Ulrike Huttar)

12 Inheritance Law

Dr. Christian Grave, Jakobljevich & Grave

Inheritance law essentially governs the fate of an estate. It is also, however, an individual's right to either partly or completely succeed a decedent to his/her legal position. The law is absolute, meaning that, like property law, with the passing of a decedent it is applicable to all that becomes available for sale and inheritance.

On the fundamental concepts of property law, the following matters apply.

12.1 The estate

The estate comprises the sum of assets and duties of the deceased. In the context of probate proceedings, the estate is identified and ultimately transferred to the heirs.

12.2 Heirs

Heirs are individuals who are entitled to acquisition of the estate. An heir is a legal successor to the deceased, and acquires the estate (or a proportion thereof) through a single act, the so-called transfer, through which he/she acquires all the rights and responsibilities of the deceased. Unlike an heir, some legatees have no claim to the entire estate or proportion thereof, but only to individual assets legally owned by the estate. Forced heirs thus possess an entitlement only for the purposes of the law of obligation.

Austrian inheritance law is founded on the principle of family succession, but to a certain extent it gives the individual testator the freedom (through a testament or inheritance contract) and thus the ability to dispose of his/her property at will. This is, however, restricted by the so-called right to a forced share, which effectively requires an individual to consider his/her next of kin. If he/she fails to do so and there are no grounds for disinheritance, the next of kin, the entitled persons (dependents and spouse or registered partner) will have a monetary claim against the estate or its heirs. If there is no valid will and the deceased did not dispose of the entire estate in his/her last will, or the heirs named by the deceased do not receive the inheritance, succession occurs in a subsidiary manner.

Austrian inheritance law thus recognizes three grounds for claiming inheritance: a will, a contract of inheritance, and the law.

12.3 Legal succession

If the deceased established neither a will nor a contract of inheritance, testamentary arrangement does not apply to the entire estate or is invalid, or the heirs appointed in the last will do not acquire the estate since they have waived their inheritance, are unable to inherit, or are themselves deceased, legal succession comes into effect. In Austria, this takes place in accordance with the so-called parentela system — a classification system of sequential inheritance. Based on this system, inheritance goes to the next relatives on the one hand and to the spouse on the other, while in each case a family or parental couple and their children form a parentela. Within a parentela (also called a line), the degree of kinship is relevant insofar as the next relation of the deceased excludes his/her own descendants.

The first parentela comprises the direct descendants of the deceased, i.e. the children and grandchildren. In the case of several children, the estate is divided by headcount. If a child is not able to claim his/her inheritance (already deceased, etc.), his/her share is not given to the other children, but he/she is instead represented by his/her own children or grandchildren. The share belonging to the child who cannot claim it is thus given to his/her children (descendants). Only if there are no more descendants will the proportion allocated to the other children increase. However, this representation takes place in a downward direction only; an heir who is a father will therefore not be represented by his own father.

The second parentela comprises the parents of the deceased and their descendants, whereby this second line benefits from the inheritance only if no one exists in the first parentela, or they do not receive the inheritance for other reasons. Both parents receive a half each. If a parent is no longer living, he/she is represented by his/her children, who do not necessarily need to be children of the surviving parent.

The third parentela constitutes the two sets of grandparents and their descendants. Each grandparent thus receives a quarter, with deceased grandparents being represented by their children. If a grandparent is no longer alive, the proportion allocated to the associated grandparent will grow. If there is no one remaining (neither a grandparent nor children), then the whole portion is allocated to the other set of grandparents.

Finally, if there is no remaining third parentela, a fourth parentela group benefits, which consists of the (eight) great-grandparents only, but not their descendants. Accordingly, in the fourth line there is no further representation by descendants.

Spouses and registered partners do not belong to a parentela. Their inheritance rights are separately justified and amount to one third of the estate, next to the first line. If there is no surviving member of the first parentela, the spouse or registered partner will receive two thirds, next to the second parentela. Next to grandparents and siblings, the spouse or registered partner will inherit everything; in addition, the proportion in this case grows to that which the descendants of the deceased parents would have received.

The right of representation therefore no longer applies to the descendants of parents after they die. The spouse or registered partner of a decedent who has no children or parents thus receives the entire estate, superseding siblings and grandparents.

If the deceased leaves no legal heirs, his/her registered partner will be subject to extraordinary succession law, provided the deceased and registered partner resided in a shared household for at least three years before the deceased passed away.

The spouse or registered partner must detail in his/her portion of inheritance anything to which he/she is entitled based on the marriage or partnership package or contract of inheritance; otherwise, he/she will receive so-called preference legacy, which consists of items belonging to the household, and the right to continue residing in the marital household or shared household, independently of whether or not he/she was named an heir. This also applies to the companion of the deceased if he/she resided in a shared household with the deceased for at least three years before the deceased passed away and was not married or in a registered partnership at the time of the death. Furthermore, the spouse or registered partner, for as long as he/she does not remarry or enter another registered partnership, holds maintenance rights toward the heirs up to the value of the inheritance with deduction of all assets received by the inheritance.

As discussed above, the legal sequence of the inheritance is disrupted by the testator's freedom principle. This may apply unilaterally through the testamentary disposition (the will) and bilaterally through legal transaction (the contract of inheritance).

12.4 The will

Crafting a valid will to manage succession in ways that deviate from standard succession law by making provisions to individuals or institutions who are not, for example, heirs, requires that the testator has testamentary capacity, which means that he/she does not lack informed consent (due to deceit, force, or error), is over the age of 18, and is of sound mind (at 14 years of age, limited testamentary capacity applies); in these cases, the creation of a will is bound to certain formal criteria. To have drawn up a valid will, it must be:

- Signed by hand, or handwritten
- Signed or written by a third party and include a handwritten amendment by the testator, stating that the document includes a last will. It also requires a record of three present witnesses, as well as their personal information (name, date of birth, address) in addition to a handwritten supplement noting their witness credentials

Other types of wills exist, including:

- An emergency will: In this case, the testament can be certified in verbal or written form, in the presence of two witnesses who are familiar with the content of the will (and attest to it unanimously), if death or a loss of testamentary capacity is imminent. A will of this kind becomes invalid three months after the threat ceases to exist

- A public will: A court or notary orders a verbal declaration or the transfer of a document
- A community will: A will of this kind may be drawn up only by the spouse, registered partner, fiancé, or fiancée, with the condition precedent of marriage, and serves the purpose of naming both registered partners, or several third parties, as heirs. This requires the form of a notarial deed

12.5 The contract of inheritance

Similarly to a will, a contract of inheritance determines the legal succession of a decedent's property among the living. It provides the strongest grounds for the appointment of heirs and therefore supersedes all other inheritances, regardless of the grounds for appointment. Inheritance contracts may be drawn up between only spouses and registered partners (or an engaged couple with marriage as a condition precedent). Through the contract of inheritance, one spouse or registered partner names the other a beneficiary, or this is done mutually. As a mutual contract, the contract of inheritance is irrevocable, but may be mutually terminated. The contract of inheritance notarial recording must be written in the form of a will and is subject to one particular limitation: one quarter of the inheritance must remain — free of debt and forced shares — at the free disposal of the deceased.

12.6 Forced shares

The law pertaining to forced shares limits testamentary freedom in favor of the next of kin. Recipients of a forced share include only the descendants and spouse or registered partner of the deceased. As with intestate succession, the forced share for the spouse or registered partner stands next to the claims to a forced share by the descendants. Parents and lateral relatives, such as uncles, aunts, siblings, etc., are not entitled to forced shares.

For a descendant and the spouse or registered partner, the forced share comprises half of what he/she would have received as a legal heir. If a forced heir is not entitled to his/her share because of a waiver of the forced share or succession, this does not generally lead to an increase in the forced share of other forced heirs. An increase in shares is created only if there is a reduced forced share, or no forced share because of other reasons such as death, debarment from succession, disinheritance, or a reduction of the forced share.

Under certain circumstances, such as if the deceased and individual entitled to a forced share (including the spouse or registered partner) have never maintained a familial relationship or did not do so for a long period before the death, the testator may divide the forced share in half.

The forced share must remain available to the forced heir, meaning that any limitations, conditions, and requirements are unlawful and invalid. The forced share is calculated based on the net inheritance, meaning the inheritance excluding any debt. This includes anything the forced heir receives as a share of the inheritance, legacy, or after succession as a beneficiary of a private foundation created by the deceased, or comparable financial assets. All types of non-monetary contributions to forced heirs, particularly gifts, are to be counted as part of the inheritance and toward the forced share.

Generally, claims to forced shares may not be circumvented if the deceased donates or gifts his/her assets to third parties while alive; the forced heir entitled to the share (only the forced heir, not his/her ancestors) is entitled to an increase in the forced share based on gifts made while the deceased was alive. Gifts made by the deceased more than two years before his/her death to individuals who are not forced heirs are not, however, included (gifts to forced heirs may be included in the share without time constraints) unless the gift was made to charitable causes, or because of moral obligation or decency. Furthermore, the deceased may exclude such gifts from the forced share at last will, or in writing, upon a mutual agreement with the recipient of the gift, but not include the gifts (creating a reduction in the forced share).

12.7 Foreign nationals: succession and international dimensions

For cases in which there is an international dimension to inheritances, for example, if a Swiss citizen dies in Austria, or if assets located in Austria are included in his/her inheritance, at least two questions arise. On the one hand is the question of which material law can be applied to the inheritance, and on the other hand is the question of which nation is responsible for handling the estate or the inheritance proceedings. If the testator died after 16 August 2016, the answer to both questions can be found in the European Succession Regulation as outlined below.

Applicable material law

The entire legal succession upon death is subject to the laws of the nation in which the deceased maintained his/her habitual residence at the time of his/her death, unless the totality of the circumstances shows that the deceased maintained a closer connection with another state; in this case, the laws of the other state apply. The deceased may choose the applicable law of the state in which he/she resides at the time of his/her death, or at the time of choosing the applicable law.

Place of jurisdiction

Since 17 August 2015, the habitual residence is a deciding factor not only in which law is applicable, but also in deciding within which jurisdiction the inheritance proceedings fall. The court in the EU member state of the last habitual place of residence has jurisdiction for all movable and immovable property, independently of the location of the property. In this case too, in the absence of a choice of law the court will apply its own law.

About the author

DR. CHRISTIAN GRAVE is a lawyer and CEO of the law firm Jakobljevich & Grave in Vienna. In a career spanning more than 25 years, he has specialized in family office planning, advising high net worth individuals, private foundation law, inheritance law, and general corporate law. Dr. Grave is the head of numerous private foundations and is on the board of directors of several Austrian companies. He has published many articles and publications on the topics of private foundation law and inheritance law.

13 Foundation Law: The Basic Legal Principles of Private Foundations

Dr. Christian Grave, Jakobljevich & Grave

Austrian law allows the establishment of private foundations, and since funding an Austrian private foundation does not rely upon the founder's citizenship and residence (at least in the context of civil law) this may be of interest to many. Questions of taxation should not, however, be disregarded in the establishment of a private foundation, which must be considered in terms of the dedicated funds and residence of the beneficiaries.

The following paragraphs explain the basic legal principles and internal organization of a foundation.

13.1 Motives for establishing a private foundation

Of course, a range of motives could drive the establishment of a private foundation, and they barely differ from those of other jurisdictions.

The primary reasons for establishing a private foundation include:

- To receive inherited or earned assets, and to protect family assets beyond generational succession from being separated or sold
- To provide for family members and potentially even third parties
- To secure corporate continuity, which could be in question in each corporate succession independently of whether successors are fit or unfit to lead the corporation

- To prevent the separation of business shares resulting from claims of forced shares
- To prevent disputes about rights of co-determination or participation at shareholder and/or management level or because of termination and disposal of business shares
- To connect the founder's name with a scientific, economic, charity-based, or social institution
- For tax-based reasons (although nowadays this is barely possible within a foundation, but can be used, for example, in the context of tax plans for countries outside Austria)

13.2 The legal status of a private foundation

A private foundation is a legal entity to which its founder dedicates assets that are used, managed, and exploited to fulfill a particular, authorized purpose set out by the founder. It is considered a legal person, but does not have property or members. It has beneficiaries, towards whom the fulfillment of its purpose is aimed. A private foundation is, therefore, generally independent of the legal fate of its founder and his/her legal successors. By reason of this independence, a private foundation is definitively distinct from corporate legal persons such as companies or associations. As legal entities, private foundations and corporations are, however, able to own property and can therefore be owners of assets.

According to the provisions of the Austrian Private Foundation Act, governance — because of a lack of membership — is shared by internal governing bodies and the commercial register, which holds a number of rights and responsibilities. Neither the establishment of a private foundation nor its management are, however, subject to control by administrative authorities.

13.3 The purpose of a private foundation

The purpose of a private foundation is an indispensable prerequisite to its establishment, because a private foundation is determined by its purpose, which may be ideational (charitable) and/or economic (self-serving), public and/or private if, and as long as, it does not violate any laws or common decency.

The following activities are, however, prohibited:

- Engaging in commercial activities that exceed subordinate employment
- The acquisition of corporate leadership in a trade company
- Holding a position as a general partner in a registered commercial partnership

A private foundation is therefore not permitted to hold shares in a general partnership,[1] or be complementary to a limited partnership.[2] A private foundation is, however, permitted to be a limited partner[3] in a limited commercial partnership.

Commercial activity is permitted as long as it does not go beyond mere subordinate activity. To date, according to § 1 of the Austrian Private Foundation Act agricultural and forestry businesses are not considered commercial businesses, which makes their operation permissible without restriction, based on current interpretation of the law. Furthermore, private foundations are permitted to participate in commercial trade as a holding foundation or the head of a limited liability company — and, therefore, even material management — provided this does not equate to commercial activity.

In practice, in general terms, the purpose is kept in the foundation's declaration of establishment. Detailed information about the purpose of the foundation and its beneficiaries is usually included in an appendix to the foundation deed or in a declaration of intent.

13.4 Founder/s, co-founder/s, and endowment contributions

Founders may include one or multiple natural or legal persons. A private foundation *causa mortis* may have only one founder.

Multiple founders form a legal community.

If the founder is a corporation, care must be taken — in addition to considering tax-based implications — to ensure that the designation of assets does not result in a reduction of assets of the founding company, which means that the dedication is made for appropriate payment. Otherwise, the issue of hidden profit distribution and/or repayment of contributions may arise. Therefore, profit distribution directly to shareholders is permitted if, at the same time, provisions for ordinary capital reduction are met.

1 *Offene Gesellschaft*
2 *Kommanditgesellschaft*
3 *Kommandist*

The establishment of a private foundation through a trust is also possible but must be disclosed to the tax authorities.

The founder alone holds certain highly personal, non-transferable rights of participation. This law does not, however, cover all rights that authorize influence on a private foundation, only those that authorize influence on the foundation's declaration of establishment. This includes, for example, the right of revocation or modification with respect to the foundation's declaration.

If the founder continues to donate additional funds to the private foundation after it has been established, this is called an endowment contribution.[4] Like a third-party donation,[5] this is a bilateral legal transaction that requires approval from the private foundation.

An additional donation of assets to the private foundation by third parties is considered a third-party donation.[6] The person providing the third-party donation does not, however, receive the founder's status as a result of his/her contribution.

13.5 Endowment of a private foundation

Assets must amount to at least EUR 70,000 and must always be dedicated in cash or in kind contributions (in kind contributions include foreign currency) in the foundation's declaration of establishment. If the minimum assets are not raised in cash, a formation audit is required.

The Austrian Private Foundation Act does not contain a regulation regarding the type of assets to be dedicated. Assets may be movable, immovable, material, immaterial, or aggregated. Only highly personal, non-transferable rights are excluded from dedication to a private foundation. Restrictions also apply insofar as that objects may be dedicated only if they have a positive value and are aligned with the activities for which the private foundation is authorized. Assets must therefore be examined for their suitability for fulfilling the foundation's purpose.

A dedication of liabilities is possible only if these liabilities are a part of aggregated assets and if there are financial assets of at least the same amount as the liabilities.

4 *Nachstiftung*
5 *Zustiftung*
6 *Zustiftung*

13.6 Beneficiaries and ultimate beneficiaries

A beneficiary is a person named as such in the foundation's declaration of establishment. If an individual is not named as a beneficiary in the declaration then the beneficiary is a person who was appointed as such by the founder or the foundation's board of directors. The beneficiary is the person for whom the foundation pursues its purpose. The purpose of a private foundation becomes apparent only through its provision for beneficiaries.

The founder may freely choose beneficiaries if they include only legal subjects. Beneficiaries may, however, include one or multiple natural or legal persons. The founder himself/herself, either individually or with other beneficiaries, may also be a beneficiary. Multiple beneficiaries must, unless otherwise determined by the foundation's declaration of establishment, be treated as equals. Even an undetermined circle of people, such as the general public, may be named as a beneficiary. If the founder wishes to transfer the selection of a beneficiary to a designated entity, this entity must be explicitly named in the foundation's declaration of establishment. The founder may freely select the entity, which could consist of legal or natural persons.

The benefit itself could consist of any type of monetary value, money, or payment in kind. If the founder does not give a definitive provision regarding the benefit to be provided to the beneficiary, the decision on this matter rests with the foundation's board of directors. The latter must then make this decision in the context of the established purpose of the foundation. The payment to the beneficiary is not a gift, because the private foundation is engaged in fulfilling its purpose, which means that payment is not a generous provision. The beneficiary must also, conclusively or explicitly, accept the donation.

For beneficiaries who are named in a foundation's declaration of establishment or the appendix to the foundation deed, beneficiary status begins with the registration of the private foundation in the commercial register, or with the birth of a beneficiary. If a concrete decision is required from an entity for the identification of a beneficiary, then beneficiary status begins when the decision is made by the appointed entity.

Beneficiary status ends with either the death of the beneficiary or renunciation of beneficiary status. Beneficiary status also ends in the case of the dissolution of the private foundation, when the dissolution is entered in the commercial register.

The ultimate beneficiary is the person who is to receive the remaining assets after the conclusion of the private foundation. This person may be named by the founder in the foundation deed or in the appendix to the foundation deed. In this case, the decision may also be made by an entity determined by the founder. Ultimate beneficiaries may be beneficiaries, but do not have to be. Furthermore, the founder may freely decide whether he/she wants to make decisions on the matter, or to leave it undecided. If the founder does not name ultimate beneficiaries, or this person does not take over the assets, and no other provisions can be gleaned from the foundation's declaration of establishment regarding this matter, then assets are transferred to the Austrian Government.

13.7 Establishment of a private foundation

A private foundation is established through a declaration of establishment, which is the basis of a private foundation; a foundation's declaration of establishment may be submitted as a unilateral act *inter vivos*, as well as *causa mortis*. The establishment of a private foundation occurs once it has been entered into the commercial register.

Declaration *inter vivos*

Foundation deed

The Austrian Private Foundation Act includes provisions regarding the minimum content to be included in a foundation's deed (such as the name, headquarters, purpose, etc.). A private foundation may be formed for a limited or an unlimited time. If it is established for a limited time, the endpoint does not necessarily have to be based on a date; termination may depend on other conditions.

Foundations that are established purely for provision and that are not considered charities must be dissolved after 100 years. Lawmakers explain this provision with the notion that, after 100 years, the relationship between the founder and beneficiaries that motivated the establishment of the foundation will cease to exist. In other words: the founder is assumed to care more deeply, for example, for those family members he/she knew during his/her lifetime, than for his/her great-great-grandchildren.

Appendix to the foundation deed[7]

If the foundation deed is missing a reference to the establishment of an appendix for its foundation, a subsequently written appendix is deemed invalid. For this reason, it is recommended that a provision of this kind is included in the initial foundation deed.

Since, in contrast to the foundation deed, the appendix to the foundation deed must not be submitted to the commercial register, the provisions of the foundation deed are often kept quite general. Detailed information on the purpose of the foundation, the beneficiaries, and the dedication of additional assets are then included in the appendix of the foundation deed.

Declaration *causa mortis*

A foundation *causa mortis* is established based on a foundation's declaration of establishment due to a testament. Because they are subject to the provisions of inheritance law, the validity and succession requirements for testamentary declarations of a foundation's establishment must be evaluated in accordance with the Austrian Civil Code, unless *leges specialis* of the Private Foundation Act apply.

Unlike other private foundations, the Private Foundation Act requires that private foundations *causa mortis* may have only one founder. In practice, this provision could be circumvented with provisions made by the individuals in the testament, such as if the person who dies first names the person who dies after as a limited heir and the private foundation as a reversionary heir, then the person who dies later donates to the private foundation by last will.

The foundation's testamentary declaration of establishment requires the form of a notarial deed and, additionally, requires the formal requirements of a last will. It may also consist of a foundation deed and an appendix of the foundation deed. The Private Foundation Act prescribes the minimum contents of a testamentary declaration of a foundation's establishment — as is the case for the declaration of establishment *inter vivos*. As in a testamentary disposition, however, the founder is free to revoke or modify the foundation's declaration of establishment at any time, even if this condition is not contained in the declaration of establishment. It should be noted, however, that the founder's rights are not transferred to his/her successors. Since a private foundation *causa mortis* is not formed until its founder is deceased, the right of revocation of the established foundation does

7 *Stiftungszusatzurkunde*

not apply. There is no obligation of a notarial deed in the case of revocation. This may be completed in the same manner as generally required for the revocation of testamentary dispositions.

Modifications to a foundation's declaration of establishment *causa mortis* are possible only if the right to modification can be transferred to third parties.

To initiate the registration process for a private foundation, a trustee — if one was requested — of the board of directors must be contacted by the probate court. If no board of directors was appointed, or registration of the private foundation cannot be expected in an appropriate timeframe because, for example, the foundation's board of directors remains inactive, the court is required to appoint a trustee *ex officio* or via written request. The trustee is tasked with the establishment of the foundation. It may therefore be necessary for him/her to appoint an initial board of directors or supervisory board for the foundation. He/she is not, however, authorized to remove an already-appointed board of directors or supervisory board and then appoint them anew. The foundation's trustee may initiate these measures only with the appropriate court. The appointment of the foundation's trustee ends upon his/her removal by the court as soon as the private foundation has been established, or if its establishment is impossible.

If the declaration of establishment contains formal or content defects by reason of death, no private foundation may be established, but a testamentary disposition may apply. In this case, attempts must be made to approximate as closely as possible the will of the testator, who is not a founder, through conversion. It is possible, for example, to convert a foundation's 'invalid' declaration of establishment into a condition to establish a foundation after a testator is deceased. This foundation is, however, considered *inter vivos*.

13.8 Formation audits

If the minimum assets are not raised in domestic currency, an audit is required to determine whether the dedicated assets total the minimum assets. This provision mirrors the requirements for formation audits in corporate law.

The law requires a formation audit if the minimum assets are fully or partially raised in in-kind contributions. To avoid a formation audit, minimum assets are generally dedicated in the foundation deed and additional assets, for example, material assets, are dedicated in the appendix of the foundation deed. The Private Foundation Act does not require formation audits for endowment contributions or third-party donations.

The formation audit determines whether the dedicated assets total the minimum asset requirement of EUR 70,000. The audit therefore includes inventory and evaluation. Whether the dedicated assets total the value indicated in the foundation deed is irrelevant provided the minimum assets are met.

13.9 The bodies of a private foundation

The bodies of a private foundation include its board of directors, auditor, and a supervisory board if applicable. Founders may also include additional bodies for the maintenance of its purpose, such as an advisory board.

The foundation's board of directors comprises at least three members. Two members must have their usual place of residence in an EU member state, or the EEA. Members of the foundation's board of directors shall be natural, fully competent individuals. Beneficiaries, their spouses or partners, and anyone related to a beneficiary in a direct line may not serve on the board of directors, nor may any relatives up to the third degree or legal persons. Individuals who were contracted by the beneficiaries, their relatives, or other excluded persons to pursue their interests are excluded from serving on the foundation's board of directors.

If the beneficiary is a legal person, he/she must be deemed the equivalent of those individuals who control the company in accordance with § 244 para 2 of the AktG. Furthermore, holding member status on the foundation's board of directors cannot be reconciled with membership of the supervisory board or appointment as a foundation auditor.

The initial foundation's board of directors is established by either the founder or, in the case of a foundation *causa mortis*, by the trustee if necessary. This provision is obligatory and may not be changed. Provisions on the appointment of additional members to the foundation's board of directors, dismissal, power of representation, and the mandate period can be included in the declaration of establishment. The authority to appoint or dismiss members to or from the foundation's board of directors may be transferred to beneficiaries in such a way that they are only granted either no authorization to dismiss, or limited authorization, for important reasons. Beneficiaries would otherwise be granted significant influence on one of the foundation's governing bodies, which would violate incompatibility rules. The supervisory board may also be granted authorization to appoint and dismiss members to or from the foundation's board of directors.

If there are no provisions regarding the appointment, dismissal, or mandate period of the foundation's board of directors in the declaration of establishment, it will then remain appointed until a reason exists according to § 27 Private Foundation Law. The court shall dismiss a member of the board of directors upon request, or *ex officio* in the event of a gross breach of duty, inability to properly complete the tasks, insolvency proceedings opening regarding the member's assets, a rejection of insolvency proceedings of this kind as a result of insufficient assets to cover the costs, or multiple failed attempts to enforce his/her assets.

The board of directors manages and represents the foundation externally and ensures that the purpose of the foundation is met. In this context, it is necessary to adhere to the provisions of the declaration of establishment. Each member of the board of directors must efficiently complete his/her tasks with the thoroughness of a diligent business manager. The board of directors is liable for any negligence. The board of directors may provide payments to beneficiaries only to meet the foundation's purposes, and only if this does not reduce the claims of creditors made to the private foundation. This does not constitute a provision to protect creditors, which is why the board of directors may not be bound by instructions. The board of directors has the binding authority to determine the amount to be disbursed, considering all the private foundation's incoming accounts payable.

If no other provisions are contained in the declaration of establishment, members of the board of directors shall receive payment for their activities appropriate to their tasks and the status of the private foundation. Unless otherwise determined in the declaration of establishment, the remuneration amount shall be set by the court upon request by the foundation body or governing body member. The consequence of this is that the court always takes part in the determination if the declaration of establishment does not contain a provision on remuneration.

The auditor is also a mandatory appointment. The primary tasks of the auditor are the end-of-year audit and the audit of accounting. Because the status report must discuss fulfillment of the foundation's purpose, this component must be included in the audit of the status report. Thus, the auditor must check if the declaration of establishment was followed with respect to the purpose of the foundation, whether the status report is in accordance with the fulfillment of the foundation's purpose, and that the status report does not create a false appearance for the status of the private foundation. The audit report must be completed in writing, submitted to the other governing entities, and include an audit opinion.

Only a certified public accountant and tax consultant, public accounting and tax consultancy firm, certified auditor and tax consultant, or auditing and tax consultancy firm can be appointed as an auditor. Excluded from appointment are beneficiaries, their spouses, anyone who is related to the beneficiary in a direct line, all relatives up to the third degree, members of other foundation bodies, and employees of the private foundation or corporations controlled by it. Furthermore, an auditor may not work with or be related to an excluded person.

The auditor is appointed by the court or by the supervisory board if one exists, regardless of whether its existence is mandatory or optional. No other entity may be tasked with the appointment of the auditor. In the case of a lack of other provisions in the declaration of establishment, the auditor's mandate period is unlimited.

The auditor is entitled to reimbursement of his/her necessary cash expenses and to appropriate remuneration for his/her activities in accordance with the fee structure. This obligatory provision may not be modified by the declaration of establishment.

The appointment of a supervisory board is mandatory if:

- The total number of foundation employees exceeds 300
- The foundation uniformly manages domestic corporations or associations and the total number of employees of these corporations or associations exceeds 300
- It controls more than 50% of those who are due an immediate share, the total number of employees of these corporations or associations exceeds 300, and — in the two latter cases — the foundation's activity is not limited to the management of the company's shares in the managed corporations

By law, the supervisory board has obligatory tasks that include monitoring the management and conduct of the foundation and representing the foundation in legal transactions with the members of the board of directors, etc. The central goal of the supervisory board's activity is ensuring that all activities are aligned with the purpose of the foundation. A legal audit is therefore conducted in addition to audits of its purpose and economic viability. If the supervisory board finds flaws within the context of its monitoring activities, the flaws must be reported to the board of directors, which could potentially request a special audit. The supervisory board may at any time request information regarding the private foundation's affairs, as well as its relationship with a large corporation. Particular transactions such as the purchase and sale of shares of corporations or companies, taking out bonds, or credit exceeding a certain amount also require the approval of the board of directors. The declaration of establishment may expand the supervisory board's areas of responsibility.

The supervisory board must consist of at least three natural persons. A member of the supervisory board and his/her relatives may not simultaneously hold a position on the board of directors or as an auditor. Beneficiaries or their relatives must not represent the majority of supervisory board members. Furthermore, individuals who are already members of the supervisory board or a comparable body of 10 other private foundations are also excluded from membership, as are individuals who were commissioned by beneficiaries or their relatives to pursue their interests on the supervisory board.

Provided the appointment of a supervisory board is mandatory, the declaration of establishment may include a provision that a mandatory supervisory board must be appointed. Once this is established, it also takes on the minimum responsibilities prescribed by the Private Foundation Act; these responsibilities are not to be eliminated in the case of an optional appointment. The expansion of its scope of responsibilities is possible if the legally required distribution of responsibilities is not violated. Both the mandatory and optional supervisory board have the right of employee participation if more than an average of 300 employees are employed in the private foundation or in a corporation controlled by the private foundation. The founder or trustee appoints the initial supervisory board for private foundations that are required to establish a supervisory board from the beginning, or if the formation of a supervisory board is set forth by a declaration of establishment. This competency is not transferable to other governing bodies. Any subsequent supervisory board must be court-appointed. This competency is also mandatory. However, third parties may be granted the right to nominate candidates, or to suggest provisions, such as candidates' required qualifications or appointment periods. If the declaration of establishment does not include a provision on the appointment period, the supervisory board must be appointed for an unlimited timeframe.

A founder may include additional governing bodies (such as an advisory board) in the declaration of establishment, and the Private Foundation Act leaves it to the founder to outline the details of this provision. In view of the absence of any provisions on the appointment, composition, internal organization, and responsibilities of the additional governing bodies, founders prefer them to supervisory boards.

Governing bodies such as the advisory board or, for example, an assembly of beneficiaries usually comprise a founder and individuals designated as beneficiaries. The Private Foundation Act does not include any provisions on the scope of responsibilities of such governing bodies. The onus is therefore on the founder to specify responsibilities. From experience it can be noted that there is an intent to prevent the factual separation of assets from the founder and his/her family. A number of rulings have nevertheless reflected that an advisory board comprising mostly beneficiaries, which holds the authority to both appoint and dismiss the foundation's board members and to exert significant influence on the management of the board of directors, is not permissible.

In some cases, these governing bodies have the right to counsel and information, but they are usually able to exert significantly more influence because they are granted the right of instruction, veto rights, the right of approval, or other rights of influence on a larger scale in the declaration of establishment and/or purpose of the foundation.

Limits to the determination of responsibilities for these governing bodies are provided if they are granted the authority of governing bodies reserved for the board of directors.

13.10 Modification and revocation of a declaration of establishment

Before a foundation is formed, the founder may modify or revoke the declaration of establishment at any time. If one of several founders steps down and the declaration of establishment does not explicitly state otherwise, the declaration of establishment may not be revoked and may be modified only if the foundation's purposes remains intact. If the only, or last, founder steps down, the board of directors may make modifications only by preserving the foundation's purpose and with consideration of previously arisen grounds for refusal and modified circumstances.

Once a foundation is established, the founder, or in the case of multiple founders, the founders, or those who are granted this right, may only change the declaration of establishment if they have reserved the right to do so in the declaration of establishment. If the only, or last, founder has stepped down, multiple founders are unable to reach an agreement, or the right to modification is not reserved, the board of directors may make modifications by maintaining the foundation's purpose and with consideration of previously arisen grounds for refusal and modified circumstances.

A founder may revoke a foundation after its establishment if he/she reserved the right of revocation. A subsequent inclusion of a revocation provision into a declaration of establishment that was approved when a private foundation was established is not permitted. Only a founder may exercise the right to revoke a private foundation. It is a strictly personal right that is non-transferable. Only the person who acted as founder upon the establishment of a private foundation may be considered the founder. The revocation of the declaration of establishment is possible at any time before a private foundation is formed.

If a foundation has multiple founders, the right of revocation may be reserved for one founder or individual founders. The right of revocation may be reserved for natural persons only; if the founder is a legal person, this person is excluded from the right of revocation. This provision's aim is to ensure that revocation is not possible without temporal restrictions. This is achieved by not transferring the right of influence to the founder's legal successors. For founders who are legal persons, a time limit would not apply. Further, the existence of a private foundation should not depend on the, at times, rapidly changing decision-makers of a legal person.

In this context, it should also be noted that a recent decision by the Austrian Supreme Court has determined that with the founder's reserved rights to modify a foundation deed and to revoke a foundation, the founder's assets do not become independent of the founder. If the founder is authorized to modify the declaration of establishment without restriction and to revoke the declaration of establishment, this right is subject to enforcement in accordance with §§ 331 et seq. of the Enforcement Code[8] if the founder is the ultimate beneficiary in the case of revocation.

13.11 Dissolution of a private foundation

The Private Foundation Act contains a tax-based list of reasons for dissolution. Based on this list, a private foundation must be dissolved for the following reasons:

Formal reasons for dissolution

1. Conclusion of the period outlined in the declaration of establishment
2. Opening of insolvency proceedings for the assets of the private foundation
3. A legal decision, as a result of which the opening of insolvency proceedings is expected to be rejected because of a lack of funds to cover insolvency proceedings regarding the assets
4. A unanimous decision made by the board of directors to dissolve the private foundation
5. A court-ordered dissolution:
   a) The court is required to dissolve the private foundation per request if the board of directors does not meet its obligation to do so
   b) The court is also required to dissolve the private foundation if:
      i) It is engaged in commercial activity exceeding a mere subordinated activity
      ii) It takes on the operational management of a trade company
      iii) It is a general partner in a registered partnership and did not meet the terms of a prohibitive injunction in a timely manner

8 *Exekutionsordnung*

Material reasons for dissolution

- Exercise of the right to revocation by the founder/s
- Attainment or unattainability of the foundation's purpose
- 100 years having passed since the date of registration in the case of a for-profit private foundation whose primary purpose is provision for natural persons
- Existence of other reasons outlined in the declaration of establishment

To protect creditors — except in the case of dissolution caused by the initiation of insolvency proceedings — liquidation proceedings must be implemented after the dissolution of a private foundation.

If there is no ultimate beneficiary, or if the beneficiary is not willing to receive the assets, and no other provision is made in the declaration of establishment, remaining assets are disbursed to the Republic of Austria. If a private foundation is dissolved as a result of revocation, and there is no other provision in the declaration of establishment, the founder will be the ultimate beneficiary. Unless otherwise prescribed by the declaration of establishment, multiple ultimate beneficiaries share equal parts of the assets.

About the author

DR. CHRISTIAN GRAVE is a lawyer and CEO of the law firm Jakobljevich & Grave in Vienna. In a career spanning more than 25 years, he has specialized in family office planning, advising high net worth individuals, private foundation law, inheritance law, and general corporate law. Dr. Grave is the head of numerous private foundations and is on the board of directors of several Austrian companies. He has published many articles and publications on the topics of private foundation law and inheritance law.

14 Taxation of Austrian Private Foundations

Mag. Gerald Huber, BDO Salzburg GmbH

Regulations concerning private foundations were first established in Austria in 1993 through the Private Foundation Act.[1] Since then, the regulations regarding the taxation of private foundations have been tightened multiple times. As such, private foundations are generally no longer used as a fiscal instrument.

Apart from the tax-free distribution of dividends from domestic and foreign subsidiary corporations to the foundation (whereby private foundations are equated with corporations), the last tax advantage that private foundations provide in Austria is the possibility for profiting from the disposal of shareholdings (particularly stocks and investments in limited liability companies) in which the foundation has held a 1% or more stake over the preceding five years, to be exempted from the 25% interim tax when the investments are transferred within 12 months[2] to another shareholding with a minimum 10% stake.

Another advantage of private foundations is their shielding effect in certain circumstances against foreign inheritance tax. For example, foreign inheritance tax can be avoided if a testator who is domiciled in Austria transfers his/her assets to an Austrian private foundation.

1 *Privatstiftungsgesetz*
2 Prof. Bruckner, PERSALDO 2/2011 30

In summary, it should be noted that fiscal aspects play only a minor role in the establishment of private foundations. Possible reasons for establishing private foundations include:

- Succession solutions for companies
- Protection of assets from outside influence
- Protection against the division of assets upon transfer to heirs; private foundations represent stable and long-term shareholders (inheritance can remain undivided and unchanged)
- The shielding effect against foreign inheritance tax

On an international level, and in German-speaking countries in particular, the Austrian private foundation is still an attractive instrument for these purposes. Alternatives either do not exist or are very difficult to find in German-speaking countries.

In Austria, efforts are now being made to make private foundations more attractive. To do this, the Private Foundation Act should be amended. A draft bill is currently available, but if and how it will be implemented remains to be seen.

14.1 Taxation of Austrian private foundations

The following statements address self-serving private foundations, as defined in the Private Foundation Act, and their beneficiaries, who are assumed to have tax liability in Austria.

Taxation of the Austrian private foundation occurs on three levels: the first level is taxation of the transfer of assets to private foundations, the second level is the taxation of the income of private foundations, and the third level deals with the taxation of distributions to beneficiaries.

Taxation of the transfer of assets to private foundations

This procedure is subject to the Austrian Foundation Entrance Tax Act,[3] which applies to gratuitous contributions made after 31 July 2008. The Foundation Entrance Tax Act applies to all gratuitous contributions to Austrian private foundations, as well as to foreign establishments that are comparable to a private foundation. As such, a person domiciled in Austria may be subject to the foundation entrance tax if he/she donates assets to a comparable foreign establishment.

3 *Stiftungseingangssteuergesetz*

The Foundation Entrance Tax Act is therefore applicable to gratuitous contributions not only within Austria. In this regard it is not important who made the contribution since contributions subject to taxation may be made by the founder or any outside party.[4]

The contribution must be gratuitous. An exchange of services does not count as gratuitous. Therefore, if the consideration does not correspond to the value of the service pursuant to the Foundation Entrance Tax Act, it could be classified as a tax-liable gratuitous contribution.[5]

In general, the foundation entrance tax amounts to 2.5%. However, the tax could increase to 25% (referred to as penalty taxation) in certain circumstances, such as:

- Lack of comparability with the Austrian private foundation structure
- Lack of disclosure of the required foundation documentation (foundation deed, declaration of foundation, etc.)
- No obligation to specify the beneficiaries
- No entry into the Austrian Commercial Register and/or any comparable foreign public register
- For foreign private foundations, no agreement on comprehensive administrative aid assistance between Austria and the foreign government

Donations of Austrian land are no longer subject to the Foundation Entrance Tax Act. As a compensation for this exclusion, a higher land transfer tax rate of up to 6% was introduced. The property value serves as the basis for assessment.

Gratuitous donations of foreign land are not subject to taxation in Austria.

In certain cases, it is possible to make tax-free contributions. In particular, this relates to those given to legal entities pursuing not-for-profit, religious, or charitable purposes or endowments *causa mortis* (those made at the time of death of the founder) for assets in the form of money deposits with credit institutions and debt securities that are subject to final taxation, provided that a public placement is made. Exceptions to this exemption from the foundation entrance tax are endowments *causa mortis* of the shares of domestic and foreign corporations.

In principle, the foundation entrance tax is calculated based on the asset value minus any liabilities and other encumbrances related thereto.

4 Burgstaller and Huemer in Cerha, Haunold, Huemer, Schuch, and Wiedermann, *Stiftungsbesteuerung* (Foundation Taxation) 33

5 Burgstaller and Huemer in Cerha, Haunold, Huemer, Schuch, and Wiedermann, *Stiftungsbesteuerung* (Foundation Taxation) 33

Taxation of the income of private foundations

Taxation of a private foundation's income is based on the legal principles that apply to the taxation of private individuals (natural persons).[6] This is so because the private foundation, with respect to the assets acquired on a gratuitous basis, is a conceptual extension of the founder as a natural person. In this regard private foundations may not conduct any direct commercial activities as defined in the Austrian Income Tax Act.[7]

Private foundations may receive income from agricultural and forestry activities, rental and leasing activities, capital assets, and 'other income' as defined in the Income Tax Act.

Even though certain favorable tax benefits no longer exist as a result of the tightened foundation regulations, the private foundation is in principle no worse off than a natural person when it comes to the taxation of income.

Insofar as income under the Income Tax Act would be taxable in the case of natural persons, private foundations are subject to the corporate income tax of 25%[8] (such as income from rental and leasing activities). Income from capital assets, however, is excluded from this to ensure that private foundations are no worse off than private individuals.

Taxation of income from capital assets

In 2000, the interim corporate income tax[9] on income from capital assets was introduced. With the introduction of this interim tax the legislature wanted to reduce or eliminate the tax-saving advantages of the reinvestment of liquid assets. Until the introduction of the interim corporate income tax certain types of income, such as interest income from bank deposits, were not subject to taxation if owned by private foundations. Since the introduction of the interim corporate income tax these sources of income have indeed been taxed, but to avoid double taxation the interim corporate income tax is credited against the withholding tax in the event of distributions to the beneficiaries so that the total tax burden remains at 27.5%.

With the 2011 Austrian Budget Supplementary Act[10] the interim corporate income tax was raised from 12.5% to 25%.

6 Cerha in Cerha, Haunold, Huemer, Schuch, and Wiedermann, *Stiftungsbesteuerung* (Foundation Taxation) 16

7 *Einkommensteuergesetz*

8 Cerha in Cerha, Haunold, Huemer, Schuch, and Wiedermann, *Stiftungsbesteuerung* (Foundation Taxation) 16

9 *Zwischenkörperschaftsteuer*

10 *Budgetbegleitgesetz*

The new taxation regulations for capital assets that were introduced with the 2011 Budget Supplementary Act also apply on a proportional basis to the private foundation's income, subject to interim taxation. This means that the following is subject to interim taxation:

- Income from the transfer of capital (interest income and other revenue from capital claims)
- Income from realized increases in value (capital appreciation)
- Income from derivatives as defined by the Income Tax Act
- Income from the sale of land

As previously mentioned in the introduction, dividends from domestic and foreign subsidiary corporations can continue to be distributed on a tax-exempt basis. The option to transfer hidden reserves in the disposal of material shareholdings also applies.

Taxation of distributions from private foundations

Distributions from private foundations fall under the Income Tax Act.[11] Accordingly, distributions from private foundations are considered income from capital assets, which are to be taxed at the special tax rate of 27.5% pursuant to the Income Tax Act.[12]

Distributions from private foundations are generally understood as gratuitous transfers of assets from the private foundation to beneficiaries or ultimate beneficiaries.[13]

Distributions to beneficiaries can have any type of monetary performance, i.e. cash benefits, compensation in kind, and use advantages.[14] As an example, the private use of any foundation assets by the founder and/or the beneficiary must be considered 'benefits in kind', which is subject to taxation. Advantages which private foundations give to the transferor through the assumption of expenses are also subject to taxation applicable to donations.[15]

Distributions can be either disclosed or undisclosed.[16]

11 S 27 para 5 No 7

12 S 27a para 1

13 Wiedermann and Migglautsch in Cerha, Haunold, Huemer, Schuch, and Wiedermann, *Stiftungsbesteuerung* (Foundation Taxation) 110

14 Arnold in Arnold, Stangl, and Tanzer, *Privatstiftungssteuerrecht* (Private Foundation Taxation Law), marginal No II/452

15 Wiedermann and Migglautsch in Cerha, Haunold, Huemer, Schuch, and Wiedermann, *Stiftungsbesteuerung* (Foundation Taxation) 110

16 *Offener* or *verdeckter*

Evidence accounts for tax purposes — tax-exempt repayment of assets

The purpose of the tax-exempt repayment of profits or assets (so-called *steuerneutrale Substanzauszahlung* in Austrian law) is to allow the founding capital/assets to be transferred tax-free to the beneficiaries.

In principle, tax-exempt repayment of assets is possible only for transfers of assets to foundations which took place after 31 July 2008.

Repayment of income and the capital from all assets donated to private foundations prior to 31 July 2008 are still subject to the capital gains tax of 27.5% of the fair market value[17] (referred to as the mousetrap effect).

A tax-exempt repayment of assets is only possible insofar as it is covered by a regularly and duly maintained evidence account for tax purposes.[18] The evidence account is increased by the value of the assets at the time of their donation[19] and reduced by the amount of the assets repaid.

The value of the assets is generally assessed as the founder's cost of acquisition, however, not the fair market value at the time of contribution. According to explicit regulations in the Income Tax Act, the following income tax values are to be taken into account as the value of the assets at the time of their donation:[20]

- The founder's cost of acquisition resulting from shareholdings in the founder's private assets that fulfill the criteria of s 31 of the previous Income Tax Act version (donations until 31 March 2012) and/or capital assets in general that are owned by the founder and that are subject to capital gains taxation pursuant to s 27 para 3 of the Income Tax Act[21]
- Carrying over of the book value for commercial establishments, operating units, and joint ventures
- All costs which were or which would have been taken as a basis for determining income

A tax-exempt repayment of assets cannot, however, be made at will. This is possible only if the contribution is higher than the decisive value (*maßgeblicher Wert*). The decisive value is understood to mean the balance sheet profit plus the earnings reserves and the hidden reserves of the foundation's assets. This means that a

17 Wiedermann and Migglautsch in Cerha, Haunold, Huemer, Schuch, and Wiedermann, *Stiftungsbesteuerung* (Foundation Taxation) 117

18 *Steuerliches Evidenzkonto*

19 *Ertragsteuerlichen Stiftungseingangswerte*

20 Wiedermann and Migglautsch in Cerha, Haunold, Huemer, Schuch, and Wiedermann, *Stiftungsbesteuerung* (Foundation Taxation) 118

21 BDO kompakt & konkret, *Erben — Schenken — Stiften* (Succession — Donation — Foundation) 54

tax-exempt repayment of assets is not possible as long as a balance sheet profit or earning reserves as defined by the Austrian Commercial Code[22] exists at the beginning of the fiscal year.[23]

Revocation or dissolution of private foundations

Should a founder be the ultimate beneficiary if a private foundation is revoked, the income from the relevant donation must be reduced, at the founder's request, by the decisive values relevant for tax purposes. This applies in particular to assets that were transferred to private foundations prior to 1 August 2008. For assets donated after 31 July 2008, the values result from those recorded at the time of their donation in the evidence account.

This reduction clause applies accordingly to the revocation of a foreign foundation or other establishment that is comparable to a private foundation provided that the values determined according to Austrian tax law are to be applied, and that the foundation entrance tax or inheritance/gift tax for the donation to the foreign foundation or establishment was paid.

Considering that the legislature has introduced stricter regulations, and considering judgements rendered in this regard since their introduction in 1993, the structure of Austrian private foundations provides few advantages. Private foundations can still be considered an attractive tool for 'asset protection' purposes nevertheless, even when compared with alternative structures existing in other countries (establishments in Liechtenstein, trusts, etc.).

It remains to be seen whether the draft amendments to the Private Foundation Act will be adopted. These planned changes would increase the attractiveness of private foundations.

22 *Unternehmensgesetzbuch*

23 Wiedermann and Migglautsch in Cerha, Haunold, Huemer, Schuch, and Wiedermann, *Stiftungsbesteuerung* (Foundation Taxation) 120

References

Arnold, Stangl, and Tanzer, *Privatstiftungs-Steuerrecht* (Private Foundation Taxation Law) (2009)

BDO kompakt & konkret, *Erben — Schenken — Stiften* (Succession — Donation — Foundation), (2nd edn)

Bruckner, PERSALDO 2/2011

Burgstaller and Huemer in Cerha, Haunold, Huemer, Schuch, and Wiedermann, *Stiftungsbesteuerung* (Foundation Taxation) (2011)

Cerha in Cerha, Haunold, Huemer, Schuch, and Wiedermann, *Stiftungsbesteuerung* (Foundation Taxation) (2011)

Wiedermann and Migglautsch in Cerha, Haunold, Huemer, Schuch, and Wiedermann, *Stiftungsbesteuerung* (Foundation Taxation) (2011)

About the author

MAG. GERALD HUBER, auditor and tax advisor, is a partner and the CEO of BDO Salzburg GmbH, an Audit and Tax Advisory firm. Mag. Huber advises national and international companies and foundations and high net worth individuals, athletes, and artists on relocation topics.

15 Banking Secrecy in Austria

Dr. Helmut Hegen & Mag. Eva-Maria Niederreiter,
HOSP, HEGEN Rechtsanwaltspartnerschaft

It will be useful for those intending to relocate to Austria to familiarize themselves with the information regarding banking secrecy that is presented in this chapter.

15.1 General information

Austrian banking secrecy is legally defined in s 38 para 1 of the Austrian Banking Act, which reads as follows (not an official translation):

> "Credit institutions, their shareholders, board members, employees and other persons acting for credit institutions must not disclose or utilize secrets entrusted to or made accessible to them exclusively on the basis of business relations with customers or on the basis of section 75 paragraph 3 (banking secrecy)."

Banking

In Austria, banking secrecy is a specially protected regulation and is privileged *vis-à-vis* 'ordinary' laws. In general, Austrian Acts can be amended by an ordinary resolution of the National Assembly (parliament). In contrast, pursuant to s 38 para 5 of the Austrian Banking Act, regulations concerning banking secrecy[1] can be amended only by a two-thirds majority and only with the attendance of at least half the members of the National Assembly. Section 38 para 5 of the Austrian Banking Act

1 S 38 paras 1–4 of the Austrian Banking Act

itself is arranged as a constitutional provision that can also be amended only under the above-mentioned conditions. In fact, the provision regarding banking secrecy as a whole[2] enjoys the same protection as other constitutional provisions in Austria.

Affected persons

Banking secrecy is aimed at two categories of persons: on the one hand, persons who are bound to banking secrecy (persons bound to banking secrecy); on the other hand, persons who are protected by banking secrecy (persons protected by banking secrecy).

Persons bound to banking secrecy

A large and extensive group of persons is bound to banking secrecy.

First, credit institutions themselves are included in this category. Credit institutions are defined as legal entities and corporations entitled to conduct banking business under the Austrian Banking Act. Bodies (management, supervisory boards, etc.), shareholders, and employees of credit institutions as well as other persons acting or working for credit institutions are also bound to banking secrecy. In this regard it is irrelevant what kind of activity an employee is conducting for a credit institution, which means that even maintenance staff, trainees, or interns of credit institutions are bound to banking secrecy.

Other persons acting for credit institutions are defined as persons who are not directly integrated into the business of a credit institution, but who are consulted by a credit institution for certain activities, for example, attorneys, tax consultants, and other occupational groups, such as IT supervisors. If facts that are subject to banking secrecy become known to these persons on the basis of their relation to a credit institution, they must also observe the secrecy of those facts pursuant to s 38 of the Austrian Banking Act.

Persons protected by banking secrecy

All customers of a credit institution benefit from banking secrecy. The term 'customer' is interpreted widely and includes any person related to a credit institution on the basis of a banking transaction.

Object, scope, and duration of banking secrecy

Austrian banking secrecy prohibits the disclosure or utilization of secrets that are entrusted to or made available to persons bound to banking secrecy on the basis of business relationships with customers.

2 S 38 of the Austrian Banking Act

Definition of 'secrets'

'Secrets' in terms of the Austrian Banking Act are defined as facts that are usually known only to customers themselves, or customers themselves as well as relatively small groups of persons, and that the customer intends to keep secret. When in doubt, it must be assumed that a fact is to be kept secret unless the customer declares otherwise.

Among others, the following facts are included by the definition of secrets: the identity of customers (name, address, date of birth, civil status, origin, etc.), occupation, financial circumstances, place of residence, payment history, relationships with other persons, education, etc.

Scope of banking secrecy

Banking secrecy prohibits the disclosure as well as the utilization of secrets.

Disclosure is defined as the transfer of facts not only to outstanding third parties but also to internal transfer within a credit institution. Within the scope of banking secrecy, customers are also entitled to claim that their secrets shall be disclosed only to those persons within the credit institution who are consulted specifically for the banking transactions of said customers. This means that customers are entitled to claim that their matters are treated as confidential even among the persons acting or working for credit institutions (who are all bound to banking secrecy themselves; so-called internal banking secrecy).

Utilization is defined as any behavior that leads to the commercial exploitation of secrets. This can occur, for example, if an employee of a credit institution discloses to a third party that a customer's property could be purchased at an attractive price because the customer is in financial distress and in urgent need of money. Passing on the customer's identity would be defined as disclosure, whereas passing on information regarding the customer's financial distress could lead to an economic benefit for the third party and would thus be defined as utilization. It is irrelevant whether the person bound to banking secrecy or the third party benefits from the utilization. A person bound to banking secrecy who is aware of the financial circumstances of customers must therefore not exploit a customer's financial distress, whether to his/her own benefit or to the benefit of a third party.

Duration of banking secrecy

The obligation to maintain banking secrecy does not result only from the conclusion of a banking transaction; even secrets that have become known in the course of contract initiation are protected by Austrian banking secrecy, even if initial consultations ultimately do not lead to a business relationship.

The obligation to maintain banking secrecy does not end because of the passage of time or because of the customer's death. Protection through banking secrecy is valid for an unlimited period and devolves to the heirs after a customer's death. Pursuant to s 38 para 2 of the Austrian Banking Act, exemptions from the obligation to maintain banking secrecy in the case of a customer's death exist only *vis-à-vis* the Probate Court and the Judicial Commissioner.

Sanctions in the case of breaches

Pursuant to s 101 of the Austrian Banking Act, persons deliberately breaching their obligation to maintain banking secrecy for the purpose of enriching themselves or a third party or for the purpose of causing damage to someone else can be charged with imprisonment of up to a year or a fine of up to 360 daily rates.

Furthermore, breaches of banking secrecy can lead to supervisory consequences as well as consequences under civil law.

15.2 Limits of banking secrecy

Naturally, protection of customers through banking secrecy is subject to certain limitations. The most important instances of limitation are set forth in s 38 para 2 of the Austrian Banking Act.

Exemptions from banking secrecy due to legal transactions

The release of the credit institution from its obligation to maintain banking secrecy by the customer is the only way of exemption from banking secrecy through legal transactions. For the sake of the customer's protection, special requirements for such a release are set forth in s 38 para 2 No. 5 of the Austrian Banking Act.

It is required by law that the customer's statement of release must be given expressively in written form. 'Expressively' means that it must not be concluded solely from the behavior of a customer that the customer (probably) wants to release the credit institution from its obligation. On the contrary, the customer's instruction must be unmistakable and clear.

According to the statutory requirement of the written form, the release must be enclosed either in a document that is personally signed by the customer or in an electronic document that has been provided with a distinctive electronic signature.

This provision intends to protect customers against rushed or inconsiderate abandonments of their protection by banking secrecy.

The Austrian Supreme Court ruled that a release from the obligation to maintain banking secrecy in the general terms and conditions[3] of a credit institution cannot be effective. In the view of the Supreme Court, such a type of release lacks explicitness and written form.

Exemptions from banking secrecy by law

Central bank account register

The introduction of the central bank account register in Austria has led to a limitation of banking secrecy. The central bank account register is a database that contains all current accounts, savings accounts, savings books, and stock deposits in Austria. The register shows the account master data, in particular the account number, the name, date of birth, and address of the account holder, information about potential authorized persons as well as the dates that the account was opened and closed. Account balances and account activities are not included in the register (see below). Credit institutions are obligated to update data continually.

The following authorities can gather information through electronic inspection of the central bank account register:

1. The Public Prosecutor's office and criminal courts for criminal investigations and prosecutions
2. Financial criminal authorities and the Federal Fiscal Court[4] for financial criminal investigations and prosecutions
3. Federal tax authorities and the Federal Fiscal Court for tax purposes if this is expedient and appropriate in the interest of the collection of revenues

The provision regarding the authorized authorities is constitutional and can therefore be amended only by a two-thirds majority and in the attendance of at least half of the members of the National Assembly (parliament).

3 AGB
4 *Bundesfinanzgericht*

Persons affected are entitled to be informed about the concrete data concerning themselves that is included in the register, for example, via the online system *FinanzOnline* (Finance Online).

During proceedings concerning the assessment of income tax, corporate income tax, and VAT, the gathering of information is permitted only in a case in which a tax authority has concerns regarding the accuracy of the assessment, initiates preliminary proceedings against a taxable person, and grants that person the opportunity to make a statement beforehand.

Every access made to the central bank account register is recorded. The recording reports must be stored for 10 years. Taxable persons are informed of every access made to their bank account data via *FinanzOnline*.

Preliminary proceedings

Under certain conditions, bank accounts can be 'opened' in the course of preliminary proceedings that have been initiated by Austrian authorities on the basis of suspected criminal offences or financial crimes. Through opening a bank account, information regarding account balances and account movements can be gathered. This investigation measure is permitted as soon as a bank customer is under investigation. This means that the opening of a bank account is allowed only if an authority has an initial suspicion attributable to specific facts. It is therefore not possible that circumstances which could lead to a suspicion are gathered only through the unsubstantiated bank enquiries of an authority.

The opening of a bank account is permitted only in cases of suspected willful criminal offences, petty offences which fall within the competence of a regional court, or willful financial offences, but not in the case of mere financial administrative offences.

Criminal investigations

The opening of a bank account during criminal investigations requires judicial approval. The court has to examine whether the requirements for the breach of banking secrecy that will be caused by the opening of the bank account are met.

The opening of a bank account during criminal investigations is permitted only if it can be assumed, based on certain facts, that:

- Goods, certificates, or documents regarding business relationships or transactions can be seized as a result of the opening, insofar as this is necessary for solving an offence
- A transaction in connection with an offence has been settled via that business relationship

In the order of the opening, which must be judicially approved, the following have to be mentioned:

- The proceedings
- The offence on which the proceedings are based
- The credit institution
- The goods, certificates, and financial assets that are to be seized
- The facts that indicate the necessity and proportionality of the opening
- The time covered by the order in the case of a request regarding transactions in connection with an offence

Credit institutions have the right to appeal against the judicial approval of an opening to a court of second instance[5] if they believe that the requirements for the breach of banking secrecy are not met. To make sure that banking secrecy is protected in such a case, the credit institution can secure documents to do with the business of the customer against unauthorized inspection or alteration in a suitable manner (for example, through sealing the envelope) and present them directly to the court of second instance. This ensures that the documents will be inspected only at the time of the court of second instance's decision.

Financial criminal investigations

Tax authorities are entitled to request certain information from credit institutions concerning business relationships if:

- They have reasonable doubt regarding the accuracy of a taxable person's statements
- It can be expected that said doubt can be clarified through the information
- It can be expected that the invasion of the bank client's legitimate interests that is associated with the request of information is not disproportionate to the purpose of the investigative measure

The Federal Fiscal Court has to decide whether a request for information is justified. A taxable person has the right to appeal against that decision. The credit institution itself has no such right. Requested information must not be exploited as evidence if the Federal Fiscal Court as appellate court rules that the request was unjustified.

During financial criminal investigations, the financial criminal authority can send requests for information to the credit institution in the form of an order. Credit institutions are obligated to provide the requested information, let the authority

5 *Oberlandesgericht*; Higher Regional Court

inspect certificates and documents, and hand over certificates and documents to the authority.

The credit institution has no right to appeal against that order. Only the accused and other persons that are entitled to dispose of the business relationship have the right to appeal. If the appellate court[6] rules that the order has been unlawful, the information gathered on the basis of the order is inadmissible as evidence. This means that the financial criminal authority must not use the information to the detriment of the accused.

Money laundering and terrorist financing

On the basis of several directives, the member states of the EU have committed themselves to combat money laundering and terrorist financing. Comprehensive obligations for credit institutions arise from the implementation of those directives into Austrian law.

In a very abridged form, money laundering can be defined as actions that are taken for the purpose of placing assets that have been obtained by a criminal offence on the market and/or for the purpose of removing them from the reach of the criminal prosecution authorities. This includes especially the disguise or concealment of the illegal origin of assets. Terrorist financing is especially defined as the provision of assets (that might also have been gathered in a legal way) for the purpose of carrying out a terrorist attack.

Pursuant to the Austrian Financial Markets Anti-Money Laundering Act,[7] credit institutions are obligated to report every suspicion of money laundering or terrorist financing immediately to the money laundering unit of the Austrian Federal Ministry of the Interior in case they gain knowledge of, suspect, or have a valid reason to think that:

- A transaction that has been attempted, is imminent, is ongoing, or that has already taken place is connected with assets that have been obtained through certain criminal offences
- An asset has been obtained through certain criminal offences
- A customer has violated his/her obligation to disclose fiduciary relationships
- A transaction that has been attempted, is imminent, is ongoing, or that has already taken place is connected to a criminal organization, a terrorist group, a terrorist offence, or to terrorist financing

6 Federal Fiscal Court; *Bundesfinanzgericht*
7 *Finanzmarkt-Geldwäschegesetz*, FM-GwG

If the credit institution submits a money laundering report, it must not conduct the affected transaction until the end of the following banking day. A decision by the money laundering unit on banning or not banning the transaction must be provided by no later than the end of that period. If the money laundering unit does not order the banning of the transaction or other measures, the credit institution is permitted to carry out the transaction. If the money laundering unit bans the transaction or orders its postponement, it must inform the Public Prosecutor's office without undue delay. The obligatory informing of the customer can be postponed for a maximum of five days if the prosecution of a transaction's beneficiary would otherwise be obstructed. The customer and other persons affected have the right to appeal to the competent administrative court against the banning order.

Moreover, credit institutions must inform the money laundering unit immediately of any applications for payments from savings books if no validation of identity concerning the savings book has taken place (anonymous savings books) and the credit balance is at least EUR 15,000 (or an amount in euro equivalent). Unless the money laundering unit orders otherwise, payments from such savings deposits must be withheld for seven calendar days starting from the day of application.

Credit institutions are furthermore obligated to provide information in the case of requests from the Austrian Federal Minister of the Interior in connection with the prevention or prosecution of money laundering and terrorist financing.

Reporting obligations in the case of capital outflows

Credit institutions are obligated to report capital outflows from bank accounts or securities accounts of natural persons of amounts of EUR 50,000 or more to the Austrian Federal Minister of Finance. Business accounts of entrepreneurs as well as escrow accounts of lawyers, notaries, and public accountants[8] are exempted from the reporting obligation. Reclassifications of existing bank accounts to business accounts and transfers from private bank accounts to business accounts are, however, classified as mandatory reportable capital outflows if they reach the minimum amount of EUR 50,000 or more.

Capital outflow is defined as:

- Payment and transfer from sight deposits, time deposits, and savings deposits
- Payment and transfer in the course of conducting payment services
- Transfer of ownership of securities through a gift within national territory
- Transfer of securities to foreign securities accounts

8 *Wirtschaftstreuhänder*

The report includes personal data, the bank account or securities account number, and the respective amount.

The obligation to report exists regardless of whether the capital outflow is carried out in a single operation or spans several operations that appear to be linked in any way.

The obligation for credit institutions to report capital outflows ends in December 2022.

Probate proceedings

After a customer's death, an exemption from banking secrecy is made *vis-à-vis* the Probate Court and the Judicial Commissioner[9] who is assigned to deal with the estate. In the course of recording a death, the Judicial Commissioner elicits the decedent's financial assets and liabilities for the settlement of probate proceedings. In practice, the Judicial Commissioner sends requests regarding the decedent's asset situation to all credit institutions that could possibly be linked to the decedent according to his/her information. The Judicial Commissioner can gain indications of links between a decedent and a credit institution through potential heirs, relatives, or documents found in the estate.

An exemption from banking secrecy *vis-à-vis* the heirs takes place only if and when they have declared taking possession of the estate after the decedent's death. As soon as the inheritance is transferred to the heirs by resolution of the Probate Court, the heirs supersede the deceased customer. From that day on, they have the same rights as the deceased customer.

Further exemptions pursuant to the Austrian Banking Act

Regarding underage customers, banking secrecy does not apply *vis-à-vis* legal representatives and the Guardianship Court.

General banking information regarding entrepreneurs may be provided to third parties. This includes, for example, a general description of the financial circumstances or the nature of a business relationship without disclosing details. Typical wording would be, for example: 'We have maintained a long-standing, smooth business relationship as the house bank of the customer. We are not aware of the customer having liquidity problems.' Every customer has the right to prohibit expressly the future provision of such information at any time.

9 *Gerichtskommissär*

In the case of a legal dispute between a credit institution and a customer, the credit institution may disclose any circumstances during that dispute that objectively appear to be necessary for law enforcement. During legal disputes between a customer and other persons, a breach of banking secrecy is not permitted.

Owing to certain supervisory requirements, credit institutions are obligated to disclose information regarding their business activities to the Financial Market Authority. The Financial Market Authority is itself bound to professional secrecy and is therefore not allowed to pass on such information.

For compliance with and proof of their own tax liability, credit institutions need to disclose partially, customers' data to the tax authorities. Owing to the protective purpose of banking secrecy, tax authorities must not misuse data gathered in this way to initiate financial (criminal) proceedings against a customer.

Exemptions of banking secrecy *vis-à-vis* foreign financial authorities

A further breach of banking secrecy regarding customers that are not exclusively tax residents in Austria exists as a result of the requirements of the OECD and the EU. On the basis of these requirements, Austria is obligated to implement common reporting standards (CRS) for the automatic exchange of data regarding financial accounts. The automatic exchange of information is expected to contribute to combating tax evasion and cross-border tax avoidance.

Pursuant to CRS, credit institutions are obligated to enquire into the tax residence of customers, save the information electronically, and submit reports to Austrian tax authorities regarding customers with foreign tax residence. Subsequently, tax authorities carry out the exchange of information with the states that take part in CRS. There are currently about 100 states worldwide that participate in CRS, including the EU member states, Switzerland, and Liechtenstein.

Inter alia, the address, telephone number, authorized signatories with foreign addresses, standing orders in another country, c/o addresses, or addresses to be held at credit institutions' counters can indicate the tax residence of a natural person.

Credit authorities must report the name and address of the holder of the bank account or securities account, his/her state of residence, tax identification number, date and place of birth, the bank account or securities account number, the account balances/deposit items to the end of the reporting period, as well as investment income, income from assets on the accounts, and sales proceeds.

Customers are obligated to provide a self-declaration and disclose their tax residence and tax identification number if they want to open a bank account or securities account at an Austrian credit institution.

Customers who are exclusively Austrian tax residents are not affected by said reporting obligations.

About the authors

DR. HELMUT HEGEN, M.B.L., is a lawyer and a partner at Salzburg law firm HOSP, HEGEN Rechtsanwaltspartnerschaft. Dr. Hegen lectures on banking law at the University of Salzburg.

MAG. EVA-MARIA NIEDERREITER is a lawyer at Salzburg law firm HOSP, HEGEN Rechtsanwaltspartnerschaft.

www.ingramcontent.com/pod-product-compliance
Lightning Source LLC
Chambersburg PA
CBHW071331230926
51849CB00002B/367
* 9 7 8 3 9 5 2 4 7 4 2 6 6 *